the food of china

the food of
china

a journey for food lovers

Photography by Jason Lowe
Recipes by Deh-Ta Hsiung and Nina Simonds

whitecap

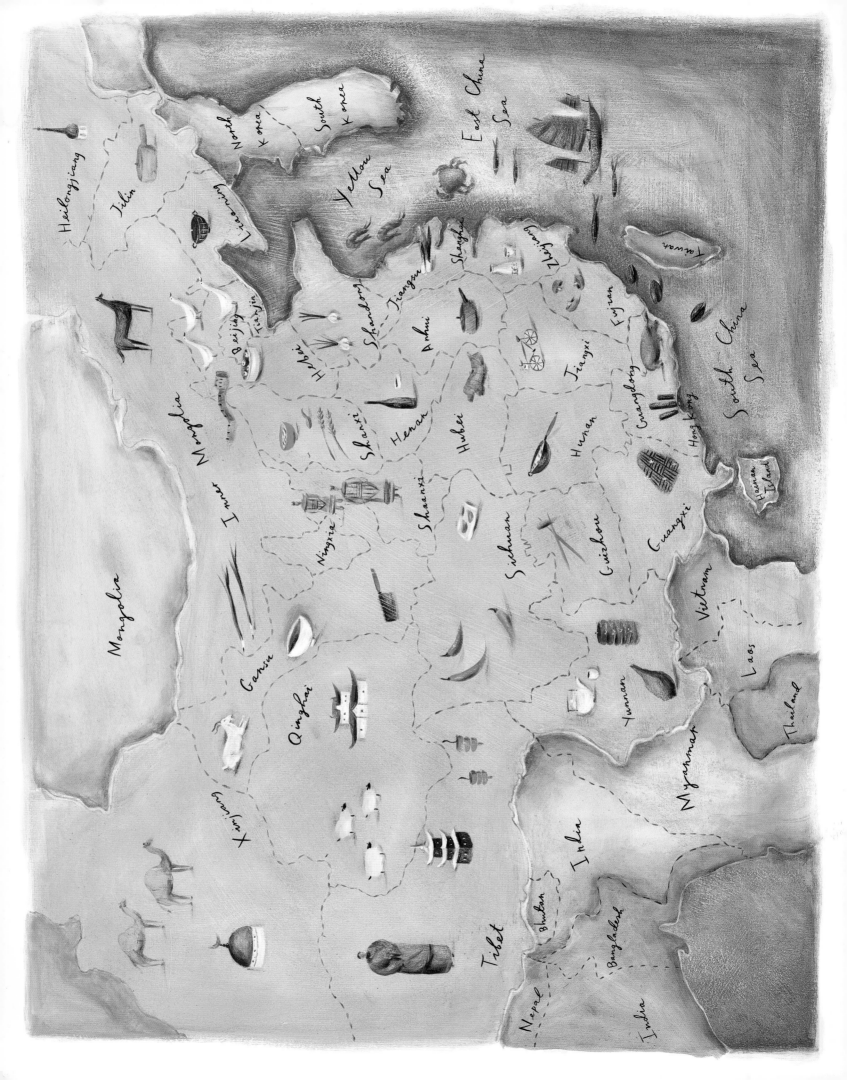

CONTENTS

THE FOOD OF CHINA   6

RECIPES

SNACKS & STARTERS   18
SOUPS   54
FISH & SEAFOOD   70
POULTRY   120
MEAT   154
TOFU   184
VEGETABLES   202
RICE & NOODLES   226
DESSERTS   262
BASICS   272

GLOSSARY OF CHINESE FOOD AND COOKING   288
INDEX   292

FOOD JOURNEYS IN CHINA

DIM SUM   From the traditional tea house to the dim sum palace   36

BANQUET   Celebrating life with food   94

PEKING DUCK   The secret of Beijing's culinary gift to the world   136

SOY   China's most versatile ingredient transformed into sauces and tofu   192

NOODLES   The ancient art of hand-made noodles   238

TEA   A connoisseur's guide to the world's finest teas   286

the food of
CHINA

AN ENORMOUS COUNTRY, WITH A LARGE POPULATION

TO FEED AND A DIVERSE GEOGRAPHY AND CLIMATE,

CHINA HAS ONE OF THE GREAT CUISINES OF THE

WORLD AND EATING PLAYS A MAJOR ROLE IN DAILY

LIFE AND IN RITUALS AND FESTIVITIES.

Chinese meals always have as their basis a staple, or fan, such as rice, wheat, maize or millet. Rice, always white and polished, is the food most associated with China and is usually steamed, while wheat grows well in the harsh climate of the North and is made into breads and noodles. In poorer areas, millet is more common, eaten as porridge. The staple is then accompanied by secondary dishes, or cai, of meat, seafood or vegetables, pickles and condiments. Snacks, from dumplings to spicy bowls of noodles, are eaten all day long, both as sustenance and to satisfy the taste buds.

INGREDIENTS

The most important factor is freshness: poultry and seafood are bought live, and a cook may make more than one trip to the market a day. Chinese cuisine developed around the foods available—often there was little meat, poultry or fish, so rice and vegetables are particularly important. However, many of the foods we associate with China today, such as chillies, capsicums (peppers) and corn, all came to China via trading routes. The Chinese also incorporate a lot of preserved vegetables and dried foods, particularly seafood, into their diet, which is especially important in areas where the climate and terrain make growing enough food a struggle.

FLAVOURS

Chinese cooking tries to reach a balance between tastes: sweet and sour, hot and cold, plain and spicy. At the heart of Chinese food is a trinity of flavours: ginger, spring onions (scallions) and garlic. Although these are not included in all Chinese dishes, they do contribute to a flavour that is seen

Snacking on noodles in the street, or feasting on steaming dumplings in a restaurant, are part of the Chinese enjoyment of food. A new sign goes up in Chengdu and a panda eats breakfast in Sichuan. Bean curd and chives are used in many dishes, while fried fish rolls served at a banquet and fried bread sold in the market both use the same cooking technique.

In the North, wheat flour is made into staples like noodles, dumplings and breads. New Year is China's most important festival, celebrated with lanterns and food, including these sweet round dumplings. In Guangxi, cormorants are still used to catch fish. All parts of the pig are sold in Chinese markets, and spring onions (scallions) are one of Chinese cooking's most essential ingredients.

8

as being quintessentially 'Chinese'. Soya bean products are another essential ingredient, and fermented tofu, soy sauce and bean sauces are tastes that define Chinese food, along with vinegars and sesame oil. In the West of the country, chilli and Sichuan pepper add heat to ingredients that are usually more simply cooked.

COOKING STYLES

A wok is without doubt the central item in a Chinese kitchen, and wok cooking, either stir-frying or deep-frying, is at the heart of China's quick style of cooking. Other techniques, such as steaming, poaching and braising, cook food more slowly. Few families own an oven, and foods that need to be oven-roasted, such as roast ducks or char siu, are instead bought from special restaurants. All food is 'prepared' in China, where salads and raw foods are not eaten, and ingredients are cooked, however briefly, or preserved. A good Chinese meal will include a mix of cooking styles so all the dishes can be ready at the same time.

EATING

A Chinese meal will also consist of a number of dishes, all made to share, that are fully prepared in the kitchen (not even carving is done at the table) and can be picked up and eaten with chopsticks. All the ingredients must be fresh and the finished food served immediately. Stir-fried dishes should still have 'wok hei' or the breath of the wok about them, indicating they have been cooked at exactly the right heat with exactly the right timing and have been served at once.

BANQUET FOOD

Food eaten at banquets is created to be the very opposite of the everyday diet of grains. The point of a banquet is eating for pleasure, not sustenance, thus rice or noodles are served only at the end, and may be left untouched. Banquet food is often symbolic and as extravagant as can be afforded with dishes such as abalone, shark's fin and whole fish.

MEDICAL

In no other cuisine is the medicinal nature of food so tied to everyday cooking. Achieving balance at every meal is an essential part of Chinese cooking. Every ingredient is accorded a nature—hot, warm, cool and neutral—and a flavour—sweet, sour, bitter, salty and pungent—and these are matched to a person's imbalances: a cooling food for a fever, warming food after childbirth. As well as the use of everyday ingredients, there is the custom of using exotic foods, such as dried lizards, wolf berries and black silky chickens, often cooked in special soups and preparations.

THE FOOD OF THE NORTH

The cuisine of the North, with Beijing at its centre, comes from an area that is generally inhospitable with, apart from Shandong, little fertile land, harsh long winters and short scorching summers. Historically the region has swung between drought and flooding from the Yellow River, 'China's Sorrow', though dams and irrigation schemes have improved things in recent years. The main crops have thus always been hardy ones: wheat and millet are eaten as noodles, breads and porridge, while in the winter, vegetables such as turnips and cabbage are supplied to the capital by farmers from neighbouring provinces, who drive in trucks to Beijing's markets and live on them until their load of vegetables has been sold. Shandong on the coast is the most fertile area and it has become a market garden of fruit and vegetables for the capital, as well as providing plentiful seafood.

Flavours are strong, with salty bean pastes and soy sauces, vinegar, spring onions (scallions) and garlic all being important ingredients. Winter vegetables are preserved or pickled, while spicy or piquant condiments are eaten with bowls of steaming noodles or rice when little else is available.

The main outside influence on the region has been the Muslim cooking of the Mongol and Manchu invaders who crossed the Great Wall from the North. Mutton and, in spring and summer, lamb, is sold as barbecued skewers on the street and stir-fried and wrapped in wheat pancakes. Steaming Mongolian hotpots and Mongolian barbecues cooked on a grill are seen everywhere.

Peking Duck, however, remains Beijing's most famous dish, and is cooked in specialist restaurants all over the city. Beggar's chicken is another local speciality, wrapped in lotus leaves and clay and baked for hours in hot ashes.

In stark contrast to the warming dumplings and hotpots of Beijing's streets is the imperial cuisine created inside the Forbidden City. The presence of the court not only encouraged a huge diversity of cooking styles in the city from every province in China, but also elevated cooking to a standard probably never seen elsewhere in the world. Food was as important to the myth surrounding the Emperor as his armies, and he employed hundreds if not thousands in his kitchens. This elaborate cuisine is no longer reproduced in its entirety, but is remembered as a set of skills, recipes and flavour combinations important today in both banquet and everyday cooking.

A little girl eats ice cream, old men play Chinese chequers, and visitors climb the steps to the Temple of Heaven despite the cold of a Beijing winter. Steaming hot buns are a staple of the North, along with cabbage, huge winter melons, red carrots and pickled vegetables. Barbecued skewers of lamb and the ubiquitous pot noodles are sold as warming street snacks.

11

Hangzhou is famous for its tea houses, while in Shanghai a woman poses for a photo in front of Yuyuan Gardens, known for its snacks and Heart of the Lake Tea House, where tea comes with an orange and a memento. High-rise Pudong towers over old Shanghai, in whose alleys a woman makes lunch and a man walks under New Year lanterns. Fish and bok choy (pak choi) are sold in markets.

THE FOOD OF THE EAST

Though the huge port city of Shanghai now dominates the East, the city is very much a modern one and it is difficult to talk of a real 'Shanghai cuisine'. Rather, the city's food reflects that of the agriculturally rich provinces that surround it on the fertile plains of the Yangtze Delta. Together they have given this area the nickname of the land of fish and rice.

With a warmer climate than the North and an all-year-round growing season, the cuisine has been shaped by the variety of available ingredients, from rice and wheat to a whole array of vegetables—bok choy (pak choi), bamboo, beans and squash, as well as some of China's finest fish—freshwater carp from the tributaries of the Yangtze, Shanghai's infamous hairy crabs and fresh seafood from the coast. Duck, chicken and pork from this region are also considered particularly good and a cured ham from Jinhua rivals that of Yunnan.

The cuisine is based on slow-braising rather than steaming or stir-frying, and thus has a reputation for being more oily than other regions. Shaoxing wine, an amber rice wine produced for both drinking and cooking in the city of Shaoxing, flavours many dishes, as does black vinegar from Chinkiang and ginger and garlic. A pinch of sugar is often added to balance these flavours, and it is in this region that sweet-and-sour dishes are most expertly cooked. Much of China's soy sauce is produced in the East, and red-cooking is a favoured cooking technique using a soy sauce and rice wine stock to braise the area's fine meat and poultry, which is also presented in the form of a mixed cold platter that begins most formal meals. Though many of the region's flavourings are strong, vegetables, fish and seafood tend to be treated simply.

The area is abundant in regional specialities, including spareribs from Wuxi cooked in soy sauce and rice wine; lion's head meatballs from Yangzhou; pressed ducks from Nanjing; and West-lake carp from Hangzhou, which also grows China's finest green tea, Dragon Well, that is sometimes used as an ingredient. The people of Shanghai love their fish and seafood, particularly the freshwater hairy crabs so associated with the city, and available for little over a month every autumn.

Snacking is an obsession, especially in Shanghai, with jiaozi, steamed buns and noodle dishes found everywhere. While rice is grown in the region, filling wheat-based breads, dumplings and noodles are favoured, particularly in winter.

13

THE FOOD OF THE WEST

The cooking of China's central and western heartlands is dominated by the spice of Sichuan, whose fertile plains are fed by the Yangtze River and its tributaries. It is famous for its hot cuisine and the sheer variety of its cooking styles, summed up in the phrase 'one hundred dishes and one hundred flavours'.

Chillies are not indigenous to China, and in fact came to Asia from South America with the Portuguese. It was therefore probably Buddhist traders and missionaries from the West who brought such ingredients and cooking techniques into Sichuan, and also left the legacy of an imaginative Buddhist vegetarian cuisine.

Sichuan pepper is the dominant spice in many dishes. Not related to Western black and white pepper, it is hot and pungent, leaving a numb sensation in the mouth. The use of chilli peppers and ginger adds additional layers of heat. Red (chilli) oil, sesame oil, various bean pastes and vinegars are common, as are nuts and sesame seeds in dishes like bang bang chicken. These flavours are uniquely Sichuanese, and are quite different from those in the rest of China.

Cooking styles are also unusual. 'Fish flavoured' (Yuxiang) sauces are made from ginger, garlic, vinegar, chilli and spring onions (scallions), usually served with vegetables like eggplant (aubergine), but never with even a hint of fish present. Other tastes include hot-and-sour (Cuan La), such as in the famous soup, and a numb-chilli flavour (Ma La), such as in the tofu dish ma po dofu with its fiery sauce. Sichuan also has its own version of the hotpot, the Chongqing hotpot, which is a heavily flavoured mix of chilli and oil and, true to the style of the region, is red-hot.

Chilli is widely used in other areas of the West, particularly in neighbouring Hunan and in Guangxi, whose Guilin chilli sauce is eaten all over China. Guangxi is also a major rice-growing region, with vast stepped terraces covering its hills.

Southwest China has the most varied mix of ethnic minorities in the country, and it is the only area in which dairy products such as goat's cheese are used. Muslim influences are also apparent and goat's meat and dried beef are available. Yunnan ham is a whole ham cured in a sweetish style, and Yunnan specialities include steampot chicken, cooked with medicinal ingredients, and crossing-the-bridge noodles, cooked in a bowl of boiling hot broth.

Modern Chengdu bustles around a statue of Mao, while a Naxi girl represents one of Yunnan's ethnic minorities. Tofu is sold on the street and used in ma po dofu, and spicy noodles are a familiar snack. Mushrooms from the mountains, red chilli bean paste, bamboo shoots and eggplants (aubergines) are all part of a rich diet. Rice grows in Guilin and sheep are farmed near the Yunnan mountains.

15

Dried food stores are found all over Hong Kong and sell many kinds of dried seafood, which is also sold fresh in the markets. Dim sum is enjoyed in Hong Kong at old-fashioned tea houses and at the famous Luk Yu Tea House, with its smart waiters, while egg noodles, steamed whole fish, oyster sauce and bowls of freshly steamed rice are all part of the varied Cantonese diet.

LUK YU TEA HOUSE

THE FOOD OF THE SOUTH

The food of the South, and especially that of Guangdong (Canton), is renowned both within and outside China as the country's finest. Guangdong has a subtropical climate that sustains rice crops and many vegetables and fruit virtually all year round, while an extensive coastline and inland waterways provide the freshest fish and shellfish.

The area also prides itself on its well-trained chefs, whose restaurants have always catered to the rich merchants of Guangzhou and Hong Kong. They insist on high-quality ingredients, which they cook in numerous ways: stir-fried, steamed or boiled, but which are usually kept simple and cooked with little oil to enhance the food's fresh flavour.

The flavours of the South are relatively simple, emphasizing the freshness of the food with just a delicate base of ginger, garlic and spring onions (scallions). Unlike the rest of China, spicy or fragrant condiments are often served with dishes, particularly sauces such as soy and chilli, so the diners can add their own flavourings. The area is responsible for the invention of oyster, hoi sin, black bean and XO sauces.

Guangzhou is known for its wonderful fish and seafood dishes, served in every restaurant. Always fresh, the customer picks from a large fish tank and specifies the cooking technique. The favoured meat of the South is without a doubt pork—often roasted or barbecued (char siu) and bought from the take-away counters of roast-meat restaurants, who hang up their wares to tempt in customers. Ducks are another favourite, bred all over the South and roasted until crispy. Dim sum is a speciality of Guangzhou and Hong Kong and these snacks, served in tea houses or dim sum restaurants, are universally popular.

The Cantonese are also known for eating just about anything—from shark's fin and snakes to monkeys and dogs. The people of this region are certainly knowledgeable and adventurous about food, though many of the more esoteric ingredients are served only at specialized restaurants or are eaten mostly for their medicinal qualities.

As well as the Cantonese cooking of Guangdong, the South is also home to the food of the Hakka people, China's gypsies, whose cooking is an earthier version of Cantonese, and Chiu Chow food from the east coast of the province, with its emphasis on seafood, goose and sauces. There are also specialities from Fujian and Taiwan.

SNACKS & STARTERS

JIAOZI

PERHAPS NO OTHER FOOD TYPIFIES THE HEARTY CHARACTERISTICS OF NORTHERN HOME-STYLE COOKING MORE THAN THESE MEAT DUMPLINGS. YOU CAN BUY GOOD-QUALITY WHEAT DUMPLING WRAPPERS AT CHINESE GROCERS, WHICH MAKES THESE A QUICK, EASY SNACK TO PREPARE.

Fold the dumplings as shown above, handling the wrappers carefully so they don't tear and making sure they don't get too wet. Squeeze the pleats firmly or they will undo as they cook.

FILLING
300 g (11 oz) Chinese cabbage, finely chopped
1 teaspoon salt
450 g (1 lb) minced (ground) pork
100 g (3 bunches) Chinese garlic chives, finely chopped
2 1/2 tablespoons light soy sauce
1 tablespoon Shaoxing rice wine
2 tablespoons roasted sesame oil
1 tablespoon finely chopped ginger
1 tablespoon cornflour (cornstarch)

50 round wheat dumpling wrappers
red rice vinegar or a dipping sauce (page 282)

MAKES 50

TO MAKE the filling, put the cabbage and salt in a bowl and toss lightly to combine. Leave for 30 minutes. Squeeze all the water from the cabbage and put the cabbage in a large bowl. Add the pork, garlic chives, soy sauce, rice wine, sesame oil, ginger and cornflour. Stir until combined and drain off any excess liquid.

PLACE a heaped teaspoon of the filling in the centre of each wrapper. Spread a little water along the edge of the wrapper and fold the wrapper over to make a half-moon shape. Use your thumb and index finger to form small pleats along the sealed edge. With the other hand, press the two opposite edges together to seal. Place the dumplings on a baking tray that has been lightly dusted with cornflour. Do not allow the dumplings to sit for too long or they will go soggy.

BRING a large saucepan of water to the boil. Add half the dumplings, stirring immediately to prevent them from sticking together, and return to the boil. For the traditional method of cooking dumplings, add 250 ml (1 cup) cold water and continue cooking over high heat until the water boils. Add another 750 ml (3 cups) cold water and cook until the water boils again. Alternatively, cook the dumplings in the boiling water for 8–9 minutes. Remove from the heat and drain the dumplings. Repeat with the remaining dumplings.

THE DUMPLINGS can also be fried. Heat 1 tablespoon oil in a frying pan, add a single layer of dumplings and cook for 2 minutes, shaking the pan to make sure they don't stick. Add 80 ml (1/3 cup) water, cover and steam for 2 minutes, then uncover and cook until the water has evaporated. Repeat with the remaining dumplings.

SERVE with red rice vinegar or a dipping sauce.

SPRING ROLLS

THE FAT, SOLID SPRING ROLLS FOUND IN MANY WESTERN RESTAURANTS ARE QUITE DIFFERENT FROM THE SLENDER AND REFINED SPRING ROLLS THAT ARE TRADITIONALLY MADE TO CELEBRATE CHINESE NEW YEAR. HERE'S AN EASY RENDITION OF THE CLASSIC.

FILLING
5 tablespoons light soy sauce
2 teaspoons roasted sesame oil
3¹/₂ tablespoons Shaoxing
    rice wine
1¹/₂ teaspoons cornflour
    (cornstarch)
450 g (1 lb) centre-cut pork loin,
    trimmed and cut into very
    thin strips
6 dried Chinese mushrooms
¹/₂ teaspoon freshly ground
    black pepper
4 tablespoons oil
1 tablespoon finely chopped ginger
3 garlic cloves, finely chopped
130 g (5 oz) Chinese cabbage,
    finely shredded
150 g (1 cup) finely shredded carrot
30 g (1 bunch) Chinese garlic
    chives, cut into 2 cm (³/₄ inch)
    lengths
180 g (2 cups) bean sprouts

1 egg yolk
2 tablespoons plain (all-purpose)
    flour
20 square spring roll wrappers
oil for deep-frying
plum sauce

MAKES 20

TO MAKE the filling, combine 2 tablespoons of the soy sauce and half the sesame oil with 1¹/₂ tablespoons of the rice wine and 1 teaspoon of the cornflour. Add the pork and toss to coat. Marinate in the fridge for 20 minutes. Meanwhile, soak the dried mushrooms in boiling water for 30 minutes, then drain and squeeze out any excess water. Remove and discard the stems and shred the caps. Combine the remaining soy sauce, sesame oil and cornflour with the black pepper.

HEAT a wok over high heat, add half the oil and heat until very hot. Add the pork mixture and stir-fry for 2 minutes, or until cooked. Remove and drain. Wipe out the wok.

REHEAT the wok over high heat, add the remaining oil and heat until very hot. Stir-fry the mushrooms, ginger and garlic for 15 seconds. Add the cabbage and carrot and toss lightly. Pour in the remaining rice wine, then stir-fry for 1 minute. Add the garlic chives and bean sprouts and stir-fry for 1 minute, or until the sprouts are limp. Add the pork mixture and soy sauce mixture and cook until thickened. Transfer to a colander and drain for 5 minutes, tossing occasionally to remove the excess liquid.

COMBINE the egg yolk, flour and 3 tablespoons water. Place 2 tablespoons of filling on the corner of a wrapper, leaving the corner itself free. Spread some of the yolk mixture on the opposite corner. Fold over one corner and start rolling, but not too tightly. Fold in the other corners, roll up and press to secure. Repeat with the remaining wrappers.

FILL a wok one-quarter full with oil. Heat the oil to 190°C (375°F), or until a piece of bread fries golden brown in 10 seconds when dropped in the oil. Cook the spring rolls in two batches, turning constantly, for 5 minutes, or until golden. Remove and drain on paper towels. Serve with plum sauce.

Spring rolls should look elegant rather than chunky, so use a small amount of filling in each and roll them neatly. Don't roll them too tightly or they may burst open as they cook.

Luk Yu Tea House,
Hong Kong

Gather in the tops of the buns as neatly as you can to make round balls. Bear in mind that they will open slightly as they cook to show their filling.

叉烧包

CHAR SIU BAU

MANTOU, OR STEAMED BUNS, ARE A FILLING STAPLE EATEN ALL OVER CHINA, BUT ESPECIALLY IN THE NORTH. HOWEVER, THESE FILLED, SLIGHTLY SWEET BUNS MADE WITH BARBECUE PORK (CHAR SIU) ARE A CANTONESE SPECIALITY, ENJOYED IN EVERY DIM SUM RESTAURANT.

1 teaspoon oil
250 g (9 oz) barbecue pork (char siu), diced
3 teaspoons Shaoxing rice wine
1 teaspoon roasted sesame oil
2 tablespoons oyster sauce
2 teaspoons light soy sauce
3 teaspoons sugar
1 quantity basic yeast dough (page 278)
chilli sauce

MAKES 12 LARGE OR
24 SMALL

HEAT the oil in a wok. Add the pork, rice wine, sesame oil, oyster sauce, soy sauce and sugar and cook for 1 minute. Leave to cool.

DIVIDE the dough into 12 or 24 portions, depending on how large you want your buns to be, and cover with a tea towel. Working with one portion at a time, press the dough into circles with the edges thinner than the centre. Place 1 teaspoon of filling on the dough for a small bun or 3 teaspoons for a large bun. Draw the sides in to enclose the filling. Pinch the top together and put each bun on a square of greaseproof paper. When you get more proficient at making these, you may be able to get more filling into the buns, which will make them less doughy. Ensure that you seal them properly. The buns can also be turned over, then cooked the other way up so they look like round balls.

PLACE the buns well apart in three steamers. Cover and steam over simmering water in a wok, reversing the steamers halfway through, for 15 minutes, or until the buns are well risen and a skewer inserted into the centre comes out hot. Serve with some chilli sauce.

荷叶糯米团

STEAMED GLUTINOUS RICE IN LOTUS LEAVES

LOR MAI GAI ARE A DIM SUM CLASSIC THAT ALSO MAKE GOOD SNACKS. WHEN STEAMED, THE RICE TAKES ON THE FLAVOURS OF THE OTHER INGREDIENTS AND FROM THE LOTUS LEAVES THEMSELVES. THE PARCELS CAN BE MADE AHEAD AND FROZEN, THEN STEAMED FROM FROZEN FOR 40 MINUTES.

600 g (3 cups) glutinous rice
4 large lotus leaves

FILLING
2 tablespoons dried shrimp
4 dried Chinese mushrooms
2 tablespoons oil
360 g (13 oz) skinless chicken
    breast fillet, cut into 1 cm
    (1/2 inch) cubes
1 garlic clove, crushed
2 Chinese sausages (lap cheong),
    thinly sliced
2 spring onions (scallions), thinly
    sliced
1 tablespoon oyster sauce
3 teaspoons light soy sauce
3 teaspoons sugar
1 teaspoon roasted sesame oil
1 tablespoon cornflour (cornstarch)
chilli sauce

MAKES 8

PLACE the rice in a bowl, cover with cold water and leave to soak overnight. Drain in a colander and place the rice in a bamboo steamer lined with a tea towel. Steam, covered, over simmering water in a wok for 30–40 minutes, or until the rice is cooked. Cool slightly before using.

SOAK the lotus leaves in boiling water for 1 hour, or until softened. Shake dry and cut the leaves in half to give eight equal pieces.

TO MAKE the filling, soak the dried shrimp in boiling water for 1 hour, then drain. Soak the dried mushrooms in boiling water for 30 minutes, then drain and squeeze out any excess water. Remove and discard the stems and finely chop the caps.

HEAT a wok over high heat, add half the oil and heat until very hot. Stir-fry the chicken for 2–3 minutes, or until browned. Add the dried shrimp, mushrooms, garlic, sausage and spring onion. Stir-fry for another 1–2 minutes, or until aromatic. Add the oyster sauce, soy sauce, sugar and sesame oil and toss well. Combine the cornflour with 185 ml (3/4 cup) water, add to the sauce and simmer until thickened.

WITH WET hands, divide the rice into 16 balls. Place the lotus leaves on a work surface, put a ball of rice in the centre of each leaf and flatten the ball slightly, making a slight indentation in the middle. Spoon one-eighth of the filling onto each rice ball, top with another slightly flattened rice ball and smooth into one ball. Wrap up firmly by folding the leaves over to form an envelope.

PLACE the parcels in three steamers. Cover and steam over simmering water in a wok, reversing the steamers halfway through, for 30 minutes. To serve, open up each leaf and eat straight from the leaf while hot with some chilli sauce.

Enclose the filling in the rice as much as possible, then neatly fold over the leaves. The leaves seal in the flavour and hold the rice in shape while cooking.

Sugar is sold loose in a market in Sichuan. This is slab sugar.

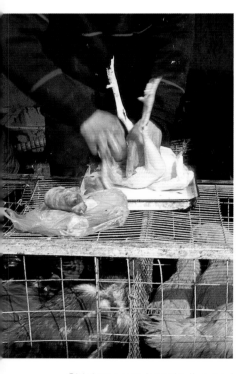

Chickens are bought live and prepared on the spot in a Beijing market to make sure they are really fresh.

焖鸡翅

BRAISED CHICKEN WINGS

THE CHINESE LOVE TO EAT EVERY PART OF THE CHICKEN AND THE WINGS, DEEP-FRIED AND CRISP, ARE A FAVOURITE SNACK. THIS RECIPE IS A SIMPLE ONE THAT MAKES A GOOD SNACK OR FIRST COURSE. YOU'LL NEED TO HAND OUT FINGER BOWLS.

24 chicken wings
3 lumps rock (lump) sugar
1 tablespoon dark soy sauce
1 tablespoon light soy sauce
1 tablespoon Shaoxing rice wine
oil for deep-frying
2 teaspoons finely chopped ginger
1 spring onion (scallion), finely
  chopped
2 tablespoons hoisin sauce
125 ml (1/2 cup) chicken stock
  (page 281)

SERVES 6

DISCARD the tip of each chicken wing. Cut each wing into two pieces through the joint. Put the wing pieces in a bowl.

PUT the rock sugar, dark soy sauce, light soy sauce and rice wine in a small jug. Mix until combined, breaking the sugar down as much as you can. Pour the mixture over the chicken wings, then marinate in the fridge for at least 1 hour, or overnight.

DRAIN the chicken wings, reserving the marinade. Fill a wok one-quarter full of oil. Heat the oil to 180°C (350°F), or until a piece of bread fries golden brown in 15 seconds when dropped in the oil. Cook the chicken wings in batches for 2–3 minutes, or until they are well browned. Drain on paper towels.

CAREFULLY POUR the oil from the wok, reserving 1 tablespoon. Reheat the wok over high heat, add the reserved oil and heat until very hot. Stir-fry the ginger and spring onion for 1 minute. Add the hoisin sauce, reserved marinade and chicken wings and cook for 1 minute, then add the stock and bring to the boil. Reduce the heat, cover the wok and cook gently for 8–10 minutes, or until the chicken wings are cooked through and tender.

INCREASE the heat and bring the sauce to the boil, uncovered. Cook until the sauce reduces to a sticky coating.

Travelling by truck in Yunnan.

STEAMED RICE NOODLE ROLLS

A DIM SUM FAVOURITE, THESE SILKY RICE NOODLES CAN BE FILLED WITH BARBECUE PORK (CHAR SIU), PRAWNS OR VEGETABLES. THE NOODLES ARE SOLD AS A LONG SHEET FOLDED INTO A ROLL. DO NOT REFRIGERATE THEM—THEY MUST BE USED AT ROOM TEMPERATURE OR THEY WILL BREAK.

Put the filling on the piece of noodle roll closest to you. Roll up carefully so you don't tear it, keeping the filling tucked inside.

PORK FILLING
350 g (12 oz) barbecue pork
  (char siu), chopped
3 spring onions (scallions), chopped
2 tablespoons chopped coriander
  (cilantro)

OR

PRAWN FILLING
250 g (9 oz) small prawns (shrimp)
1 tablespoon oil
3 spring onions (scallions), chopped
2 tablespoons chopped coriander
  (cilantro)

OR

VEGETABLE FILLING
300 g (11 oz) Chinese broccoli
  (gai lan)
1 teaspoon light soy sauce
1 teaspoon roasted sesame oil
2 spring onions (scallions), chopped

4 fresh rice noodle rolls
oyster sauce

MAKES 4

TO MAKE the pork filling, combine the pork with the spring onion and coriander.

TO MAKE the prawn filling, peel and devein the prawns. Heat a wok over high heat, add the oil and heat until very hot. Stir-fry the prawns for 1 minute, or until they are pink and cooked through. Season with salt and white pepper. Add the spring onion and coriander and mix well.

TO MAKE the vegetable filling, wash the broccoli well. Discard any tough-looking stems and chop the rest of the stems. Put on a plate in a steamer, cover and steam over simmering water in a wok for 3 minutes, or until the stems and leaves are just tender. Combine the Chinese broccoli with the soy sauce, sesame oil and spring onion.

CAREFULLY UNROLL the rice noodle rolls (don't worry if they crack or tear a little at the sides). Trim each one into a neat rectangle about 15 x 18 cm (6 x 7 inches) (you may be able to get two out of one roll if they are very large). Divide the filling among the rolls, then re-roll the noodles. Put the rolls on a plate in a large steamer, cover and steam over simmering water in a wok for 5 minutes. Serve the rolls cut into pieces and drizzled with the oyster sauce.

香辣椒盐排骨

SPICY SALT AND PEPPER SPARERIBS

1 kg (2 lb 4 oz) Chinese-style pork
  spareribs
1 egg, beaten
2–3 tablespoons plain (all-purpose)
  flour
oil for deep-frying
2 spring onions (scallions), finely
  chopped
2 small red chillies, finely chopped

MARINADE
1/2 teaspoon ground Sichuan
  peppercorns
1/2 teaspoon five-spice powder
1/2 teaspoon salt
1 tablespoon light soy sauce
1 tablespoon Shaoxing rice wine
1/4 teaspoon roasted sesame oil

SERVES 4

ASK the butcher to cut the spareribs crosswise
into thirds that measure 4–5 cm (11/2–2 inches) in
length, or use a cleaver to do so yourself. Cut the
ribs between the bones to separate them.

TO MAKE the marinade, combine the ingredients
in a bowl. Add the ribs and toss lightly. Marinate in
the fridge for at least 3 hours, or overnight.

MIX the egg, flour and a little water to form a
smooth batter the consistency of thick cream.
Fill a wok one-quarter full of oil. Heat the oil to
180°C (350°F), or until a piece of bread fries
golden brown in 15 seconds when dropped in the
oil. Dip the ribs in the batter and fry in batches for
5 minutes until they are crisp and golden, stirring
to separate them, then remove and drain. Reheat
the oil and fry the ribs for 1 minute to darken the
colour. Remove and drain on paper towels.

SOAK the spring onion and chilli in the hot oil (with
the heat off) for 2 minutes. Remove with a wire
strainer or slotted spoon and sprinkle over the ribs.

A cleaver is the only knife heavy
enough to easily cut through the
bones of spareribs.

烤排骨

BARBECUE SPARERIBS

1.5 kg (3 lb 5 oz) Chinese-style
  pork spareribs

MARINADE
125 ml (1/2 cup) hoisin sauce
3 tablespoons light soy sauce
3 tablespoons Shaoxing rice wine
2 tablespoons sugar
3 tablespoons tomato sauce
  (ketchup)
4 garlic cloves, finely chopped
3 tablespoons finely chopped
  ginger

SERVES 6

ASK the butcher to cut the spareribs crosswise
into thirds that measure 4–5 cm (11/2–2 inches) in
length, or use a cleaver to do so yourself.

PLACE the spareribs in a large clay pot, casserole
or saucepan and cover with water. Bring to the
boil, then reduce the heat to a simmer. Cook for
20 minutes, drain and allow the ribs to cool. Cut
the ribs between the bones to separate them.

TO MAKE the marinade, combine the ingredients
in a bowl. Add the ribs and toss lightly. Marinate in
the fridge for at least 3 hours, or overnight.

PREHEAT the oven to 180°C (350°F/Gas 4). Put
the ribs and marinade on a baking tray lined with
foil. Bake for 45 minutes, turning once, until golden.

BARBECUE SPARERIBS

豆腐卷

TOFU ROLLS

THESE DELICATE ROLLS MAKE A CHANGE TO SPRING ROLLS AND ARE OFTEN SERVED AS DIM SUM. TOFU SKINS CAN BE PURCHASED EITHER VACUUM-PACKED AND READY TO USE, OR DRIED. THE DRIED TOFU SKINS NEED TO BE HANDLED CAREFULLY AS THEY BREAK EASILY.

4 dried Chinese mushrooms
100 g (3¹/₂ oz) fresh or canned
    bamboo shoots, rinsed and
    drained
1 small carrot
3 tablespoons oil
300 g (10¹/₂ oz) firm tofu, drained
    and diced
200 g (7 oz) bean sprouts
¹/₂ teaspoon salt
¹/₂ teaspoon sugar
2 spring onions (scallions), finely
    shredded
1 tablespoon light soy sauce
1 teaspoon roasted sesame oil
1 tablespoon plain (all-purpose)
    flour
12 sheets soft or dried tofu skins
oil for deep-frying
red rice vinegar, soy sauce or a
    dipping sauce (page 282)

MAKES 12

SOAK the dried mushrooms in boiling water for 30 minutes, then drain and squeeze out any excess water. Remove and discard the stems and finely shred the caps. Cut the bamboo shoots and carrot into thin strips about the size of the bean sprouts.

HEAT a wok over high heat, add the oil and heat until very hot. Stir-fry the carrot, tofu and bean sprouts for 1 minute. Add the mushrooms and bamboo shoots, toss, then add the salt, sugar and spring onion. Stir-fry for 1 minute, then add the soy sauce and sesame oil, and blend well. Remove the mixture from the wok and drain off the excess liquid. Leave to cool. Combine the flour with a little cold water to make a paste.

IF YOU are using dried tofu skins, soak them in cold water until they are soft. Peel off a sheet of tofu skin and trim to a 15 x 18 cm (6 x 7 inch) rectangle. Place 2 tablespoons of the filling at one end of the skin, and roll up to make a neat parcel, folding the sides in as you roll. Brush the skin with some of the flour paste to seal the flap firmly. Repeat with the remaining tofu skins and filling.

FILL a wok one-quarter full of oil. Heat the oil to 180°C (350°F), or until a piece of bread fries golden brown in 15 seconds when dropped in the oil. Cook the rolls in batches for 3–4 minutes, or until golden. Serve with some red rice vinegar, soy sauce or a dipping sauce.

As the tofu skins are rather thin, spread them out well before you roll them up.

CITY HALL CHINESE RESTAURANT is one of Hong Kong's busiest dim sum restaurants, appealing to the building's civil servants during the week and long queues of families at the weekends. The dim sum are stacked on trolleys that are wheeled from table to table, and are also found at 'stations' throughout the room, such as the one above frying turnip cake and noodles to order.

DIM SUM

DIM SUM ARE SNACKS AND DUMPLINGS THAT 'TOUCH THE HEART' AND ARE CENTRAL TO THE CANTONESE TEA HOUSE TRADITION OF YUM CHA. YUM CHA MEANS SIMPLY 'TO DRINK TEA', BUT EATING DIM SUM, READING NEWSPAPERS AND CATCHING UP WITH FRIENDS AND FAMILY ARE ALL PART OF THE EXPERIENCE.

The Chinese love to snack and each region has its favourites, from mantou and jiaozi in the North to little spicy Sichuan dishes. But it is in Guangzhou and Hong Kong's tea houses that dim sum—China's most famous snacks—are found.

TEA HOUSES

Traditional tea houses are almost like a pub. Regulars, mostly older men, spend their early mornings sipping tea, eating just a few dim sum and reading the newspapers. In a few tea houses, the men are accompanied by their song birds, whose cages are hung up around the room. Today, most tea houses are bright, dim sum palaces. Often huge, multi-level restaurants, they work at a frantic, noisy pace, with office workers or families eating a whole meal of dim sum.

EATING DIM SUM

Dim sum is usually eaten mid-morning, but it can be found at any time, and even enjoyed as a midnight snack in busy Hong Kong. The meal begins by choosing a tea, usually pu'er (a black tea), jasmine or chrysanthemum. In fact, yum cha is the only meal where the tea is drunk with the food rather than before or afterwards. Anyone from the table can

THIS TRADITIONAL TEA HOUSE in Sham Shui Po, Hong Kong, opens as early as 5 o'clock in the morning for its regulars, almost all of whom are men. The dim sum are brought around in trays hung from the server's neck and are mostly large and filling. Just one or two items are chosen to supplement the important business of tea drinking, gossiping and catching up on the racing form.

top up the tea cups during the meal, and they are thanked by tapping your fingers on the table, expressing gratitude even when mouths are full. To get the pot refilled, the lid is lifted to the side so the waiters can see that it is empty.

Sometimes dim sum is ordered from a menu, but in the most busy places it is usually taken around the tables in trays or trolleys hot from the kitchen. Servers shout out the name of the dishes they have and people lift up the lids to peak at what is on offer. There may also be 'stations' where noodles are fried and vegetables cooked. Dim sum mostly come in small steamers or dishes, usually three servings to a portion.

Dim sum are rarely made at home and restaurants prize their chefs, who make everything by hand. These chefs undergo an apprenticeship of 3 years, and take another 5 years on average to become fully qualified dim sum chefs.

THE BILL for a dim sum meal is calculated from a card kept on each table. Each time a dish is ordered, the server marks the card with a stamp called a chop.

A traditional tea house in Hong Kong.

烧卖

SIU MAI

SOME SIU MAI PURISTS CONSIDER THE ADDITION OF SEAFOOD TO THE TRADITIONAL ALL-MEAT FILLING TO BE OUTRAGEOUS. HOWEVER, THE PRAWNS (SHRIMP) ADD DEPTH AND CONTRAST TO THE FLAVOUR OF THE PORK AND IT IS NOW COMMON PRACTICE IN DIM SUM KITCHENS.

FILLING
180 g (6 oz) prawns (shrimp)
80 g (1/2 cup) peeled water
  chestnuts
450 g (1 lb) minced (ground) pork
2 tablespoons light soy sauce
1 1/2 tablespoons Shaoxing
  rice wine
2 teaspoons roasted sesame oil
1/4 teaspoon freshly ground
  black pepper
2 tablespoons finely chopped
  ginger
1 spring onion (scallion), finely
  chopped
1 egg white, lightly beaten
2 tablespoons cornflour (cornstarch)

30 square or round egg dumpling
  wrappers
1 tablespoon shrimp roe (optional)
a dipping sauce (page 282)

MAKES 30

TO MAKE the filling, peel and devein the prawns. Place in a tea towel and squeeze out as much moisture as possible, then roughly chop.

BLANCH the water chestnuts in a pan of boiling water for 1 minute, then refresh in cold water. Drain, pat dry and roughly chop them. Place the prawns, water chestnuts, minced pork and the remaining filling ingredients in a large bowl and stir until well combined.

PLACE 1 tablespoon of filling in the centre of a dumpling wrapper. Gather up the edges of the wrapper around the filling. Holding the dumpling between your thumb and index finger, lightly squeeze it to form a 'waist', while at the same time pushing up the filling from the bottom with the other hand to create a flat base. Smooth the surface of the filling with a knife dipped in water.

PLACE the dumplings well apart in four steamers lined with greaseproof paper punched with holes. Put a small dot of shrimp roe in the centre of the filling in each dumpling if using. Cover and steam over simmering water in a wok, reversing the steamers halfway through, for 15 minutes. Serve with a dipping sauce.

Hold the siu mai firmly in your hand and smooth the surface of the filling with a knife dipped in water to prevent it sticking.

虾饺

HAR GAU

HAR GAU ARE THE BENCHMARK DIM SUM BY WHICH RESTAURANTS ARE MEASURED AND THEY ARE NOT EASY TO MAKE. THE WHEAT STARCH DOUGH IS HARD TO HANDLE AND NEEDS TO BE KEPT WARM WHILE YOU WORK WITH IT, BUT THE RESULTS ARE VERY SATISFYING.

FILLING
500 g (1 lb 2 oz) prawns (shrimp)
45 g (1¹/₂ oz) pork or bacon fat
    (rind removed), finely chopped
40 g (1¹/₂ oz) fresh or tinned
    bamboo shoots, rinsed, drained
    and finely chopped
1 spring onion (scallion), finely
    chopped
1 teaspoon sugar
3 teaspoons light soy sauce
¹/₂ teaspoon roasted sesame oil
1 egg white, lightly beaten
1 teaspoon salt
1 tablespoon cornflour (cornstarch)

WRAPPER DOUGH
170 g (1¹/₃ cups) wheat starch
3 teaspoons cornflour (cornstarch)
2 teaspoons oil

soy sauce, chilli sauce or a dipping
    sauce (page 282)

MAKES 24

TO MAKE the filling, peel and devein the prawns and cut half of them into 1 cm (¹/₂ inch) chunks. Chop the remaining prawns until finely minced. Combine all the prawns in a large bowl. Add the pork or bacon fat, bamboo shoots, spring onion, sugar, soy sauce, sesame oil, egg white, salt and cornflour. Mix well and drain off any excess liquid.

TO MAKE the dough, put the wheat starch, cornflour and oil in a bowl. Add 250 ml (1 cup) boiling water and mix until well combined. Add a little extra wheat starch if the dough is too sticky.

ROLL the dough into a long cylinder, divide it into 24 pieces and cover with a hot damp tea towel. Working with one portion at a time, roll out the dough using a rolling pin or a well-oiled cleaver. If using a rolling pin, roll the dough into a 9–10 cm (3¹/₂–4 inch) round between two pieces of oiled plastic wrap. If using a cleaver, place the blade facing away from you and gently press down on the flat side of the blade with your palm, squashing the dough while twisting the handle to form a round shape. Fill each wrapper as you make it.

PLACE a heaped teaspoon of the filling in the centre of each wrapper. Spread a little water along the edge of the wrapper and fold the wrapper over to make a half-moon shape. Use your thumb and index finger to form small pleats along the top edge. With the other hand, press the two opposite edges together to seal. Place the har gau in four steamers lined with greaseproof paper punched with holes. Cover the har gau as you make them to prevent them from drying out.

COVER AND steam the har gau over simmering water in a wok, reversing the steamers halfway through, for 6–8 minutes, or until the wrappers are translucent. Serve with soy sauce, chilli sauce or a dipping sauce.

Har gau pastry is more delicate to handle than noodle-type wrappers. To make it easier, keep the pastry warm and pliable while you are working with it.

TURNIP CAKE

ONE OF THE MORE COMMON DIM SUM, TURNIP CAKE IS SOLD BY WOMEN PUSHING HOT PLATES ON TROLLEYS. EACH PORTION OF THE TURNIP CAKE IS FRESHLY FRIED TO ORDER. SERVE WITH LIGHT SOY SAUCE OR A CHILLI SAUCE FOR DIPPING.

900 g (2 lb) Chinese turnip, grated
30 g (1 oz) dried shrimp
20 g (2 cups) dried Chinese
　mushrooms
150 g (5¹/₂ oz) Chinese sausage
　(lap cheong)
1 tablespoon oil
3 spring onions (scallions), thinly
　sliced
3 teaspoons sugar
3 teaspoons Shaoxing rice wine
¹/₄ teaspoon freshly ground
　white pepper
2 tablespoons finely chopped
　coriander (cilantro)
290 g (1²/₃ cups) rice flour
oil for frying

MAKES 6

PLACE the turnip in a large bowl and cover with boiling water for 5 minutes. Drain, reserving any liquid, then leave the turnip to drain in a colander. When it is cool enough to handle, squeeze out any excess liquid. Place in a large bowl.

SOAK the dried shrimp in boiling water for 1 hour, then drain, adding any soaking liquid to the reserved turnip liquid.

SOAK the dried mushrooms in boiling water for 30 minutes, then drain, adding any soaking liquid to the reserved turnip liquid. Squeeze out any excess water from the mushrooms. Remove and discard the stems and finely dice the caps.

PLACE the sausage on a plate in a steamer. Cover and steam over simmering water in a wok for 10 minutes, then finely dice it.

HEAT a wok over high heat, add the oil and heat until very hot. Stir-fry the sausage for 1 minute, then add the shrimp and mushrooms and stir-fry for 2 minutes, or until fragrant. Add the spring onion, sugar, rice wine and pepper, then add the turnip, coriander and rice flour and toss to combine. Add 500 ml (2 cups) of the reserved liquid. Mix well.

PLACE the mixture in a greased and lined 25 cm (10 inch) square cake tin (or in two smaller tins if your steamers are small). Place the tin in a steamer. Cover and steam over simmering water in a wok for 1¹/₄–1¹/₂ hours, or until firm, replenishing with boiling water during cooking. Remove the tin and cool in the fridge overnight. Take the cake from the tin and cut into 5 cm (2 inch) squares that are 1 cm (¹/₂ inch) thick.

HEAT a wok over high heat, add 2 tablespoons of the oil and heat until very hot. Cook the turnip cakes in batches, adding more oil between batches if necessary, until golden and crispy.

In dim sum restaurants, turnip cake is always fried to order.

葱油饼

SPRING ONION PANCAKES

ONE OF THE MOST POPULAR SNACKS IN NORTHERN CHINA IS CRISP SPRING ONION PANCAKES EATEN

STRAIGHT FROM THE HOT OIL. SOME RESTAURANTS ALSO MAKE BIG, THICK ONES THAT THEY CUT INTO

WEDGES AND SERVE AS AN ACCOMPANIMENT TO A MEAL.

250 g (2 cups) plain (all-purpose)
   flour
1/2 teaspoon salt
1 tablespoon oil
3 tablespoons roasted sesame oil
2 spring onions (scallions), green
   part only, finely chopped
oil for frying

MAKES 24

PLACE the flour and salt in a mixing bowl and stir to combine. Add the oil and 220 ml (8 fl oz) boiling water and, using a wooden spoon, mix to a rough dough. Turn the dough out onto a lightly floured surface and knead for 5 minutes, or until smooth and elastic. If the dough is very sticky, knead in a little more flour. Cover the dough with a cloth and let it rest for 20 minutes.

ON a lightly floured surface, use your hands to roll the dough into a long roll. Divide the dough into 24 pieces. Working with one portion of dough at a time, place the dough, cut edge down, on the work surface. Using a small rolling pin, roll it out to a 10 cm (4 inch) circle. Brush the surface generously with the sesame oil and sprinkle with some spring onion. Starting with the edge closest to you, roll up the dough and pinch the ends to seal in the spring onion and sesame oil. Lightly flatten the roll, then roll it up again from one end like a snail, pinching the end to seal it. Repeat with the remaining dough, sesame oil and spring onion. Let the rolls rest for 20 minutes.

PLACE EACH roll flat on the work surface and press down with the palm of your hand. Roll out to a 10 cm (4 inch) circle and place on a lightly floured tray. Stack the pancakes between lightly floured sheets of baking paper and leave to rest for 20 minutes.

HEAT a frying pan over medium heat, brush the surface with oil, and add two or three of the pancakes at a time. Cook for 2–3 minutes on each side, turning once, until the pancakes are light golden brown and crisp. Remove and drain on paper towels. Serve immediately.

YOU CAN reheat the pancakes, wrapped in foil, in a 180°C (350°F/Gas 4) oven for 15 minutes.

Spread the spring onion (scallion) through the dough by first rolling up the pancake and spring onion, then rolling this into a snail shape, and finally by rolling the snail into a pancake again.

蒸馒头

STEAMED BREADS

THE BASIC YEAST DOUGH CAN BE USED TO MAKE LOTS OF DIFFERENT STEAMED BUNS, CALLED MANTOU IN CHINA. FLOWER ROLLS ARE ONE OF THE SIMPLEST SHAPES, WHILE SILVER THREAD ROLLS REQUIRE MORE DEXTERITY. THESE BREADS ARE DELICIOUS WITH RED-COOKED MEATS INSTEAD OF RICE.

1 quantity basic yeast dough
 (page 278)
3 tablespoons roasted sesame oil

MAKES 12 FLOWER ROLLS
OR 6 SILVER THREAD LOAVES

Folding sesame oil into the dough means that when the breads are steamed, the layers will spring open.

Steaming mantou being sold in the streets in Beijing.

CUT the dough in half and, on a lightly floured surface, roll out each half to form a 30 x 10 cm (12 x 4 inch) rectangle. Brush the surface of the rectangles liberally with the sesame oil. Place one rectangle directly on top of the other, with both oiled surfaces facing up. Starting with one of the long edges, roll up the dough swiss-roll style. Pinch the two ends to seal in the sesame oil.

LIGHTLY FLATTEN the roll with the heel of your hand and cut the roll into 5 cm (2 inch) pieces. Using a chopstick, press down on the centre of each roll, holding the chopstick parallel to the cut edges. (This will cause the ends to 'flower' when they are steamed.) Arrange the shaped rolls well apart in four steamers lined with greaseproof paper punched with holes. Cover and let rise for 15 minutes.

COVER AND steam each steamer separately over simmering water in a wok for 15 minutes, or until the rolls are light and springy. Keep the rolls covered until you are about to eat them to make sure they stay soft.

THE DOUGH can also be shaped in other ways, one of the most popular being silver thread bread. Divide the dough in half and roll each half into a sausage about 3 cm (1¼ inches) in diameter, then cut each sausage into six pieces. Roll six of the pieces into rectangles 20 x 10 cm (8 x 4 inches) and set aside. Roll the remaining pieces into rectangles 20 x 10 cm (8 x 4 inches), brush each with a little sesame oil and fold in half to a 10 cm (4 inch) square. Brush with more sesame oil and fold in half again. Cut into thin strips crossways. Place one of the rectangles on the work surface and stretch the strips so they fit down the centre. Fold the ends and sides in to completely enclose the strips. Repeat with the remaining dough until you have six loaves. Steam as for the flower rolls for 20–25 minutes.

茶叶蛋

TEA EGGS

TEA EGGS, BRAISED IN A FRAGRANT TEA AND SOY SAUCE MIXTURE, ARE EASY TO MAKE AND GREAT FOR SNACKS—THEY CAN BE REHEATED AND TASTE EQUALLY GOOD HOT OR COLD. IN CHINA, THEY ARE FOUND IN TEA HOUSES AND ROADSIDE STALLS, OFTEN BUBBLING AWAY IN VATS FULL OF HOT TEA.

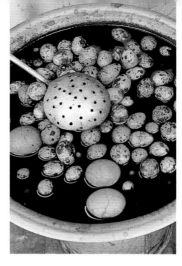

Tea eggs sold warm as a snack.

10 very fresh eggs or 20 quail eggs

TEA COOKING MIXTURE
3 tablespoons light soy sauce
3 tablespoons Shaoxing rice wine
1 star anise
1 tablespoon sugar
1 cinnamon stick
3 slices ginger, smashed with the flat side of a cleaver
3 tablespoons Chinese black tea leaves

MAKES 10 EGGS OR
20 QUAIL EGGS

PLACE the eggs in a saucepan with enough cold water to cover. Bring the water to the boil, then reduce the heat to low and let the eggs simmer for 10 minutes, or until they are hard-boiled. Refresh the eggs in cold water. Drain the eggs and lightly tap and roll the shells on a hard surface to crack them. Do not remove the shells.

PUT the tea cooking mixture ingredients in a heavy-based clay pot, casserole or saucepan with 1 litre (4 cups) water and heat until boiling. Reduce the heat to low and simmer for 20 minutes. Add the cooked eggs and simmer for 45 minutes. Turn off the heat and let the eggs sit in the tea mixture until cool enough to handle. Remove the shells and serve the eggs warm or cold, cut into wedges, with some of the cooking mixture on top.

脆皮猪耳沙律

CRISPY FRIED PIG'S EAR

EVERY PART OF THE PIG IS USED IN ONE WAY OR ANOTHER IN CHINESE COOKING. HERE PIG'S EARS ARE SLOW-COOKED WHOLE TO BRING OUT THEIR MELTING, GELATINOUS QUALITIES, THEN SHREDDED AND FRIED TO GIVE THEM A CRISP COATING. EAT AS A SNACK WITH DRINKS OR AS A STARTER.

1 pig's ear
1 tablespoon Shaoxing rice wine
1 tablespoon oil
2 garlic cloves, crushed
4 spring onions (scallions), thinly sliced
2 tablespoons light soy sauce
1/2 teaspoon salt
2 teaspoons chilli oil
2 teaspoons roasted sesame oil

SERVES 4 AS A SNACK

SCRAPE the pig's ear thoroughly to get rid of any bristles and rinse. Put it in a clay pot, casserole or saucepan, cover with water, add the rice wine and bring to the boil. Reduce the heat and simmer for 40 minutes, or until tender. Drain and leave to cool.

SLICE the ear diagonally into thin strips and finely shred the strips. Heat a wok over high heat, add the oil and heat until very hot. Cook the strips until very crisp. Add the garlic and spring onion and toss together. Add the soy sauce, salt, chilli and sesame oils and toss together. Serve immediately.

CRISPY FRIED PIG'S EAR

四川腌黄瓜

SICHUAN PICKLED CUCUMBER

THE COMPLEXITY OF FLAVOURS IN THIS SIMPLE PICKLE IS UNUSUAL. THE SEASONINGS COMBINE TO CREATE

A TASTE THAT IS SIMULTANEOUSLY SWEET, SOUR, HOT AND NUMBING.

200 g (7 oz) cucumbers
1/2 teaspoon salt
30 g (1 oz) ginger, finely shredded
1/2 small red chilli, seeded and
    finely shredded
3 tablespoons roasted sesame oil
1/2 teaspoon Sichuan peppercorns
6 dried chillies, seeded and cut into
    5 mm (1/4 inch) lengths
11/2 tablespoons clear rice vinegar
11/2 tablespoons sugar

SERVES 6 AS A SNACK

CUT the cucumbers in half lengthways, remove the seeds, and cut into 6 cm (21/2 inch) long, 2 cm (3/4 inch) thick slices. Place in a bowl, add the salt, toss lightly and leave for 30 minutes. Soak the ginger in a bowl of cold water for 20 minutes.

POUR OFF any water that has accumulated with the cucumber, rinse the cucumber lightly, then drain thoroughly and pat dry. Place the cucumber in a bowl with the drained ginger and chilli.

HEAT a wok over high heat, add the sesame oil and heat until very hot. Add the peppercorns and stir-fry for 15 seconds until fragrant. Add the dried chilli and stir-fry for 15 seconds, or until dark. Pour into the bowl with the cucumber, toss lightly and leave to cool. Add the vinegar and sugar, toss to coat, then leave in the fridge for at least 6 hours or overnight. Serve cold or at room temperature.

A wide variety of hot pickles are sold in the markets in Sichuan.

CANTONESE PICKLED
VEGETABLES

广东腌菜

CANTONESE PICKLED VEGETABLES

VARIATIONS OF PICKLED VEGETABLE SALADS ARE FOUND ALL OVER CHINA. THIS SWEET-AND-SOUR

VERSION FROM THE SOUTH IS GOOD ALONE OR WITH SWEET-AND-SOUR PRAWNS (SHRIMP) OR PORK.

200 g (7 oz) Chinese turnip, peeled
2 carrots
1 cucumber
1/2 teaspoon salt
100 g (31/2 oz) sugar
100 ml (31/2 fl oz) clear rice vinegar
5 thin slices ginger, smashed with
    the flat side of a cleaver

SERVES 6 AS A SNACK

CUT the turnip in half lengthways, then cut lengthways into thirds and diagonally cut into 2 cm (3/4 inch) pieces. Diagonally cut the carrots into 2 cm (3/4 inch) pieces. Cut the cucumber in half lengthways, remove any seeds and cut lengthways into thirds. Diagonally cut into 2 cm (3/4 inch) pieces. Lightly toss the vegetables and salt in a bowl. Set aside for 1 hour. Dry thoroughly.

COMBINE the sugar and vinegar and stir until the sugar has dissolved. Add to the vegetables with the ginger and toss lightly to coat. Leave in the fridge for at least 6 hours, or overnight.

盐水蚕豆

SALTED SOYA BEAN PODS

300 g (10¹/₂ oz) fresh soya bean
 pods
1 tablespoon coarse sea salt
4 star anise

SERVES 4 AS A SNACK

TOP AND tail the soya bean pods, then place in a bowl with the salt and rub some of the fuzz off the skin. Rinse the pods. Place in a saucepan of salted water with the star anise and bring to the boil. Reduce the heat and simmer for 20 minutes, or until tender. Drain and leave to cool.

TO EAT, suck the beans out of the pods and throw the pods away. Serve as a snack.

SALTED SOYA BEAN PODS

油炸花生米

FRIED PEANUTS

1 tablespoon Sichuan peppercorns
4 star anise
1 tablespoon sugar
1 teaspoon salt
450 g (1 lb) shelled peanuts, skins on
3 tablespoons roasted sesame oil

SERVES 8 AS A SNACK

PUT the spices, sugar, salt and 750 ml (3 cups) water in a saucepan and bring to the boil. Add the peanuts and simmer for 5 minutes. Turn off the heat and leave the peanuts to cool in the liquid.

DRAIN AND dry the peanuts, removing the whole spices. Heat the sesame oil in a wok and fry the peanuts until brown. Serve warm or cold as a snack.

FRIED PEANUTS

蜜饯核桃仁

CANDIED WALNUTS

250 g (9 oz) sugar
450 g (1 lb) shelled walnut halves
oil for deep-frying

SERVES 8 AS A SNACK

DISSOLVE the sugar in 100 ml (3¹/₂ fl oz) water, then bring to the boil and cook for 2 minutes.

BLANCH the walnuts in a pan of boiling water briefly, then drain. Tip immediately into the syrup, stirring to coat. Cool for 5 minutes, then drain.

FILL a wok one-quarter full of oil. Heat the oil to 190°C (375°F), or until a piece of bread fries golden brown in 10 seconds when dropped in the oil. Add the walnuts in batches, stirring to brown evenly. As soon as they brown, remove with a wire sieve or slotted spoon and put on some foil, making sure they are well spaced. Do not touch as they will be hot. When cool, drain on paper towels. Serve as a snack or at the start of a meal.

CANDIED WALNUTS

SOUPS

Stripping corn cobs in Yunnan.

CHICKEN AND
MUSHROOM SOUP

港式玉米汤

CANTONESE CORN SOUP

THIS DELECTABLE SOUP IS A CANTONESE CLASSIC. YOU NEED TO USE A GOOD-QUALITY CAN OF CREAMED CORN WITH A SMOOTH TEXTURE, OR ALTERNATIVELY, IF IT IS QUITE COARSE, QUICKLY BLEND YOUR CREAMED CORN IN A BLENDER OR FOOD PROCESSOR TO MAKE IT EXTRA SMOOTH.

250 g (9 oz) skinless chicken breast
  fillet, minced (ground)
150 ml (5 fl oz) Shaoxing rice wine
400 g (14 oz) canned creamed
  corn
1.5 litres (6 cups) chicken stock
  (page 281)
1 teaspoon salt
2¹/₂ tablespoons cornflour
  (cornstarch)
2 egg whites, lightly beaten
1 teaspoon roasted sesame oil

SERVES 6

PLACE the chicken in a bowl, add 3 tablespoons of the rice wine and stir to combine. In a large clay pot or saucepan, combine the creamed corn, stock, remaining rice wine and salt. Bring to the boil, stirring. Add the chicken and stir to separate the meat. Return to the boil and skim any scum from the surface.

COMBINE the cornflour with enough water to make a paste, add to the soup and simmer until thickened. Remove from the heat. Mix 2 tablespoons water into the egg white, then slowly add to the clay pot or saucepan in a thin stream around the edge of the pan. Stir once or twice, then add the sesame oil. Check the seasoning, adding more salt if necessary. Serve immediately.

蘑菇鸡汤

CHICKEN AND MUSHROOM SOUP

FOR THIS SOUP YOU CAN USE EITHER BUTTON OR CHINESE MUSHROOMS. CHINESE MUSHROOMS ARE USUALLY LABELLED SHIITAKE (THE JAPANESE NAME FOR THEM) WHEN FRESH AND WILL ADD MORE FLAVOUR TO THE FINISHED SOUP.

2 tablespoons cornflour (cornstarch)
3–4 egg whites, beaten
1 teaspoon salt
100 g (3¹/₂ oz) skinless chicken
  breast fillet, thinly sliced
750 ml (3 cups) chicken and meat
  stock (page 281)
100 g (3¹/₂ oz) button or Chinese
  (shiitake) mushrooms, thinly sliced
1 teaspoon roasted sesame oil
chopped spring onion (scallion)

SERVES 4

COMBINE the cornflour with enough water to make a paste. Mix 1 teaspoon each of the egg white and cornflour paste and a pinch of salt with the chicken. Blend the remaining egg white and cornflour mixture to a smooth paste.

BRING the stock to a rolling boil in a large clay pot or saucepan. Add the chicken and return to the boil, then add the mushrooms and salt. Return to the boil then, very slowly, pour in the egg white and cornflour mixture, stirring constantly. As soon as the soup has thickened, add the sesame oil. Serve sprinkled with the spring onion.

鱼翅汤

SHARK'S FIN SOUP

ONE OF THE MOST EXPENSIVE AND PRIZED OF ALL CHINESE DELICACIES, SHARK'S FIN IS SERVED ON SPECIAL OCCASIONS AND AT BANQUETS. IF POSSIBLE, MAKE THE STOCK A DAY IN ADVANCE AND STORE IN THE FRIDGE. THIS WILL IMPROVE THE FLAVOURS AND ALLOW ANY FAT TO EASILY BE SKIMMED OFF.

Shark's fin is available ready-prepared, usually compressed and shrink-wrapped in packages. It just needs to be soaked and simmered to soften it.

300 g (10½ oz) ready-prepared
  shark's fin
400 g (14 oz) bacon or ham bones
500 g (1 lb 2 oz) chicken bones
500 g (1 lb 2 oz) beef bones
4 slices ginger
300 g (10½ oz) skinless chicken
  breast fillet, minced (ground)
1 egg white, lightly beaten
4 tablespoons cornflour (cornstarch)
1 tablespoon light soy sauce
red rice vinegar

SERVES 6

PLACE the shark's fin in a large bowl and cover with cold water. Leave to soak overnight. Strain the shark's fin and rinse gently to remove any remaining sand and sediment. Bring a stockpot of water to the boil. Add the shark's fin, reduce the heat and simmer, covered, for 1 hour. Strain and set aside.

PLACE the bacon or ham bones, chicken bones and beef bones in a large stockpot with the ginger slices and 2 litres (8 cups) water. Bring to the boil, then reduce the heat and simmer, covered, for 2 hours. Skim off any scum and fat during cooking. Strain the stock, discarding the bones. Measure the stock—you will need 1.5–1.75 litres (6–7 cups). If you have more, return the stock to the pan and reduce it further until you have the correct amount.

COMBINE the chicken, egg white and 1 tablespoon of the cornflour. Set aside in the fridge.

PUT the prepared shark's fin and stock in a large clay pot or saucepan and simmer, covered, for 30 minutes. Add the chicken mixture and stir to separate the meat. Simmer for 10 minutes, or until the chicken is cooked.

SEASON the soup with the soy sauce and some salt and white pepper. Combine the remaining cornflour with 125 ml (½ cup) water, add to the soup and simmer until thickened.

SERVE the soup with some red rice vinegar, which can be added to the soup to taste.

To see if they have been fertilized, eggs are checked at the market by placing them above a light.

Scalding the tomatoes in boiling water makes it very easy to slip off their skins.

TOMATO AND EGG SOUP

THIS DELICIOUS AND NUTRITIOUS SOUP IS SIMPLICITY ITSELF AND IS SOMETIMES KNOWN AS AN EGG DROP SOUP BECAUSE THE EGG IS SLOWLY POURED IN NEAR THE END OF COOKING. MAKE SURE YOU USE RIPE TOMATOES OR BOTH THE COLOUR AND FLAVOUR WILL BE INSIPID.

250 g (9 oz) firm ripe tomatoes
2 eggs
1 spring onion (scallion), finely
  chopped
1 tablespoon oil
1 litre (4 cups) vegetable or chicken
  and meat stock (page 281)
1 tablespoon light soy sauce
1 tablespoon cornflour (cornstarch)

SERVES 4

SCORE a cross in the bottom of each tomato. Plunge into boiling water for 20 seconds, then drain and peel the skin away from the cross. Cut into slices or thin wedges, trimming off the core. Beat the eggs with a pinch of salt and a few pieces of spring onion.

HEAT a wok over high heat, add the oil and heat until very hot. Stir-fry the spring onion for a few seconds to flavour the oil, then pour in the stock and bring to the boil. Add the tomato and return to the boil. Add the soy sauce and very slowly pour in the beaten eggs, stirring as you pour. Return to the boil.

COMBINE the cornflour with enough water to make a paste, add to the soup and simmer until thickened.

TOMATO AND EGG SOUP

TOFU AND SPINACH SOUP

THIS SIMPLE BUT BEAUTIFUL SOUP IS ALSO KNOWN AS 'EMERALD AND WHITE JADE SOUP' IN CHINESE. IT IS A CLEAR SOUP, WHICH REQUIRES A VERY GOOD STOCK FOR FLAVOUR, WHILE PIECES OF SOFT TOFU ADD TEXTURE AND THE SPINACH ADDS COLOUR AND FLAVOUR.

120 g (4 oz) soft tofu, drained
100 g (3¹/2 oz) baby English
  spinach leaves
1 litre (4 cups) chicken and meat
  stock (page 281)
1 tablespoon light soy sauce

SERVES 4

CUT the tofu into small slices about 5 mm (¹/4 inch) thick. Chop the baby spinach leaves roughly if they are large.

BRING the stock to a rolling boil in a large clay pot or saucepan, then add the tofu slices and soy sauce. Return to the boil, then reduce the heat and simmer gently for 2 minutes. Skim any scum from the surface. Add the spinach and cook for 1–2 minutes. Season with salt and white pepper. Serve hot.

冬瓜火腿汤

WINTER MELON AND HAM SOUP

ALTHOUGH IT LOOKS LIKE A WATERMELON, A WINTER MELON IS REALLY A MARROW OR WAX GOURD. IT IS SAID THAT WINTER MELONS WITH A GOOD COVERING OF WHITE POWDER ARE BEST. THE DELICATE FLESH BECOMES ALMOST TRANSLUCENT WHEN COOKED AND TASTES A LITTLE LIKE MARROW.

1 tablespoon dried shrimp
250 g (9 oz) winter melon, rind and
 seeds removed
750 ml (3 cups) chicken and meat
 stock (page 281)
150 g (5¹/₂ oz) Chinese ham or
 prosciutto, chopped

SERVES 4

SOAK the dried shrimp in boiling water for 1 hour, then drain. Cut the winter melon into small pieces.

BRING the stock to a rolling boil in a large clay pot or saucepan. Add the dried shrimp, winter melon and ham. Return to the boil, then reduce the heat and simmer for 2 minutes. Season with salt and white pepper. Serve hot.

什锦菜汤

MIXED VEGETABLE SOUP

ALMOST ANY TYPE OF VEGETABLE CAN BE USED FOR THIS SOUP. CHOOSE THREE OR FOUR DIFFERENT ITEMS FROM THE INGREDIENTS LIST DEPENDING ON WHAT'S IN SEASON, BEARING IN MIND THAT THEY SHOULD CREATE A HARMONY IN COLOUR AND TEXTURES.

500 g (1 lb 2 oz) mixed vegetables,
 such as carrots, baby corn,
 bamboo shoots, Chinese
 (shiitake) or button mushrooms,
 asparagus, English spinach
 leaves, lettuce, cucumber,
 Chinese cabbage or tomato
120 g (4 oz) soft tofu, drained
750 ml (3 cups) vegetable or
 chicken stock (page 281)
1 tablespoon light soy sauce
¹/₂ teaspoon roasted sesame oil
chopped spring onion (scallion)
 or chives

SERVES 4

CUT YOUR selection of vegetables and the tofu into a roughly uniform shape and size. You can cut into shreds, cubes or slices, but the pieces should be small enough for a spoonful of soup to include several at once, giving a balance of flavours.

BRING the stock to a rolling boil in a large clay pot or saucepan. Add your selection of the carrots, corn, bamboo shoots and mushrooms first and cook for 2–3 minutes, then add any other vegetables and the tofu and cook for 1 minute. Do not overcook the vegetables or they will become soggy and lose their crispness and delicate flavour.

SEASON WITH salt and white pepper. Add the soy sauce, drizzle with the sesame oil and sprinkle with the spring onion or chives.

WINTER MELON AND
HAM SOUP

鱼片香菜汤

SLICED FISH AND CORIANDER SOUP

THE CHINESE OFTEN USE A CHICKEN AND MEAT STOCK WHEN COOKING SEAFOOD. HOWEVER, IF YOU

PREFER, YOU CAN USE A VEGETABLE OR FISH STOCK FOR THIS RECIPE.

250 g (9 oz) firm white fish fillets, such as cod, halibut or monkfish, skin removed
2 teaspoons egg white, beaten
1 teaspoon Shaoxing rice wine
2 teaspoons cornflour (cornstarch)
750 ml (3 cups) chicken and meat stock (page 281)
1 tablespoon light soy sauce
40 g (1¹/₂ oz) coriander (cilantro) leaves

SERVES 4

CUT the fish into 2 x 3 cm (³/₄ x 1¹/₄ inch) slices. Blend the egg white, rice wine and cornflour to make a smooth paste, and use it to coat each fish slice.

BRING the stock to a rolling boil in a large clay pot or saucepan. Add the fish slices one by one, stir gently and return to the boil. Reduce the heat and simmer for 1 minute, then add the soy sauce and coriander leaves. Return to the boil, season with salt and white pepper and serve immediately.

Using a cornflour (cornstarch) mixture to coat seafood before cooking is called 'velveting'. The coating adds a silky texture to the cooked food as well as protecting it and keeping it moist.

西湖牛肉汤

WEST LAKE BEEF SOUP

THERE IS A WEST LAKE (AND OFTEN A NORTH, SOUTH OR EAST LAKE) IN MOST CITIES IN CHINA, SO

THIS SOUP IS MORE LIKELY NAMED AFTER A LAKE IN ITS PROVINCE OF ORIGIN, GUANGZHOU, THAN THE

FAMOUS WEST LAKE OF HANGZHOU.

150 g (5¹/₂ oz) rump or fillet steak
1 teaspoon salt
1 teaspoon sugar
1 tablespoon light soy sauce
1 tablespoon Shaoxing rice wine
2 tablespoons cornflour (cornstarch)
¹/₂ teaspoon roasted sesame oil
750 ml (3 cups) chicken and meat stock (page 281)
100 g (3¹/₂ oz) peas, fresh or frozen
1 egg, lightly beaten
1 chopped spring onion (scallion)

SERVES 4

TRIM the fat off the steak and cut the steak into small pieces, about the size of the peas. Combine the beef with a pinch of the salt, about half the sugar, 1 teaspoon each of the soy sauce, rice wine and cornflour and the sesame oil. Marinate in the fridge for at least 20 minutes.

BRING the stock to a rolling boil in a large clay pot or saucepan. Add the beef and stir to separate the meat, then add the peas and the remaining salt, sugar, soy sauce and rice wine. Return to the boil, then stir in the egg. Combine the remaining cornflour with enough water to make a paste, add to the soup and simmer until thickened. Garnish with the spring onion.

WEST LAKE BEEF SOUP

十宝炖汤

TEN-TREASURE SOUP

THIS MEAL-IN-ONE SOUP IS ALMOST A KIND OF STEW, WHERE THE INGREDIENTS SIMMER TOGETHER SO THAT THE FLAVOURS MIX. TRADITIONALLY THIS SOUP HAS TEN MAIN INGREDIENTS, BUT THE EXACT NUMBER DOES NOT MATTER AND YOU CAN VARY THE INGREDIENTS DEPENDING ON WHAT'S AVAILABLE.

400 g (14 oz) Chinese cabbage
2 tablespoons oil
4 garlic cloves, smashed with the
   flat side of a cleaver
125 ml (1/2 cup) Shaoxing rice wine
1.5 litres (6 cups) chicken stock
   (page 281)
1 teaspoon salt
250 g (9 oz) centre-cut pork loin,
   trimmed
2 teaspoons light soy sauce
1/2 teaspoon roasted sesame oil
450 g (1 lb) prawns (shrimp)
3 slices ginger, smashed with the
   flat side of a cleaver
30 g (1 oz) bean thread noodles
6 dried Chinese mushrooms
450 g (1 lb) firm tofu, drained and
   cut into 2.5 cm (1 inch) squares
2 carrots, cut into 2 cm (3/4 inch)
   pieces
200 g (1/2 bunch) baby English
   spinach leaves
3 spring onions (scallions), green
   part only, cut diagonally into 1 cm
   (1/2 inch) lengths

SERVES 6

REMOVE the stems from the cabbage and cut the leaves into 5 cm (2 inch) squares. Separate the hard cabbage pieces from the leafy ones. Heat a wok over high heat, add the oil and heat until very hot. Add the hard cabbage pieces and the garlic. Toss lightly over high heat, adding 1 tablespoon of the rice wine. Stir-fry for several minutes, then add the leafy cabbage pieces. Stir-fry for 1 minute, then add 4 tablespoons of the rice wine, the stock and half of the salt. Bring to the boil, then reduce the heat to low and cook for 30 minutes. Transfer to a clay pot or saucepan.

CUT the pork across the grain into slices about 2 mm (1/8 inch) thick. Place the pork in a bowl, add the soy sauce and sesame oil, and toss lightly. Marinate in the fridge for 20 minutes.

PEEL and devein the prawns, then place in a bowl with the ginger, remaining rice wine and salt and toss lightly. Marinate in the fridge for 20 minutes. Remove and discard the ginger.

SOAK the bean thread noodles in hot water for 10 minutes, then drain and cut into 15 cm (6 inch) lengths. Soak the dried mushrooms in boiling water for 30 minutes, then drain and squeeze out any excess water. Remove and discard the stems.

ARRANGE the pork slices, tofu, mushrooms, noodles and carrot in separate piles on top of the cabbage in the casserole, leaving some space in the centre for the prawns and spinach. Cover and cook over medium heat for 20 minutes. Arrange the prawns and spinach in the centre and sprinkle with the spring onion. Cover and cook for 5 minutes, or until the prawns are pink and cooked through. Season with salt if necessary. Serve directly from the pot.

Use the flat side of a cleaver to smash the garlic cloves and the blade for cutting the carrots.

Adding the egg to the hot soup forms egg drops. Pour it in in an even stream.

酸辣汤

HOT-AND-SOUR SOUP

THIS SOUP SHOULD NOT CONTAIN HOT CHILLIES—THE HOTNESS COMES FROM GROUND WHITE PEPPER, WHICH, IN ORDER TO GET A GOOD FLAVOUR, MUST BE VERY FRESHLY GROUND.

4 dried Chinese mushrooms
2 tablespoons dried black fungus
   (wood ears)
100 g (3¹/₂ oz) lean pork, shredded
1 tablespoon cornflour (cornstarch)
120 g (4 oz) firm tofu, drained
60 g (¹/₄ cup) fresh or tinned bamboo
   shoots, rinsed and drained
1 litre (4 cups) chicken and meat
   stock (page 281)
1 teaspoon salt
1 tablespoon Shaoxing rice wine
2 tablespoons light soy sauce
1–2 tablespoons Chinese black
   rice vinegar
2 eggs, beaten
1–2 teaspoons freshly ground white
   pepper
1 chopped spring onion (scallion)

SERVES 4

SOAK the dried mushrooms in boiling water for 30 minutes, then drain and squeeze out any excess water. Remove and discard the stems and shred the caps. Soak the dried black fungus in cold water for 20 minutes, then drain and squeeze out any excess water. Shred the black fungus.

COMBINE the pork, a pinch of salt and 1 teaspoon of the cornflour. Thinly shred the tofu and bamboo shoots to the same size as the pork.

BRING the stock to the boil in a large clay pot or saucepan. Add the pork and stir to separate the meat, then add the mushroom, fungus, tofu and bamboo. Return to the boil and add the salt, rice wine, soy and vinegar. Slowly pour in the egg, whisking to form thin threads, and cook for 1 minute. Combine the remaining cornflour with enough water to make a paste, add to the soup and simmer until thickened. Put the pepper in a bowl, pour in the soup and stir. Garnish with spring onion.

LAMB AND CUCUMBER SOUP

羊肉黄瓜汤

LAMB AND CUCUMBER SOUP

250 g (9 oz) lamb fillet
1 tablespoon Shaoxing rice wine
1 tablespoon light soy sauce
1 teaspoon roasted sesame oil
¹/₂ cucumber
750 ml (3 cups) chicken and meat
   stock (page 281)
2 teaspoons Chinese black rice
   vinegar, or to taste
coriander (cilantro) leaves

SERVES 4

CUT the lamb into very thin slices and combine with the rice wine, soy sauce and sesame oil. Marinate in the fridge for at least 15 minutes. Halve the cucumber lengthways, discarding the seeds, and cut it into thin slices.

BRING the stock to a rolling boil in a large clay pot or saucepan. Add the lamb and stir to separate the meat. Return to the boil, then add the cucumber and rice vinegar, and season with salt and white pepper. Return to the boil. Serve garnished with the coriander leaves.

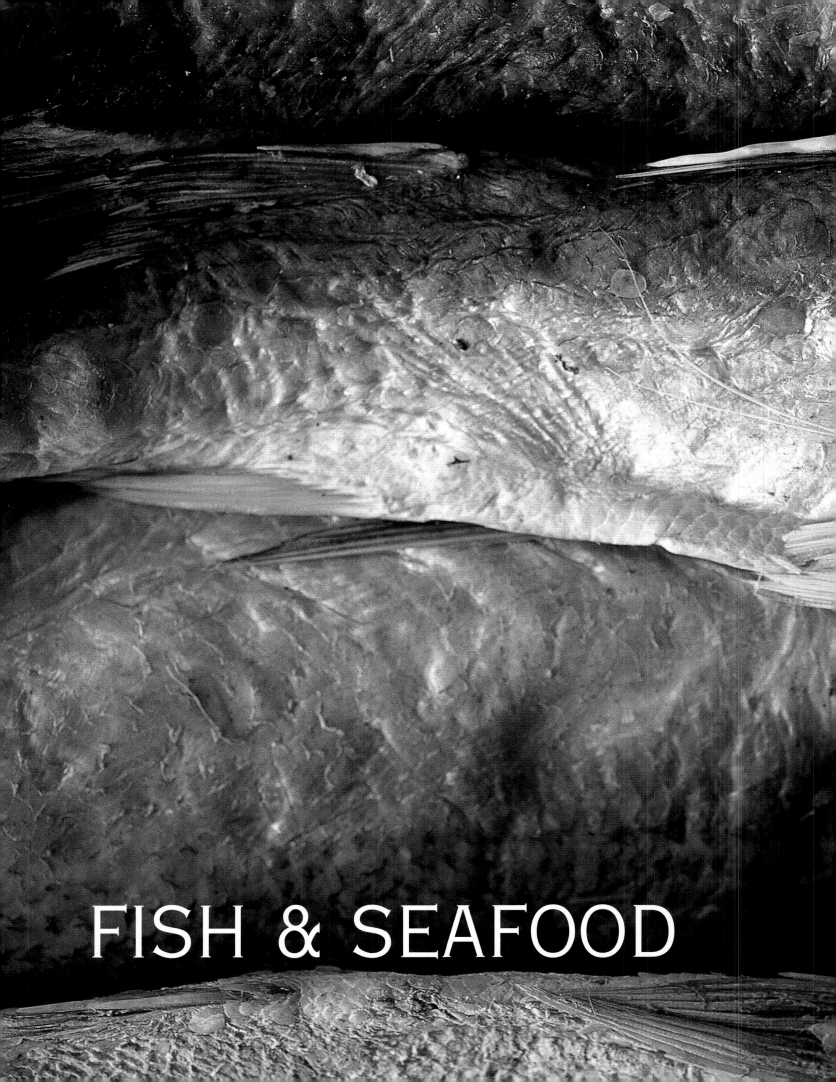

FISH & SEAFOOD

极品海鲜（鲍鱼、焖荷兰豆和凤尾菇）

ABALONE, SNOWPEAS AND OYSTER MUSHROOMS

ABALONE IS EATEN IN CHINA AT FESTIVAL TIMES, ESPECIALLY AT NEW YEAR AS THE CHINESE NAME BAU YU SOUNDS JUST LIKE THE WORDS FOR 'GUARANTEED WEALTH'. DRIED ABALONE IS OFTEN USED IN CHINA, BUT FRESH OR TINNED ABALONE IS MUCH EASIER TO PREPARE.

Remove the meat from the abalone by severing the muscle that holds it to the shell. Trim off any hard patches.

New Year fireworks over Beijing.

1.3 kg (3 lb) fresh abalone (450 g/
   1 lb prepared weight) or 450 g
   (1 lb) tinned abalone
300 g (10$^1/_2$ oz) snowpeas
   (mangetout), ends trimmed
150 g (5$^1/_2$ oz) oyster mushrooms
2 tablespoons oil
2 garlic cloves, finely chopped
2 teaspoons finely chopped ginger
2 tablespoons oyster sauce
2 teaspoons light soy sauce
1 teaspoon sugar
3 teaspoons cornflour (cornstarch)

SERVES 4

PREPARE the fresh abalone by removing the meat from the shell using a sharp knife. Wash the meat under cold running water, rubbing well to remove any dark-coloured slime. Trim off any hard outer edges and the mouth as well as any hard patches on the bottom of the foot. Pound the meat with a mallet for 1 minute to tenderize it, but be careful not to break the flesh.

PLACE the fresh abalone in a saucepan of simmering water and cook, covered, for about 2 hours, or until the meat is tender (test it by seeing if a fork will pierce the meat easily). Drain the abalone and, when it is cool enough to handle, cut it into thin slices.

IF YOU are using tinned abalone, simply drain, reserving the juice, and cut into thin slices.

CUT any large snowpeas in half diagonally. Halve any large oyster mushrooms.

HEAT a wok over medium heat, add the oil and heat until hot. Stir-fry the snowpeas and mushrooms for 1 minute. Add the garlic and ginger and stir for 1 minute, or until aromatic.

REDUCE the heat slightly and add the oyster sauce, soy sauce, sugar and the sliced abalone. Stir well to combine. Combine the cornflour with enough water (or the reserved abalone juice if using tinned abalone) to make a paste, add to the sauce and simmer until thickened.

极品海鲜（鲍鱼、焖荷兰豆和凤尾菇）

CANTONESE-STYLE STEAMED FISH

ALL CHINESE COOKS, BUT PARTICULARLY THE CANTONESE, DEMAND THE FRESHEST INGREDIENTS. THE LUSH LAND OF GUANGZHOU PROVIDES FRESH VEGETABLES, AND SINCE THE REGION IS BORDERED BY THE SEA AND HAS MANY RIVERS AND LAKES, FISH IS SOLD LIVE AND KILLED JUST BEFORE COOKING.

750 g–1 kg (1 lb 10 oz–2 lb 4 oz) whole fish, such as carp, bream, grouper or sea bass
2 tablespoons Shaoxing rice wine
1¹/₂ tablespoons light soy sauce
1 tablespoon finely chopped ginger
1 teaspoon roasted sesame oil
2 tablespoons oil
2 spring onions (scallions), finely shredded
3 tablespoons finely shredded ginger
¹/₄ teaspoon freshly ground black pepper

SERVES 4

Test if the flesh of the fish is cooked by pressing it to see if it feels or looks flaky—you can either use a pair of chopsticks or your fingers.

IF YOU do manage to buy a swimming (live) fish, then ask the fishmonger to gut it through the gills. This is harder than gutting through the stomach, but leaves the fish looking whole. If you are gutting the fish yourself, make a cut from the throat to the tail and pull out the guts through the stomach. Remove any scales with a fish scaler or the back of a knife. Check that the gills have been cut out, then rinse the fish under cold, running water and drain thoroughly in a colander.

PLACE the fish in a large bowl. Add the rice wine, soy sauce, chopped ginger and sesame oil, and toss lightly to coat. Cover with plastic wrap and leave to marinate in the fridge for 10 minutes.

ARRANGE the fish on a heatproof plate, with the marinade, and place in a steamer. Steam over simmering water in a covered wok for 5–8 minutes, or until the fish flakes when the skin is pressed firmly or the dorsal fin pulls out easily. Remove the fish from the steamer and place on a heatproof platter.

HEAT a wok over high heat, add the oil and heat until smoking. Sprinkle the steamed fish with the spring onion, shredded ginger and pepper, and slowly pour the hot oil over the fish. This will cause the skin to crisp, and cook the garnish.

Scrub off any barnacles from the mussels, then remove the beards (byssus) by tugging on them firmly.

豆豉蒸蚌

STEAMED MUSSELS WITH BLACK BEAN SAUCE

MUSSELS ARE NOT EATEN AS MUCH IN CHINA AS CLAMS, HOWEVER, THEY ARE ENJOYED IN SEASIDE AREAS. THIS RECIPE WORKS EQUALLY WELL WITH CLAMS IF YOU PREFER.

1 kg (2 lb 4 oz) mussels
1 tablespoon oil
1 garlic clove, finely chopped
1/2 teaspoon finely chopped ginger
2 spring onions (scallions), finely chopped
1 red chilli, chopped
1 tablespoon light soy sauce
1 tablespoon Shaoxing rice wine
1 tablespoon salted, fermented black beans, rinsed and mashed
2 tablespoons chicken and meat stock (page 281)
few drops of roasted sesame oil

SERVES 4

SCRUB the mussels, remove any beards, and throw away any that do not close when tapped on the work surface.

PLACE the mussels in a large dish in a steamer. Steam over simmering water in a covered wok for 4 minutes, discarding any that do not open after this time.

MEANWHILE, HEAT the oil in a small saucepan. Add the garlic, ginger, spring onion and chilli and cook, stirring, for 30 seconds. Add the remaining ingredients, and blend well. Bring to the boil, then reduce the heat and simmer for 1 minute.

TO SERVE, remove and discard the top shell of each mussel, pour 2 teaspoons of the sauce into each mussel and serve on the shell.

CLAMS IN YELLOW BEAN SAUCE

豆酱焖蛤

CLAMS IN YELLOW BEAN SAUCE

CLAMS ARE IMMENSELY POPULAR IN CHINA AND ARE SEEN AS A SYMBOL OF GOOD FORTUNE AS THEIR SHELLS ARE SAID TO LOOK LIKE COINS. THIS IS A VERY SIMPLE RECIPE FOR THEM.

1.5 kg (3 lb 5 oz) hard-shelled clams (vongole)
1 tablespoon oil
2 garlic cloves, crushed
1 tablespoon grated ginger
2 tablespoons yellow bean sauce
125 ml (1/2 cup) chicken stock (page 281)
1 spring onion (scallion), sliced

SERVES 4

WASH the clams in several changes of cold water, leaving them for a few minutes each time to remove any grit. Scrub the clams well, discarding any that remain open. Drain well.

HEAT a wok over high heat, add the oil and heat until very hot. Stir-fry the garlic and ginger for 30 seconds, then add the bean sauce and clams and toss together. Add the stock and stir for 3 minutes until the clams have opened, discarding any that do not open after this time. Season with salt and white pepper. Transfer the clams to a plate and sprinkle with spring onion.

The Li River in Guangxi.

Fishermen on the Li River use tame cormorants to catch fish.

 熏鱼

SMOKED FISH

IN FACT, THE FISH IN THIS DISH IS NOT SMOKED AT ALL. INSTEAD IT ACQUIRES A SMOKY FLAVOUR FROM BEING MARINATED AND BRAISED IN A SPICY SAUCE, THEN BEING DEEP-FRIED AND MARINATED IN THE SAUCE ONCE MORE BEFORE SERVING.

2 tablespoons light soy sauce
1 tablespoon dark soy sauce
3 tablespoons Shaoxing rice wine
2 tablespoons rock (lump) sugar
2 teaspoons five-spice powder
1 spring onion (scallion), finely chopped
2 teaspoons finely chopped ginger
450 g (1 lb) firm white fish fillets, such as haddock, monkfish or sea bass, skin on
310 ml (1¼ cups) chicken and meat stock (page 281)
oil for deep-frying
coriander (cilantro) leaves

SERVES 6

MIX together the soy sauces, rice wine, sugar, five-spice powder, spring onion and ginger. Pat dry the fish and leave in the marinade for 1 hour. Transfer the fish and marinade to a clay pot or saucepan. Add the stock and bring to the boil. Reduce the heat and simmer gently for 10 minutes, or until the fish is cooked through, then drain the fish, reserving the marinade.

FILL a wok one-quarter full of oil. Heat the oil to 190°C (375°F), or until a piece of bread fries golden brown in 10 seconds when dropped in the oil. Carefully cook the fish in batches for 3–4 minutes, or until golden and crisp (it will spit a little). Remove the fish from the oil and return it to the marinade. Leave to cool for 2–3 hours.

REMOVE the fish from the marinade and leave to dry for a few minutes. Cut the fish into thin slices and serve cold, sprinkled with coriander leaves.

THE MARINADE can be reused as a 'Master Sauce' (see page 290).

Score the inside of the squid with fine lines in a crisscross pattern before cutting into pieces.

STIR-FRIED SQUID FLOWERS WITH CAPSICUM

油炸椒盐苏东

DEEP-FRIED SQUID FLOWERS WITH SPICY SALT

500 g (1 lb 2 oz) squid tubes
1 teaspoon ginger juice (page 285)
1 tablespoon Shaoxing rice wine
oil for deep-frying
2 teaspoons spicy salt and pepper
  (page 285)
coriander (cilantro) leaves

SERVES 4

OPEN UP the squid tubes and scrub off any soft jelly-like substance, then score the inside of the flesh with a fine crisscross pattern, making sure you do not cut all the way through. Cut the squid into 3 x 5 cm (1¼ x 2 inch) pieces.

BLANCH the squid in a pan of boiling water for 25–30 seconds—each piece will curl up and the crisscross pattern will open out, hence the name 'squid flower'. Remove and refresh in cold water, then drain and dry well. Marinate the squid in the ginger juice and rice wine for 25–30 minutes.

FILL a wok one-quarter full of oil. Heat the oil to 180°C (350°F), or until a piece of bread fries golden brown in 15 seconds when dropped in the oil. Cook the squid for 35–40 seconds, then remove and drain well. Sprinkle with the spicy salt and pepper and toss to coat. Serve sprinkled with the coriander.

辣椒炒苏东

STIR-FRIED SQUID FLOWERS WITH CAPSICUM

400 g (14 oz) squid tubes
3 tablespoons oil
2 tablespoons salted, fermented
  black beans, rinsed and mashed
1 small onion, cut into small cubes
1 small green capsicum (pepper),
  cut into small cubes
3–4 small slices ginger
1 spring onion (scallion), cut into
  short lengths
1 small red chilli, chopped
1 tablespoon Shaoxing rice wine
½ teaspoon roasted sesame oil

SERVES 4

OPEN UP the squid tubes and scrub off any soft jelly-like substance, then score the inside of the flesh with a fine crisscross pattern, making sure you do not cut all the way through. Cut the squid into 3 x 5 cm (1¼ x 2 inch) pieces.

BLANCH the squid in a pan of boiling water for 25–30 seconds—each piece will curl up and the crisscross pattern will open out, hence the name 'squid flower'. Remove and refresh in cold water, then drain and dry well.

HEAT a wok over high heat, add the oil and heat until very hot. Stir-fry the black beans, onion, green capsicum, ginger, spring onion and chilli for 1 minute. Add the squid and rice wine, mix together and stir for 1 minute. Sprinkle with the sesame oil.

西湖鱼

WEST LAKE FISH

HANGZHOU IN THE EAST OF CHINA IS FAMOUS FOR ITS REFINED CUISINE AND EXQUISITE SCENERY. A SPECIALITY OF THIS REGION IS WEST LAKE FISH MADE WITH FRESHWATER CARP. THE POACHING METHOD IS UNIQUE AND QUITE INGENIOUS AS THE FISH IS COOKED OFF THE HEAT.

1 x 1.75 kg (4 lb) whole fish,
    such as carp, bream, grouper or
    sea bass
4 tablespoons Shaoxing rice wine
2 teaspoons salt
4 slices ginger, smashed with the
    flat side of a cleaver
4 spring onions (scallions), sliced
    and smashed with the flat side
    of a cleaver
1 tablespoon oil
2 tablespoons finely shredded
    ginger
1 spring onion (scallion), finely
    shredded
1 red chilli, seeded and finely
    shredded
1/2 teaspoon freshly ground white
    pepper
2 1/2 tablespoons light soy sauce
2 tablespoons sugar
2 tablespoons Chinese black rice
    vinegar
1 tablespoon cornflour (cornstarch)

SERVES 6

IF YOU do manage to buy a swimming (live) fish, then ask the fishmonger to gut it through the gills. This is harder than gutting through the stomach, but leaves the fish looking whole. If you are gutting the fish yourself, make a cut from the throat to the tail and pull out the guts through the stomach. Remove any scales with a fish scaler or the back of a knife. Check that the gills have been cut out, then rinse the fish under cold, running water and drain thoroughly in a colander. Diagonally score both sides of the fish, cutting through as far as the bone at 2 cm (3/4 inch) intervals.

COMBINE 1 tablespoon of the rice wine, 1 teaspoon of the salt, the ginger slices and smashed spring onions. Pinch the ginger slices and the spring onions in the marinade repeatedly for several minutes to impart their flavours into the marinade. Rub the marinade all over the outside of the fish and into the slits. Leave the fish to marinate in the refrigerator for 30 minutes.

BRING 4 litres (16 cups) water to the boil in a wok with the oil and remaining rice wine. Gently lower the fish into the poaching liquid and return to the boil. Turn off the heat, cover, and leave for 20 minutes, or until the fish flakes when the skin is pressed firmly or the dorsal fin pulls out easily. If the fish is not cooked through, cook over low heat for 5 minutes. Using slotted spoons, carefully transfer the fish to a platter. Reserve 375 ml (1 1/2 cups) of the poaching liquid. Sprinkle the shredded ginger, shredded spring onion, chilli and white pepper over the fish.

ADD the soy sauce, remaining salt, sugar and black vinegar to the liquid. Heat the wok over high heat, add the liquid and bring to the boil. Combine the cornflour with enough water to make a paste, add to the sauce and simmer until thickened. Pour the sauce over the fish.

Rinse the fish thoroughly, making sure that all the scales are washed off—scales left on will be hard and unpalatable. Marinating the fish not only adds flavour but also makes it aromatic and less 'fishy' tasting.

青菜炒干贝
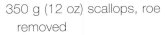

STIR-FRIED SCALLOPS WITH CHINESE GREENS

THIS DISH EMPHASIZES THE FRESHNESS AND DELICATE SEASONING THAT GIVE CANTONESE CUISINE ITS REPUTATION. CHINESE BROCCOLI (GAI LAN) OR BOK CHOY (PAK CHOI) IS TRADITIONALLY USED, BUT YOU COULD USE REGULAR BROCCOLI.

350 g (12 oz) scallops, roe removed
2 tablespoons Shaoxing rice wine
1 tablespoon roasted sesame oil
1 teaspoon finely chopped ginger
1/2 spring onion (scallion), finely chopped
200 g (7 oz) Chinese broccoli (gai lan) or bok choy (pak choi)
80 ml (1/3 cup) chicken stock (page 281)
1/2 teaspoon salt
1/4 teaspoon sugar
1/4 teaspoon freshly ground white pepper
1 teaspoon cornflour (cornstarch)
1 tablespoon oil
1 tablespoon finely shredded ginger
1 spring onion (scallion), finely shredded
1 garlic clove, very thinly sliced

SERVES 6

SLICE the small, hard white muscle off the side of each scallop and pull off any membrane. Rinse the scallops and drain. Holding a knife blade parallel to the cutting surface, slice each scallop in half horizontally. Place the scallops in a bowl with 1 tablespoon of the rice wine, 1/4 teaspoon of the sesame oil and the chopped ginger and spring onion. Toss lightly, then leave to marinate for 20 minutes.

WASH the broccoli well. Discard any tough-looking stems and diagonally cut into 2 cm (3/4 inch) pieces through the stem and the leaf. Blanch the broccoli in a pan of boiling water for 2 minutes, or until the stems and leaves are just tender, then refresh in cold water and dry thoroughly.

COMBINE the chicken stock, salt, sugar, white pepper, cornflour and the remaining rice wine and sesame oil.

HEAT a wok over high heat, add the oil and heat until very hot. Add the scallops and stir-fry for 30 seconds, then remove. Add the shredded ginger, shredded spring onion and the garlic and stir-fry for 10 seconds. Add the stock mixture and cook, stirring constantly, until the sauce thickens. Add the Chinese broccoli and scallops. Toss lightly to coat with the sauce.

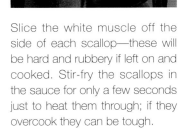

Slice the white muscle off the side of each scallop—these will be hard and rubbery if left on and cooked. Stir-fry the scallops in the sauce for only a few seconds just to heat them through; if they overcook they can be tough.

A fresh produce market in Sichuan.

酸甜素菜拌虾

SWEET-AND-SOUR PRAWNS WITH VEGETABLES

SWEET AND SOUR IS PROBABLY ONE OF THE MOST ABUSED CHINESE DISHES, BUT WHEN WELL DONE
IT CAN BE ONE OF THE MOST PLEASING. THE KEY IS THE SAUCE, WHICH HAS EQUAL AMOUNTS OF RICE
VINEGAR AND SUGAR TO GIVE IT ITS SWEET-AND-SOUR FLAVOUR.

Bottles of condiments and
sauces for sale in a grocery shop
in Beijing.

700 g (1 lb 9 oz) prawns (shrimp)
2 tablespoons Shaoxing rice wine
2 slices ginger, smashed with the
    flat side of a cleaver
3 teaspoons roasted sesame oil
1 1/2 tablespoons cornflour
    (cornstarch)
125 ml (1/2 cup) oil
2 spring onions (scallions), white
    part only, finely chopped
1 tablespoon finely chopped ginger
2 garlic cloves, finely chopped
1 red capsicum (pepper), diced
1 green capsicum (pepper), diced
2 1/2 tablespoons tomato sauce
    (ketchup)
2 tablespoons clear rice vinegar
2 tablespoons sugar
1 teaspoon light soy sauce
1/2 teaspoon salt

SERVES 6

PEEL the prawns, score each one along the
length of the back so the prawns will 'butterfly'
when cooked, and devein them. Place the
prawns in a bowl and add the rice wine, ginger,
2 teaspoons of the sesame oil and 1 tablespoon
of the cornflour. Pinch the ginger slices in the
marinade repeatedly for several minutes to impart
the flavour into the marinade. Toss lightly, then
leave to marinate for 20 minutes. Discard the
ginger slices and drain the prawns.

HEAT a wok over high heat, add 2 tablespoons
of the oil and heat until very hot. Add half the
prawns and toss lightly over high heat for about
1 1/2 minutes, or until the prawns turn pink and
curl up. Remove with a wire sieve or slotted spoon
and drain. Repeat with another 2 tablespoons of
the oil and the remaining prawns. Pour off the oil
and wipe out the wok.

REHEAT the wok over high heat, add the
remaining oil and heat until very hot. Add the
spring onion, chopped ginger and garlic and
stir-fry for 15 seconds, or until fragrant. Add the
red and green capsicum and stir-fry for 1 minute.
Combine the tomato sauce, rice vinegar, sugar,
soy sauce, salt and the remaining sesame oil
and cornflour with 125 ml (1/2 cup) water, add to
the sauce and simmer until thickened. Add the
prawns and toss lightly to coat.

芙蓉龙虾

LOBSTER FU RONG

THE WORDS 'FU RONG' MEAN EGG WHITES AND IN RECIPES DENOTE A CLASSIC CANTONESE COOKING METHOD, THOUGH THE TERM IS OFTEN ASSOCIATED WITH THE QUITE DIFFERENT EGG FOO YOUNG OF WESTERN CHINESE RESTAURANTS. THIS DISH CAN BE MADE WITH ANY KIND OF SEAFOOD.

450 g (1 lb) lobster meat
3 tablespoons Shaoxing rice wine
3 teaspoons finely chopped ginger
1¹/₂ teaspoons salt
12 egg whites
¹/₂ teaspoon cream of tartar
oil for deep-frying
125 ml (¹/₂ cup) chicken stock
　(page 281)
¹/₄ teaspoon freshly ground white
　pepper
1 teaspoon roasted sesame oil
1 teaspoon cornflour (cornstarch)
2 spring onions (scallions), finely
　chopped
2 spring onions (scallions), green
　part only, sliced

SERVES 6

CUT the lobster meat into pieces, put in a bowl with 1 tablespoon of the rice wine, 1 teaspoon of the ginger and ¹/₂ teaspoon of the salt and toss lightly to coat. Beat the egg whites and cream of tartar using a balloon whisk or electric beaters until stiff. Fold the lobster into the egg white mixture.

FILL a wok one-quarter full of oil. Heat the oil to 190°C (375°F), or until a piece of bread fries golden brown in 10 seconds when dropped in the oil. Pour the lobster into the wok in batches—do not stir, otherwise it will scatter, but gently stir the oil from the bottom of the wok so that the 'fu rong' rises to the surface. Remove each batch as soon as it is set, without letting it go too brown, and drain well. Pour the oil from the wok, leaving 2 tablespoons.

COMBINE the chicken stock, remaining rice wine and salt, white pepper, sesame oil and cornflour.

REHEAT the reserved oil over high heat until very hot and stir-fry the finely chopped spring onion and the remaining ginger for 10 seconds, or until fragrant. Add the stock mixture and cook, stirring constantly to prevent lumps, until thickened. Add the cooked lobster mixture and carefully toss it in the sauce. Transfer to a serving platter, sprinkle with the sliced spring onion and serve.

海蜇鸡丝沙律

JELLYFISH AND CHICKEN SALAD

JELLYFISH ARE ONLY EVER EATEN ONCE THEY HAVE BEEN PRESERVED AND DRIED. THEY HAVE A CRUNCHY TEXTURE AND ARE NOT LIKE JELLY. YOU CAN BUY THEM DRIED, CUT INTO STRIPS OR WHOLE, AND ALSO ALREADY RECONSTITUTED IN VACUUM PACKS. THE LATTER ARE MUCH EASIER TO USE.

375 g (13 oz) dried or ready-
  prepared jellyfish
1.3 kg (3 lb) chicken
2 celery stalks, cut into 5 cm
  (2 inch) lengths and finely
  shredded
1 carrot, cut into 5 cm (2 inch)
  lengths and finely shredded
1 tablespoon oyster sauce
2 teaspoons light soy sauce
2 teaspoons roasted sesame oil
25 g (³/4 cup) coriander (cilantro)
  leaves
3 teaspoons sesame seeds

DRESSING
185 ml (³/4 cup) clear rice vinegar
55 g (¹/4 cup) sugar
1 tablespoon finely chopped ginger
3 spring onions (scallions), thinly
  sliced

SERVES 8

TO PREPARE dried jellyfish, remove from the packet, cover with tepid water and soak overnight. Drain, then rinse to remove any sand and sediment. Drain well. Cut into strands using a pair of scissors, then cut any long strands into shorter lengths. If you are using ready-prepared jellyfish, remove it from the packet and rinse.

RINSE the chicken, drain, and remove any fat from the cavity opening and around the neck. Cut off and discard the parson's nose. Bring a large saucepan of water to the boil. Add the chicken and bring the water to a gentle simmer. Cook, covered, for 25–30 minutes, or until the chicken is cooked through. Remove the chicken from the saucepan and plunge into cold water. When cool enough to handle, remove the skin and bones from the chicken and finely shred the meat.

PLACE the chicken in a large bowl and add the jellyfish, celery, carrot, oyster sauce, soy sauce, sesame oil and coriander. Mix well to combine.

TO MAKE the dressing, place the vinegar and sugar in a bowl and stir until dissolved. Stir in the ginger and spring onion.

TOAST the sesame seeds by dry-frying in a pan until brown and popping. Sprinkle the salad with the sesame seeds and serve cold with the dressing alongside.

It is easiest to cut the jellyfish using a pair of scissors. Make sure you keep the strands roughly the same width.

Cut the last two joints off the crab legs as these don't contain much meat.

辣椒螃蟹

CHILLI CRAB

4 x 250 g (9 oz) live crabs
3 tablespoons oil
1 tablespoon Guilin chilli sauce
2 tablespoons light soy sauce
3 teaspoons clear rice vinegar
4 tablespoons Shaoxing rice wine
1/2 teaspoon salt
2 tablespoons sugar
2 tablespoons chicken stock
   (page 281)
1 tablespoon grated ginger
2 garlic cloves, crushed
2 spring onions (scallions), finely
   chopped

SERVES 4

TO KILL the crabs humanely, put them in the freezer for 1 hour. Bring a large saucepan of water to the boil. Plunge the crabs into boiling water for about 1 minute, then rinse them in cold water. Twist off and discard the upper shell, and remove and discard the spongy grey gill tissue from inside the crab. Rinse the bodies and drain well. Cut away the last two hairy joints of the legs. Cut each crab into four to six pieces, cutting so that a portion of the body is attached to one or two legs. Crack the crab claws using crab crackers or the back edge of a cleaver—this will help the flavouring penetrate the crab meat.

HEAT a wok over high heat, add 1 tablespoon of the oil and heat until very hot. Add half the crab and fry for several minutes to cook the meat right through. Remove and drain. Repeat with another tablespoon of the oil and the remaining crab.

COMBINE the chilli sauce, soy sauce, rice vinegar, rice wine, salt, sugar and stock.

REHEAT the wok over high heat, add the remaining oil and heat until very hot. Stir-fry the ginger, garlic and spring onion for 10 seconds. Add the sauce mixture to the wok and cook briefly. Add the crab pieces and toss lightly to coat with the sauce. Cook, covered, for 5 minutes, then serve immediately.

CRAB IS best eaten with your hands, so supply finger bowls as well as special picks to help remove the meat from the crab claws.

AT A WEDDING BANQUET food is often presented in pairs, like these dumplings and wrapped lettuce parcels, to symbolize marriage. Ducks represent fidelity in Chinese culture because mandarin ducks live in couples for their whole lives. They are used to symbolize a pair that is not identical but belongs together. Here two egg white ducks float on top of a soup.

BANQUET

FOOD PLAYS AN IMPORTANT PART IN THE CHINESE FESTIVALS THAT MARK THE PASSING OF THE YEAR AND LIFE ITSELF, FROM CHINESE NEW YEAR TO THE MOON FESTIVAL, AND FROM BIRTH THROUGH TO MARRIAGE AND EVEN DEATH.

A banquet can be a social or commercial event to celebrate anything from a graduation to a successful business deal. Dishes are chosen carefully as different foods symbolize instantly recognizable meanings to the guests, while the number of courses and even the colour of the food (red and yellow are particularly lucky colours) are important.

Banquets can consist of 10 to 15 courses or even more, though often eight dishes are served as in Chinese the word 'eight' sounds like the word for prosperity and success, or sometimes nine as this word sounds like long-lasting. As each course is served, the host respectfully offers the choice pieces to the honoured guest or perhaps the eldest. The banquet traditionally starts with a beautifully arranged cold platter of sliced meats, seafood and nuts, to be picked at during the toasts. This is followed by some deep-fried, steamed or stir-fried dishes, then shark's fin or another special soup. Next come the main dishes featuring the most expensive and prestigious ingredients: poultry, usually whole, or possibly a roast suckling pig. At New Year, a fish course will be served last so that some may remain on the table for the start of the next year. Simple rice and noodle dishes come at the end to fill up any gaps. Finally fresh fruit, a sweet soup or the equivalent of petits fours are served.

THE LUNAR NEW YEAR is welcomed in with a huge family feast—each dish promising good luck and happiness for the year to come. Shops and homes are decorated in red and yellow and on New Year's Day, envelopes of lucky money and tangerines are exchanged with family and friends. The Lantern Festival marks the end of the festivities, with tiny dumplings and fireworks.

BIRTHDAYS AND MARRIAGES

A child's first celebration occurs at a month old and is a big family affair, with healing dishes of chicken and pig's trotters for the mother. Birthdays are then only celebrated enthusiastically after the age of 60 and every decade thereafter. A marriage is usually an extravagant affair, with a banquet following the ceremony that may involve hundreds of guests. The couple traditionally perform a tea ceremony for their parents.

FESTIVALS

The New Year is the most important festival: houses are cleaned, debts paid and special food prepared. The New Year's Eve meal is a family affair at home, after which the festival continues with 2 weeks of visiting family and friends and eating. The Qing Ming and Hungry Ghosts Festivals honour the dead, offering food to placate the spirits, and moon cakes, pastries filled with egg yolk, are eaten at the Moon Festival.

DURING CHINESE NEW YEAR gods are pasted on the doors of houses along with sayings that wish for happiness, wealth, longevity and fertility, the most longed-for states.

A market stall in Sichuan.

川 式 焖虾

SICHUAN-STYLE BRAISED PRAWNS

ALSO KNOWN AS CHILLI OR SPICY PRAWNS, THIS IS ONE OF THE MOST POPULAR DISHES IN CHINESE RESTAURANTS. USE UNCOOKED, UNPEELED PRAWNS (SHRIMP) WITH THEIR HEADS AND TAILS STILL ATTACHED FOR THE BEST RESULTS, AS THE SHELLS ADD FLAVOUR TO THE SAUCE.

16 king prawns (shrimp)
oil for deep-frying
1 tablespoon oil, extra
1 garlic clove, finely chopped
1/2 teaspoon finely chopped ginger
1 tablespoon light soy sauce
1 tablespoon Shaoxing rice wine
1 tablespoon chilli bean paste
   (toban jiang)
1 teaspoon sugar
3–4 tablespoons chicken and meat
   stock (page 281)
1 teaspoon clear rice vinegar
1 spring onion (scallion), finely
   chopped
2 red chillies, finely chopped
1/4 teaspoon roasted sesame oil
2 teaspoons cornflour (cornstarch)
coriander (cilantro) leaves

SERVES 4

PULL OFF the legs from the prawns, but leave the body shells on. Using a pair of scissors, cut each prawn along the back to devein it.

FILL a wok one-quarter full of oil. Heat the oil to 190°C (375°F), or until a piece of bread fries golden brown in 10 seconds when dropped in the oil. Cook the prawns in batches for 2 minutes, or until they turn bright orange. Remove and drain. It is important to keep the oil hot for each batch or the shells with not turn crisp. Pour off the oil and wipe out the wok.

REHEAT the wok over high heat, add the extra oil and heat until very hot. Cook the garlic and ginger for a few seconds to flavour the oil. Add the soy sauce, rice wine, chilli bean paste, sugar and stock. Stir to combine, then bring to the boil. Add the prawns and cook for 1 minute, then add the rice vinegar, spring onion, chilli and sesame oil, stirring constantly. Combine the cornflour with enough water to make a paste, add to the sauce and simmer until thickened. Serve sprinkled with the coriander leaves, and provide finger bowls.

Loosen the prawn's (shrimp's) dark, vein-like digestive tract with the point of some scissors, then gently pull it out.

上海式五柳鱼

SHANGHAI-STYLE FIVE-WILLOW FISH

THIS IS A VARIATION ON THE CLASSIC SWEET-AND-SOUR FISH (SEE PAGE 117). THE 'FIVE-WILLOW' REFERS TO THE FIVE SHREDDED VEGETABLES USED FOR THE SAUCE, WHILE THE AROMATICS TRADITIONALLY REMOVED ANY 'FISHY' TASTE FROM THE FRESHWATER FISH.

3–4 dried Chinese mushrooms
750 g–1 kg (1 lb 10 oz–2 lb 4 oz) whole fish, such as carp, bream, grouper or sea bass
1 teaspoon salt
oil for deep-frying
2 tablespoons oil, extra
1 tablespoon shredded ginger
2 spring onions (scallions), shredded
1/2 small carrot, shredded
1/2 small green capsicum (pepper), shredded
1/2 celery stalk, shredded
2 red chillies, seeded and finely shredded
2 tablespoons light soy sauce
3 tablespoons sugar
3 tablespoons Chinese black rice vinegar
1 tablespoon Shaoxing rice wine
125 ml (1/2 cup) chicken and meat stock (page 281)
1 tablespoon cornflour (cornstarch)
1/2 teaspoon roasted sesame oil

SERVES 4

SOAK the dried mushrooms in boiling water for 30 minutes, then drain and squeeze out any excess water. Remove and discard the stems. Finely shred the caps.

IF YOU do manage to buy a swimming (live) fish, then ask the fishmonger to gut it through the gills. This is harder than gutting through the stomach, but leaves the fish looking whole. If you are gutting the fish yourself, make a cut from the throat to the tail and pull out the guts through the stomach. Remove any scales with a fish scaler or the back of a knife. Check that the gills have been cut out, then rinse the fish under cold, running water and drain thoroughly in a colander.

DIAGONALLY score both sides of the fish, cutting through as far as the bone at intervals of 2 cm (3/4 inch). Rub the salt all over the inside and outside of the fish and into the slits.

FILL a wok one-quarter full of oil. Heat the oil to 190°C (375°F), or until a piece of bread fries golden brown in 10 seconds when dropped in the oil. Holding the fish by its tail, gently and carefully lower it into the oil. Cook the fish for 3–4 minutes on each side, or until the fish flakes when the skin is pressed firmly or the dorsal fin pulls out easily. Remove from the wok and drain on paper towels, then place on a dish and keep warm in a low oven. Pour off the oil and wipe out the wok.

REHEAT the wok over high heat, add the extra oil and heat until very hot. Stir-fry the mushrooms, ginger, spring onion, carrot, green capsicum, celery and chilli for 1 1/2 minutes. Add the soy sauce, sugar, rice vinegar, rice wine and stock, and bring to the boil. Combine the cornflour with enough water to make a paste, add to the sauce and simmer until thickened. Add the sesame oil, blend well and spoon over the fish.

The Oriental Pearl Tower in Pudong, Shanghai.

SEA CUCUMBER WITH MUSHROOMS

SEA CUCUMBER, OR BECHE-DE-MER, IS SOLD DRIED OR READY-PREPARED (RECONSTITUTED). THE DRIED ONES NEED A LOT OF SOAKING TO REHYDRATE AND BECOME GELATINOUS IN TEXTURE. SEA CUCUMBER HAS NO FLAVOUR OF ITS OWN, BUT ABSORBS FLAVOURS FROM WHATEVER IT IS COOKED WITH.

3 dried or ready-prepared
   sea cucumbers
24 dried Chinese mushrooms
4 tablespoons oil
1 skinless chicken breast fillet,
   cut into 2 cm (³/4 inch) cubes
1 egg white
3–4 tablespoons cornflour
   (cornstarch)
1 tablespoon light soy sauce
3 tablespoons oyster sauce
3 teaspoons sugar
2 spring onions (scallions), cut into
   2 cm (³/4 inch) lengths

SERVES 4

TO PREPARE the dried sea cucumbers, allow up to 4 days for them to rehydrate. On the first day, soak the cucumbers in water overnight. Drain and cook in a saucepan of simmering water for 1 hour, then drain again. Re-soak overnight and repeat the cooking and soaking process at least three times to allow the sea cucumbers to soften. Once softened, cut the sea cucumbers in half lengthways, scrape out and discard the insides and cut into chunks. If you are using ready-prepared sea cucumbers, they only need to be rinsed, drained and have the insides discarded before cutting into chunks.

PLACE the dried mushrooms in a saucepan and add 500 ml (2 cups) water and half the oil. Cover, bring to the boil, then reduce the heat and simmer for 1 hour. Drain the mushrooms, reserving 250 ml (1 cup) of the liquid. Remove and discard the stems.

COMBINE the chicken with the egg white and 1 tablespoon of the cornflour until it is completely coated. Heat a wok over high heat, add the remaining oil and heat until very hot. Stir-fry the chicken pieces in batches for 3 minutes, or until browned. Return all the chicken to the wok and add the sea cucumber, mushrooms, reserved liquid, soy sauce, oyster sauce, sugar and spring onion. Stir to combine, then cook for 2 minutes.

COMBINE the remaining cornflour with enough water to make a paste, add to the sauce and simmer until thickened.

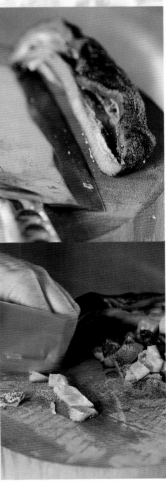

Slice the sea cucumber in half and scrape out the insides, leaving the cavity clean. Cut the sea cucumber into chunks.

A theatrical wedding in progress
in Hangzhou.

鸳鸯大虾

LOVE BIRDS PRAWNS

THE CHINESE NAME FOR THIS DISH, YUAN YANG XIA, REFERS TO MANDARIN DUCKS KNOWN AS 'LOVE

BIRDS' BECAUSE THEY ARE ALWAYS SEEN TOGETHER, SYMBOLIZING AFFECTION AND HAPPINESS. DISHES

WITH ONE MAIN INGREDIENT PRESENTED IN TWO WAYS OFTEN REPRESENT THIS IN CHINESE COOKING.

600 g (1 lb 5 oz) tiger prawns
  (shrimp)
1 tablespoon cornflour (cornstarch)
$^1/_2$ egg white, beaten
oil for deep-frying
150 g (5$^1/_2$ oz) snowpeas
  (mangetout), ends trimmed
$^1/_2$ teaspoon salt
$^1/_2$ teaspoon sugar
1 spring onion (scallion), finely
  chopped
1 teaspoon finely chopped ginger
1 tablespoon light soy sauce
1 tablespoon Shaoxing rice wine
$^1/_2$ teaspoon roasted sesame oil
1 tablespoon chilli bean paste
  (toban jiang)
1 tablespoon tomato paste (purée)

SERVES 4

PEEL and devein the prawns, leaving the tails intact. Combine the cornflour with enough water to make a paste. Stir in the egg white and a pinch of salt, then stir in the prawns.

FILL a wok one-quarter full of oil. Heat the oil to 180°C (350°F), or until a piece of bread fries golden brown in 15 seconds when dropped in the oil. Cook the prawns for 1 minute, stirring to separate them. Remove the prawns from the wok with a wire sieve or slotted spoon as soon as the colour changes, then drain. Pour the oil from the wok, leaving 1 tablespoon.

REHEAT the reserved oil over high heat until very hot and stir-fry the snowpeas with the salt and sugar for 1$^1/_2$ minutes. Remove and place in the centre of a serving platter.

REHEAT the wok again and stir-fry the spring onion and ginger for a few seconds. Add the prawns, soy sauce and rice wine, blend well and stir-fry for about 30 seconds, then add the sesame oil. Transfer about half of the prawns to one end of the serving platter.

ADD the chilli bean paste and tomato paste to the remaining prawns, blend well, tossing to coat the prawns, then transfer the prawns to the other end of the platter.

酸甜鱼片

SWEET-AND-SOUR FISH FILLETS

THIS SWEET-AND-SOUR DISH IS SUBTLY VINEGARY AND HAS JUST A FAINT TOUCH OF SWEETNESS.
SWEET-AND-SOUR FISH IS EATEN ALL OVER CHINA, OFTEN USING A WHOLE DEEP-FRIED FISH, BUT
THIS RECIPE COMES FROM THE SOUTH-EAST AND IS A GREAT WAY TO COOK FISH FILLETS.

450 g (1 lb) firm white fish fillets,
   such as haddock, monkfish or
   sea bass, skin removed
$1/2$ teaspoon salt
$1^1/2$ tablespoons Shaoxing rice
   wine
1 egg, beaten
3–4 tablespoons plain (all-purpose)
   flour
oil for deep-frying
$1/2$ teaspoon chopped ginger
1 spring onion (scallion), finely
   chopped
125 ml ($1/2$ cup) chicken and meat
   stock (page 281)
2 tablespoons light soy sauce
1 tablespoon sugar
2 tablespoons clear rice vinegar
1 red chilli, finely chopped (optional)
1 tablespoon cornflour (cornstarch)
$1/2$ teaspoon roasted sesame oil
coriander (cilantro) leaves

SERVES 4

PAT DRY the fish, cut into 3 cm ($1^1/4$ inch) cubes
and marinate with the salt and 2 teaspoons of the
rice wine for about 15–20 minutes.

MEANWHILE, blend the egg and flour with a little
water to form a smooth batter the consistency of
thick cream. Coat the fish cubes with the batter.

FILL a wok one-quarter full of oil. Heat the oil to
180°C (350°F), or until a piece of bread fries
golden brown in 15 seconds when dropped in the
oil. Carefully lower the pieces of fish, one by one,
into the hot oil and stir gently to make sure they
do not stick together. Cook for about 3 minutes,
or until golden. Remove and drain well on
crumpled paper towels. Pour off the oil, leaving
1 tablespoon, and wipe out the wok.

REHEAT the reserved oil over high heat until very
hot and add the ginger, spring onion, stock, soy
sauce, remaining rice wine, sugar and half the rice
vinegar. Bring to the boil, then reduce the heat
and simmer for 30 seconds. Add the fish pieces
and cook for 2 minutes. Add the chilli, if using,
and the remaining rice vinegar. Combine the
cornflour with enough water to make a paste, add
to the sauce and simmer until thickened.

SPRINKLE the fish with the sesame oil and the
coriander leaves to serve.

You can use your wok for deep-
frying, but make sure that it is
really steady on the wok burner.
A wire sieve drains away far more
oil than a slotted spoon and
leaves the batter less greasy.

Dried fish in the market in Guangzhou.

Carefully lower the whole fish into the hot oil. If you like you can gently hold the fish open with a fish slice so the oil can get inside the cavity easily.

A girl in a traditional headdress in Dali, Yunnan.

豆醬金目鱸

WHOLE FISH WITH YELLOW BEAN SAUCE

750 g–1 kg (1 lb 10 oz–2 lb 4 oz) whole fish, such as carp, bream, grouper or sea bass
1 tablespoon light soy sauce
1 tablespoon Shaoxing rice wine
oil for deep-frying
1 tablespoon shredded ginger
2 spring onions (scallions), thinly shredded
1 teaspoon sugar
1 tablespoon dark soy sauce
2 tablespoons yellow bean sauce
125 ml (1/2 cup) chicken and meat stock (page 281)
1/2 teaspoon roasted sesame oil

SERVES 4

IF YOU do manage to buy a swimming (live) fish, then ask the fishmonger to gut it through the gills. This is harder than gutting through the stomach, but leaves the fish looking whole. If you are gutting the fish yourself, make a cut from the throat to the tail and pull out the guts through the stomach. Remove any scales with a fish scaler or the back of a knife. Check that the gills have been cut out, then rinse the fish under cold, running water and drain thoroughly in a colander.

DIAGONALLY score both sides of the fish, cutting through as far as the bone at intervals of 2 cm (3/4 inch). Place the fish in a shallow dish with the light soy sauce and rice wine and leave to marinate for 10–15 minutes, then drain off any liquid, reserving the marinade.

FILL a wok one-quarter full of oil. Heat the oil to 190°C (375°F), or until a piece of bread fries golden brown in 10 seconds when dropped in the oil. Holding the fish by its tail, gently and carefully lower it into the oil, bending the body so that the cuts open up. Cook for 5 minutes, or until golden brown, tilting the wok so that the entire fish is cooked in the oil. Remove and drain on crumpled paper towels and keep warm in a low oven. Pour the oil from the wok, leaving 1 1/2 tablespoons.

REHEAT the reserved oil over high heat until very hot. Add the ginger, spring onion, sugar, dark soy sauce, yellow bean sauce and reserved marinade. Stir for a few seconds, add the stock, bring to the boil and add the fish. Cook for 4–5 minutes, basting constantly and turning the fish once after 2 minutes.

TURN the fish over and sprinkle with the sesame oil. Serve with the sauce poured over.

蒸虾奶油羹

STEAMED PRAWN CUSTARDS

4 eggs
310 ml (1¼ cups) chicken stock
  (page 281)
16 prawns (shrimp)
1 spring onion (scallion), finely
  chopped
1 tablespoon light soy sauce
1 tablespoon oil

SERVES 4

BEAT the eggs and chicken stock together and season with salt and white pepper. Peel and devein the prawns, then roughly chop the prawn meat.

DIVIDE the prawns among four small heatproof bowls. Pour the egg and stock mixture over the prawns. Put the bowls in a steamer, and steam over simmering water in a covered wok for 10 minutes. The custards should be just set. Shake them gently to see if the centre is set. If you overcook them they will be rubbery.

SPRINKLE the custards with the spring onion and soy sauce. Heat the oil in a wok until very hot and pour a little over each custard (it will spit as it hits the surface). Serve immediately.

酱油蒸蚌

STEAMED MUSSEL CUSTARDS

450 g (1 lb) mussels
2 tablespoons Shaoxing rice wine
1 tablespoon finely chopped ginger
6 eggs
1 teaspoon salt

SERVES 6

SCRUB the mussels, remove any beards, and throw away any that do not close when tapped on the work surface. Put the mussels in a wok with 250 ml (1 cup) water, the rice wine and ginger. Cook, covered, over high heat for 1 minute, or until boiling. Reduce the heat to low and cook, covered, for 2 minutes, or until the mussels have opened, shaking the pan so that they cook evenly. Discard any that do not open after 2 minutes.

REMOVE the mussels with a wire sieve or slotted spoon, reserving the liquid, and allow to cool. Remove the mussels from their shells and divide among six small heatproof bowls. Lightly beat the eggs, salt and 250 ml (1 cup) of the reserved liquid, then pour over the mussels.

PUT the bowls in a steamer and steam over simmering water in a covered wok for 10 minutes. The custards should be just set. Shake them gently to see if the centre is set. If you overcook them they will be rubbery. Serve immediately.

STEAMED MUSSEL CUSTARDS

STEAMED PRAWN CUSTARDS

川式辣焖鱼

SICHUANESE BRAISED FISH IN SPICY SAUCE

Scoring the fish through the flesh allows the heat to penetrate much more easily.

Renmin Park in Chengdu.

1 x 1.75 kg (4 lb) whole fish, such as carp, bream, grouper or sea bass
2¹/₂ tablespoons Shaoxing rice wine
2¹/₂ tablespoons finely chopped ginger
¹/₂ teaspoon salt
15 g (¹/₂ oz) dried black fungus (wood ears)
oil for deep-frying
2 spring onions (scallions), finely chopped
4 garlic cloves, finely chopped
1¹/₂ teaspoons chilli bean paste (toban jiang)
500 ml (2 cups) chicken stock (page 281)
1¹/₂ tablespoons light soy sauce
2 teaspoons sugar
1 tablespoon Chinese black vinegar
1 tablespoon cornflour (cornstarch)
2 spring onions (scallions), green part only, finely chopped

SERVES 6

IF YOU do manage to buy a swimming (live) fish, then ask the fishmonger to gut it through the gills. This is harder than gutting through the stomach, but leaves the fish looking whole. If you are gutting the fish yourself, make a cut from the throat to the tail and pull out the guts through the stomach. Remove any scales with a fish scaler or the back of a knife. Check that the gills have been cut out, then rinse the fish under cold, running water and drain thoroughly in a colander.

DIAGONALLY score both sides of the fish, cutting through as far as the bone at intervals of 2 cm (³/₄ inch). Combine 1 tablespoon of the rice wine, 2 teaspoons of the ginger and the salt. Place the fish in a dish and rub the mixture all over the outside of the fish and into the slits. Marinate for 30 minutes, then drain.

SOAK the dried fungus in cold water for 20 minutes, drain, squeeze out any excess water, and shred.

FILL a wok one-quarter full of oil. Heat the oil to 190°C (375°F), or until a piece of bread fries golden brown in 10 seconds when dropped in the oil. Holding the fish by its tail, gently and carefully lower it into the oil, bending the body so that the cuts open up. Cook for 5 minutes, or until golden brown, tilting the wok so that the entire fish is cooked in the oil. Remove and drain on crumpled paper towels and keep warm in a low oven. Pour the oil from the wok, leaving 1¹/₂ tablespoons.

REHEAT the reserved oil over high heat until very hot and stir-fry the spring onion, remaining ginger, garlic and chilli bean paste for 10 seconds. Toss in the fungus, then the remaining rice wine, stock, soy, sugar and vinegar and bring to the boil. Add the fish, return to the boil, then reduce the heat and cook, covered, for 12 minutes, or until the fish flakes when the skin is pressed firmly or the dorsal fin pulls out easily. Remove the fish.

SKIM ANY scum from the sauce and bring to the boil. Combine the cornflour with enough water to make a paste, add to the sauce and simmer until thickened. Pour over the fish with the spring onion.

椒盐软壳蟹

SALT AND PEPPER SOFT-SHELL CRABS

THESE CRABS ARE A DELIGHT TO EAT AS YOU CAN DEVOUR THE ENTIRE CREATURE—SHELLS AND ALL.

THEY ARE EATEN WHEN THEY HAVE JUST SHED THEIR OLD SHELL AND BEFORE A NEW SHELL HARDENS.

4 soft-shell crabs
1 teaspoon spicy salt and pepper (page 285)
1 tablespoon Shaoxing rice wine
1 egg, beaten
1 tablespoon plain (all-purpose) flour
oil for deep-frying
1 spring onion (scallion), chopped
2 small red chillies, chopped

SERVES 4

TO KILL the crabs humanely, put them in the freezer for 1 hour. Bring a large saucepan of water to the boil. Plunge the crabs into boiling water for about 1 minute, then rinse them in cold water. Marinate in the spicy salt and pepper and rice wine for 10–15 minutes, then coat with the egg and dust with the flour.

FILL a wok one-quarter full of oil. Heat the oil to 190°C (375°F), or until a piece of bread fries golden brown in 10 seconds when dropped in the oil. Cook the crabs for 3–4 minutes, or until golden. Remove and drain, reserving the oil. Cut each crab in half and arrange on a serving plate.

SOAK the spring onion and chilli in the hot oil (with the heat turned off) for 2 minutes. Remove with a wire sieve or slotted spoon and sprinkle over the crabs.

芙蓉蟹肉

CRABMEAT FU RONG

250 g (9 oz) crabmeat, picked over
1/2 teaspoon salt
4 egg whites, beaten
1 tablespoon cornflour (cornstarch)
4 tablespoons milk
oil for deep-frying
125 ml (1/2 cup) chicken and meat stock (page 281)
1/2 spring onion (scallion), finely chopped
1/2 teaspoon grated ginger
2 tablespoons peas
1 teaspoon Shaoxing rice wine
1/4 teaspoon roasted sesame oil
coriander (cilantro) leaves

SERVES 4

FLAKE the crabmeat and mix with the salt, egg white, cornflour and milk. Blend well.

FILL a wok one-quarter full of oil and heat to 190°C (375°F), or until a piece of bread fries golden brown in 10 seconds when dropped in the oil. Pour the crabmeat into the wok in batches—do not stir, otherwise it will scatter, but gently stir the oil from the bottom of the wok so that the 'fu rong' rises to the surface. Remove each batch as soon as it is set, without letting it go too brown, and drain. Pour off the oil and wipe out the wok.

REHEAT the wok over high heat until very hot, add the stock, bring to the boil and add the spring onion, ginger, peas and rice wine. Add the sesame oil. Pour over the fu rong and sprinkle with coriander.

CRABMEAT FU RONG

酱油炒干贝

SCALLOPS WITH BLACK BEAN SAUCE

1 kg (2 lb 4 oz) large scallops
2 tablespoons salted, fermented
   black beans, rinsed and mashed
2 garlic cloves, crushed
3 teaspoons finely chopped ginger
2 teaspoons sugar
2 teaspoons light soy sauce
2 tablespoons oyster sauce
2 tablespoons oil
2 spring onions (scallions), cut into
   2 cm (³/4 inch) lengths

SERVES 6

SLICE the small, hard white muscle off the side of each scallop and pull off any membrane. Rinse the scallops and drain. Pull off the roes if you prefer.

PLACE the black beans, garlic, ginger, sugar, soy and oyster sauces in a bowl and mix together.

HEAT a wok over high heat, add the oil and heat until very hot. Stir-fry the scallops and roes for 2 minutes, or until the scallops are cooked through and opaque. Just before the scallops are cooked, add the spring onion. Transfer the mixture to a sieve to drain.

REHEAT the wok over medium heat. Stir-fry the black bean mixture for 1–2 minutes, or until aromatic. Return the scallops and spring onion to the wok and toss together to combine.

SCALLOPS WITH BLACK
BEAN SAUCE

海鲜沙锅

SEAFOOD CLAY POT

8 scallops
12 prawns (shrimp)
12 hard-shelled clams (vongole)
8 oysters, shucked
4 slices ginger
2 tablespoons Shaoxing rice wine
1 teaspoon roasted sesame oil
140 g (5 oz) bean thread noodles
140 g (5 oz) Chinese cabbage
1 spring onion (scallion), thinly
   sliced
310 ml (1¹/4 cups) chicken stock
   (page 281)
coriander (cilantro) sprigs

SERVES 4

SLICE the small, hard white muscle off the side of each scallop and pull off any membrane. Rinse the scallops and drain. Pull off the roes if you prefer. Peel and devein the prawns. Wash the clams in several changes of cold water, leaving them for a few minutes each time to remove any grit. Scrub the clams well, discarding any that remain open. Drain well.

PUT the scallops, prawns, clams and oysters in a bowl with the ginger, rice wine and sesame oil. Marinate for 30 minutes. Soak the bean thread noodles in hot water for 10 minutes, then drain.

CUT the cabbage into small squares, put in a clay pot with the spring onion and place the noodles on top. Remove the ginger from the marinade and put the seafood and marinade on top of the noodles. Pour the stock over. Slowly bring to the boil, then simmer, covered, for 10 minutes. Stir once, season and cook for 8 minutes. Serve from the pot, sprinkled with coriander.

酸甜鲤鱼

SWEET-AND-SOUR FISH

PEOPLE TEND TO THINK THAT SWEET-AND-SOUR DISHES ARE CANTONESE, BUT IN FACT COOKS IN THE YELLOW RIVER VALLEY INVENTED THEM TO SUPPRESS THE MUDDY TASTE OF CARP FROM THE YELLOW RIVER. THIS RECIPE REPRESENTS WHAT MAY BE THE ORIGINAL 'SWEET-AND-SOUR SAUCE'.

750 g–1 kg (1 lb 10 oz–2 lb 4 oz) whole fish, such as sea bass, carp, grouper or bream
1 teaspoon salt
2 tablespoons plain (all-purpose) flour
20 g (³/₄ oz) dried black fungus (wood ears)
3–4 peeled water chestnuts
oil for deep-frying
2 tablespoons oil, extra
¹/₂ teaspoon chopped garlic
1 tablespoon shredded ginger
2 spring onions (scallions), shredded
60 g (¹/₄ cup) fresh or tinned bamboo shoots, rinsed and drained, shredded
3 tablespoons rice vinegar
150 ml (5 fl oz) chicken and meat stock (page 281)
3 tablespoons sugar
2 tablespoons light soy sauce
2 tablespoons Shaoxing rice wine
2 teaspoons cornflour (cornstarch)
coriander (cilantro) leaves

SERVES 4

IF YOU do manage to buy a swimming (live) fish, then ask the fishmonger to gut it through the gills. This is harder than gutting through the stomach, but leaves the fish looking whole. If you are gutting the fish yourself, make a cut from the throat to the tail and pull out the guts through the stomach. Remove any scales with a fish scaler or the back of a knife. Check that the gills have been cut out, then rinse the fish under cold, running water and drain thoroughly in a colander.

DIAGONALLY score both sides of the fish, cutting through as far as the bone at intervals of 2 cm (³/₄ inch). Rub a little salt then a little flour all over the outside of the fish and into the slits. Put the remaining flour in a dish and coat the whole fish, from head to tail on both sides, with flour. Soak the dried black fungus in cold water for 20 minutes then drain, squeeze out any excess water, and shred. Blanch the water chestnuts in a pan of boiling water for 1 minute, then refresh in cold water. Drain, pat dry and roughly chop them.

FILL a wok one-quarter full of oil. Heat the oil to 190°C (375°F), or until a piece of bread fries golden brown in 10 seconds when dropped in the oil. Holding the fish by the tail, carefully lower it into the oil, bending the body so that the cuts open up. Cook the fish for 5 minutes, or until golden brown. Remove and drain on crumpled paper towels and keep warm in a low oven. Pour off the oil and wipe out the wok.

REHEAT the wok over high heat, add the extra oil and heat until very hot. Stir-fry the garlic, ginger, spring onion, bamboo shoots, water chestnuts and black fungus for 30 seconds, then add the vinegar, stock, sugar, soy and rice wine. Combine the cornflour with enough water to make a paste, add to the sauce and simmer until thickened. Pour over the fish and sprinkle with coriander.

Peeling water chestnuts with a cleaver requires some dexterity.

Coating the fish in flour soaks up any moisture and gives it a very crisp surface when fried.

A rice wine store in Beijing.

米酒蘑菇蒸比目鱼

SOLE WITH MUSHROOMS AND RICE WINE

THIS DISH IS SURPRISINGLY SIMILAR TO THE FRENCH SOLE BONNE FEMME (SOLE WITH MUSHROOMS AND WINE SAUCE), THOUGH THE CHINESE VERSION IS MUCH SIMPLER TO MAKE. YOU COULD USE ANY WHITE FISH INSTEAD OF THE FLAT FISH.

450 g (1 lb) flat fish fillets, such as sole, plaice, flounder or brill
1 egg white, beaten
1 tablespoon cornflour (cornstarch)
250 g (9 oz) button mushrooms
oil for deep-frying
1 garlic clove, thinly shredded
2 spring onions (scallions), thinly shredded
1 teaspoon shredded ginger
1 teaspoon salt
1 teaspoon sugar
1 tablespoon light soy sauce
2 tablespoons Shaoxing rice wine
1 tablespoon Chinese spirit (Mou Tai) or brandy
125 ml (1/2 cup) chicken and meat stock (page 281)
1/2 teaspoon roasted sesame oil
coriander (cilantro) leaves

SERVES 4

TRIM the soft bones along the edges of the fish, but leave the skin on. Cut each fillet into three or four slices if large, two or three if small. Mix the egg white with half the cornflour and 1 teaspoon of water. Add the fish slices and toss to coat thoroughly. Thinly slice the mushrooms.

FILL a wok one-quarter full of oil. Heat the oil to 180°C (350°F), or until a piece of bread fries golden brown in 15 seconds when dropped in the oil. Cook the fish slices for 1 minute, or until golden brown. Stir gently to make sure the slices do not stick together. Remove and drain on paper towels and keep warm in a low oven. Pour the oil from the wok, leaving 2 tablespoons.

REHEAT the reserved oil over high heat until very hot and stir-fry the garlic, spring onion, ginger and mushrooms for 1 minute. Add the salt, sugar, soy sauce, wine, Chinese spirit and stock, and bring to the boil. Return the fish slices to the sauce, blend well and simmer for 1 minute.

COMBINE the remaining cornflour with enough water to make a paste, add to the sauce and simmer until thickened. Sprinkle the fish with the sesame oil and coriander leaves.

Posters of the gods are pasted on front doors over the New Year period to bring good luck and good fortune.

POULTRY

Dried jujubes, or Chinese dates.

Chopping ginger outside a shop in Chengdu.

云南气锅鸡

YUNNAN POT CHICKEN

A YUNNAN POT IS AN EARTHENWARE SOUP POT WITH A CHIMNEY. THE POT COOKS FOOD BY 'CLOSED STEAMING', WHICH GIVES A CLEARER, MORE INTENSELY FLAVOURED STOCK THAN ORDINARY STEAMING. INSTEAD OF A YUNNAN POT, YOU CAN USE A CLAY POT OR CASSEROLE INSIDE A STEAMER.

25 jujubes (dried Chinese dates)
1.5 kg (3 lb 5 oz) chicken
6 wafer-thin slices dang gui (dried angelica)
6 slices ginger, smashed with the flat side of a cleaver
6 spring onions (scallions), ends trimmed, smashed with the flat side of a cleaver
60 ml (1/4 cup) Shaoxing rice wine
1/2 teaspoon salt

SERVES 6

SOAK the jujubes in hot water for 20 minutes, then drain and remove the stones.

RINSE the chicken, drain, and remove any fat from the cavity opening and around the neck. Cut off and discard the parson's nose. Using a cleaver, cut the chicken through the bones into square 4 cm (1½ inch) pieces. Blanch the chicken pieces in a pan of boiling water for 1 minute, then refresh in cold water and drain thoroughly.

ARRANGE the chicken pieces, jujubes, dang gui, ginger and spring onions in a clay pot or casserole about 24 cm (9½ inches) in diameter. Pour the rice wine and 1 litre (4 cups) boiling water over the top and add the salt. Cover the clay pot or casserole tightly, adding a layer of wet muslin between the pot and lid to form a good seal if necessary, and place it in a steamer.

STEAM over simmering water in a covered wok for about 2 hours, replenishing with boiling water during cooking.

REMOVE the pot from the steamer and skim any fat from the surface of the liquid. Discard the dang gui, ginger and spring onions. Taste and season if necessary. Serve directly from the pot.

香菜炒乳鸽

STIR-FRIED SQUAB IN LETTUCE LEAVES

THIS DISH IS A CANTONESE CLASSIC, SOMETIMES CALLED SAN CHOY BAU, AND THE LITTLE PARCELS, WITH THE CONTRAST BETWEEN THEIR WARM FILLING AND THE COLD LETTUCE, ARE WONDERFUL. IF SQUAB IS UNAVAILABLE, CHICKEN MAY BE USED INSTEAD.

12 soft lettuce leaves, such as butter lettuce
250 g (9 oz) squab or pigeon breast meat
450 g (1 lb) centre-cut pork loin, trimmed
80 ml ($^1/_3$ cup) light soy sauce
$3^1/_2$ tablespoons Shaoxing rice wine
$2^1/_2$ teaspoons roasted sesame oil
8 dried Chinese mushrooms
240 g ($1^1/_2$ cups) peeled water chestnuts
125 ml ($^1/_2$ cup) oil
2 spring onions (scallions), finely chopped
2 tablespoons finely chopped ginger
1 teaspoon salt
1 teaspoon sugar
1 teaspoon cornflour (cornstarch)

SERVES 6

RINSE the lettuce and separate the leaves. Drain thoroughly, then lightly pound each leaf with the flat side of a cleaver. Arrange the flattened leaves in a basket or on a platter and set aside.

MINCE the squab meat in a food processor or chop very finely with a sharp knife. Mince the pork to the same size as the squab. Place the squab and pork in a bowl with 2 tablespoons of the soy sauce, $1^1/_2$ tablespoons of the rice wine and 1 teaspoon of the sesame oil, and toss lightly. Marinate in the fridge for 20 minutes.

SOAK the dried mushrooms in boiling water for 30 minutes, then drain and squeeze out any excess water. Remove and discard the stems and chop the caps. Blanch the water chestnuts in a pan of boiling water for 1 minute, then refresh in cold water. Drain, pat dry and roughly chop them.

HEAT a wok over high heat, add 3 tablespoons of the oil and heat until very hot. Stir-fry the meat mixture, mashing and separating the pieces, until browned. Remove and drain. Reheat the wok, add 3 tablespoons more of the oil and heat until very hot. Stir-fry the spring onion and ginger, turning constantly, for 10 seconds, or until fragrant. Add the mushrooms and stir-fry for 5 seconds, turning constantly. Add the water chestnuts and stir-fry for 15 seconds, or until heated through. Add the remaining soy sauce, rice wine and sesame oil with the salt, sugar, cornflour and 125 ml ($^1/_2$ cup) water. Stir-fry, stirring constantly, until thickened. Add the cooked meat mixture and toss lightly.

TO SERVE, place some of the stir-fried meat in a lettuce leaf, roll up and eat.

Like all poultry, pigeons are sold live in the markets so there is no doubt as to how fresh they are.

A restaurant in Beijing.

Preparing spring onions (scallions) in a kitchen in Beijing.

Selling vegetables in Yunnan.

香菇蒸鸡

STEAMED CHICKEN WITH MUSHROOMS

THIS DISH IS TRADITIONALLY COOKED USING PIECES OF CHICKEN WITH BOTH THE BONE AND SKIN STILL ATTACHED, BUT YOU CAN ALSO USE CHICKEN FILLET, IN WHICH CASE THE THIGH MEAT HAS MORE FLAVOUR THAN BREAST MEAT.

450 g (1 lb) skinless chicken thigh
  fillet or 1.5 kg (3 lb 5 oz) chicken
1 teaspoon salt
1/2 teaspoon sugar
1 tablespoon Shaoxing rice wine
1 teaspoon cornflour (cornstarch)
3–4 dried Chinese mushrooms
1 tablespoon shredded ginger
a pinch of ground Sichuan
  peppercorns
1 teaspoon roasted sesame oil

SERVES 4

CUT the chicken thigh fillet into bite-size pieces. For a whole chicken, rinse, drain, and remove any fat from the cavity opening and around the neck. Cut off and discard the parson's nose. Using a cleaver, cut the chicken through the bones into square 4 cm (1 1/2 inch) pieces. Combine with the salt, sugar, rice wine and cornflour.

SOAK the dried mushrooms in boiling water for 30 minutes, then drain and squeeze out any excess water. Discard the stems and shred the caps.

GREASE a shallow heatproof dish and place the chicken pieces on the plate with the mushrooms, ginger, Sichuan peppercorns and sesame oil on top. Put the plate in a steamer. Steam over simmering water in a covered wok for 20 minutes.

芹菜炒鸡丝

SHREDDED CHICKEN WITH CELERY

250 g (9 oz) skinless chicken
  breast fillet
1/4 egg white, beaten
2 teaspoons cornflour (cornstarch)
3 Chinese celery or celery stalks
400 ml (14 fl oz) oil
1 tablespoon shredded ginger
2 spring onions (scallions), shredded
1 red chilli, shredded (optional)
1 teaspoon salt
1/2 teaspoon sugar
1 tablespoon light soy sauce
1 tablespoon Shaoxing rice wine
2 tablespoons chicken and meat
  stock (page 281)
1/4 teaspoon roasted sesame oil

SERVES 4

CUT the chicken into matchstick-size shreds. Combine with a pinch of salt, the egg white and cornflour. Shred the celery.

HEAT a wok over high heat. Add the oil and heat until hot, then turn off the heat. Blanch the chicken in the oil for 1 minute. Stir to separate the shreds, then remove and drain. Pour the oil from the wok, leaving 2 tablespoons.

REHEAT the reserved oil over high heat until very hot and stir-fry the ginger, spring onion, celery and chilli for 1 minute. Add the salt and sugar, blend well, then add the chicken with the soy sauce, rice wine and stock. Stir thoroughly and stir-fry for 1 minute. Sprinkle with the sesame oil to serve.

Roast meat stall in Kunming.

Steaming the duck and then frying it keeps the meat very moist and allows the marinade flavours to penetrate. For serving, poultry is traditionally chopped into bite-size pieces, rather than jointed, so that the pieces can be picked up with chopsticks.

脆皮鸭

CRISPY SKIN DUCK

NORTHERN CHEFS HAVE THEIR FAMOUS PEKING DUCK, BUT IN SICHUAN, CRISPY SKIN DUCK IS EQUALLY POPULAR. THIS DISH CAN ALSO BE MADE WITH BONELESS DUCK BREASTS, JUST ADJUST THE COOKING TIMES. SERVE THE DUCK WITH MANDARIN PANCAKES OR STEAMED FLOWER ROLLS.

2.25 kg (5 lb) duck
8 spring onions (scallions), ends trimmed, smashed with the flat side of a cleaver
8 slices ginger, smashed with the flat side of a cleaver
3 tablespoons Shaoxing rice wine
2 tablespoons salt
2 teaspoons Sichuan peppercorns
1 star anise, smashed with the flat side of a cleaver
2 tablespoons light soy sauce
125 g (1 cup) cornflour (cornstarch)
oil for deep-frying
hoisin sauce
Mandarin pancakes (page 277) or steamed breads (page 46)

SERVES 6

RINSE the duck, drain, and remove any fat from the cavity opening and around the neck. Cut off and discard the parson's nose. Combine the spring onion, ginger, rice wine, salt, Sichuan peppercorns and star anise. Rub the marinade all over the inside and outside of the duck. Place, breast side down, in a bowl with the remaining marinade and leave in the fridge for at least 1 hour. Put the duck and the marinade, breast side up, on a heatproof plate in a steamer, or cut into halves or quarters and put in several steamers.

STEAM over simmering water in a covered wok for 1 1/2 hours, replenishing with boiling water during cooking. Remove the duck, discard the marinade, and let cool. Rub the soy sauce over the duck and then dredge in the cornflour, pressing lightly to make it adhere to the skin. Let the duck dry in the fridge for several hours until very dry.

FILL a wok one-quarter full of oil. Heat the oil to 190°C (375°F), or until a piece of bread fries golden brown in 10 seconds when dropped in the oil. Lower the duck into the oil and fry, ladling the oil over the top, until the skin is crisp and golden.

DRAIN the duck and, using a cleaver, cut the duck through the bones into pieces. Serve plain or with hoisin sauce and pancakes or bread.

Cook the spinach for just a short amount of time so that it keeps its rich colour.

Roasting sesame oil outside a shop where it is sold in Chengdu.

宫保鸡丁

KUNG PAO CHICKEN

KUNG PAO IS ONE OF THE MOST CLASSIC HOT-AND-SOUR SICHUANESE SAUCES, AND CAN BE STIR-FRIED WITH SEAFOOD, PORK OR VEGETABLES AS WELL AS CHICKEN. THE SEASONINGS ARE FRIED IN OIL OVER HIGH HEAT, INTENSIFYING THE SPICINESS AND FLAVOURING THE OIL.

350 g (12 oz) skinless chicken breast fillet
3 tablespoons light soy sauce
3 tablespoons Shaoxing rice wine
2 teaspoons roasted sesame oil
1 tablespoon cornflour (cornstarch)
120 g (3/4 cup) peeled water chestnuts
3 tablespoons oil
450 g (1 lb) baby English spinach leaves
1/2 teaspoon salt
3 garlic cloves, finely chopped
120 g (3/4 cup) unsalted peanuts
1 spring onion (scallion), finely chopped
1 tablespoon finely chopped ginger
1 teaspoon chilli sauce
1 tablespoon sugar
1 teaspoon Chinese black rice vinegar
60 ml (1/4 cup) chicken stock (page 281)

SERVES 6

CUT the chicken into 2.5 cm (1 inch) cubes. Place the cubes in a bowl, add 2 tablespoons of the soy sauce, 2 tablespoons of the rice wine, 1 teaspoon of the sesame oil and 2 teaspoons of the cornflour, and toss lightly. Marinate in the fridge for at least 20 minutes.

BLANCH the water chestnuts in a pan of boiling water, then refresh in cold water. Drain, pat dry and cut into thin slices.

HEAT a wok over high heat, add 1 teaspoon of the oil and heat until very hot. Stir-fry the spinach, salt, 2 teaspoons of the garlic and 2 teaspoons of the rice wine, turning constantly, until the spinach is just becoming limp. Remove the spinach from the wok, arrange around the edge of a platter, cover and keep warm.

REHEAT the wok over high heat, add 1 tablespoon of the oil and heat until very hot. Stir-fry half the chicken pieces, turning constantly, until the meat is cooked. Remove with a wire sieve or slotted spoon and drain. Repeat with 1 tablespoon of oil and the remaining chicken. Wipe out the pan.

DRY-FRY the peanuts in the wok or a saucepan until browned.

REHEAT the wok over high heat, add the remaining oil and heat until very hot. Stir-fry the spring onion, ginger, remaining garlic and the chilli sauce for 10 seconds, or until fragrant. Add the sliced water chestnuts and stir-fry for 15 seconds, or until heated through. Combine the sugar, black vinegar, chicken stock and remaining soy sauce, rice wine, sesame oil and cornflour, add to the sauce and simmer until thickened. Add the cooked chicken and the peanuts. Toss lightly to coat with the sauce. Transfer to the centre of the platter and serve.

海 南 鸡 饭

HAINAN CHICKEN

HAINAN CHICKEN IS A MEAL OF CHICKEN, RICE AND SOUP, EATEN WITH A SPRING ONION (SCALLION) OR CHILLI SAUCE. ORIGINALLY FROM HAINAN ISLAND IN THE SOUTH OF CHINA, THIS DISH WAS BROUGHT TO SINGAPORE BY IMMIGRANTS AND IS NOW A SINGAPOREAN CLASSIC.

1.2 kg (2 lb 12 oz) chicken
2 spring onions (scallions), cut into
    5 cm (2 inch) lengths
5 coriander (cilantro) sprigs
3/4 teaspoon salt
4 slices ginger, smashed with the
    flat side of a cleaver
1/4 teaspoon black peppercorns
finely chopped spring onion
    (scallion)

DIPPING SAUCES
2 spring onions (scallions), sliced
1 tablespoon finely grated ginger
1 teaspoon salt
3 tablespoons oil
3 tablespoons light soy sauce
1–2 red chillies, sliced

SERVES 4

RINSE the chicken, drain, and remove any fat from the cavity opening and around the neck. Cut off and discard the parson's nose. Place the chicken in a large clay pot or casserole. Add the spring onion, coriander, salt, ginger, peppercorns and enough water to cover the chicken. Cover and bring to the boil, then reduce the heat and simmer very gently for 30 minutes. Turn off the heat and leave the chicken for 10 minutes. Remove the chicken from the pot and drain well. Skim off any scum from the liquid and strain the liquid.

TO MAKE the dipping sauces, combine the spring onion, ginger and salt in one small heatproof or metal bowl.

HEAT a wok over high heat, add the oil and heat until smoking. Allow it to cool slightly, then pour over the spring onion mixture. The mixture will splatter. Stir well. Combine the soy sauce and chilli in another small bowl.

USING a cleaver, cut the chicken through the bones into bite-size pieces. Pour the stock into soup bowls, sprinkle with the finely chopped spring onion, and serve with the chicken along with bowls of rice and the dipping sauces.

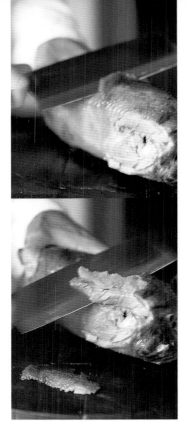

Carve the duck so that each slice has some crispy skin and tender meat. The skin can also be eaten separately, wrapped in the pancakes, while the meat is used in a stir-fry.

Commercially made pancakes are available in Asian shops, fresh or frozen, or from restaurants that sell take-away ducks and barbecued meat.

北京烤鴨

PEKING DUCK

THIS DISH OWES ITS REPUTATION NOT SO MUCH TO THE WAY IT IS COOKED, BUT TO THE WAY IT IS THEATRICALLY CARVED AND EATEN ROLLED INTO PANCAKES. IN RESTAURANTS, THE DUCK IS COOKED IN A SPECIAL OVEN, BUT THIS RECIPE HAS BEEN MODIFIED FOR THE HOME KITCHEN.

2.5 kg (5 lb 8 oz) duck
2 tablespoons maltose or honey, dissolved in 2 tablespoons water
125 ml (1/2 cup) hoisin sauce or plum sauce
24 Mandarin pancakes (page 277)
6–8 spring onions (scallions), shredded
1/2 cucumber, shredded

SERVES 6

CUT the wing tips off the duck with a pair of poultry shears. Rinse the duck, drain, and remove any fat from the cavity opening and around the neck. Cut off and discard the parson's nose. Plunge the duck into a pot of boiling water for 2–3 minutes to tighten the skin. Remove and drain, then dry thoroughly.

WHILE the skin is still warm, brush the duck all over with the maltose or honey and water solution, then hang it up to dry in a cool and airy place for at least 6 hours, or overnight, or leave it uncovered in the fridge.

PREHEAT the oven to 200°C (400°F/Gas 6). Place the duck, breast side up, on a rack in a roasting tin, and cook without basting or turning for 1 1/2 hours. Check to make sure the duck is not getting too dark and, if it is, cover it loosely with foil.

TO SERVE, remove the crispy duck skin in small slices by using a sharp carving knife, then carve the meat, or carve both together. Arrange on a serving plate.

TO EAT, spread about 1 teaspoon of the hoisin sauce or plum sauce in the centre of a pancake, add a few strips of spring onion, cucumber, duck skin and meat, roll up the pancake and turn up the bottom edge to prevent the contents from falling out.

THE QUANJUDE ROAST DUCK RESTAURANTS are perhaps the most famous Peking duck restaurants in Beijing. Established as early as 1864, the name Quanjude means 'everything is included'. More than just Peking duck restaurants, these restaurants specialize in all-duck dinners. Originally the menu included just four items: roast duck, stuffed duck neck, duck soup and stir-fried duck, but at the Quanjude

PEKING DUCK

DUCK DISHES HAVE ALWAYS BEEN CLASSICS OF THE CHINESE KITCHEN: ROASTED IN GUANGZHOU, CAMPHOR AND TEA-SMOKED IN SICHUAN, AND PRESSED IN NANJING, BUT IT IS IN THE CAPITAL THAT PEKING DUCK, PERHAPS CHINA'S MOST FAMOUS DISH, ORIGINATED.

True Peking duck must be made with a white-feathered mallard called a Peking duck. These ducks are bred on farms around Beijing and fattened up with grain for a few months to produce tender meat.

MAKING PEKING DUCK

The dish is prepared in different ways by different restaurants, though there are some principles that remain the same. After the duck is plucked, air is pumped in between the skin and body to inflate the bird, then the duck is blanched in boiling water. The crispy skin is formed by washing the duck with a maltose solution and leaving it to dry in a cool, dry place. The maltose, made from fermented barley, turns a dark reddish brown when cooked to give the bird a lacquered effect.

The duck is filled with boiling water to steam it from the inside and roasted in a specially made kiln-like oven. Inside the oven, the ducks are hung vertically or spit-roasted over fruit wood at very high temperatures for a relatively short time—this produces a truly crisp skin, but prevents the meat from drying out.

today you can order from more than 200 duck dishes, using every conceivable part of the duck, from deep-fried hearts to webs with mustard sauce and stewed tongues. The branch in Wangfujing has two duck kitchens, two pancake kitchens and two general kitchens for a restaurant that seats 800. The chefs are trained at the Beijing Culinary Institute for 3 years before working their way up through the kitchens.

PERFECT PEKING DUCK

The quality of the ingredients is paramount to the flavour of Peking duck. The Peking duck is specially bred to be plump and tender and is reared on a grain diet. Some restaurants add flavourings to the duck by varying the ingredients of the maltose solution or adding flavourings to the boiling water inside the cavity. However, Peking duck should not have a spicy or sweet aroma, instead the natural flavour of the duck juices and crispy skin should dominate.

Crispy skin is the true test of perfect Peking duck. This is achieved by separating the skin from the flesh, then drying the skin thoroughly before the duck is cooked. The wood-fired oven uses its high heat to cook the skin quickly, which also causes most of the fat to melt and run out, while the liquid that has been put inside the duck heats up and steams the flesh from the inside, keeping the meat moist.

THE WEATHER can be an important factor with Peking and roast ducks, and ducks can be seen hanging up outside all over China when it is cold and dry. To form a really crisp skin, the ducks must be thoroughly dried in air with a low humidity until the skin is like paper.

盐锅鸡

SALT-BAKED CHICKEN

THIS IS ANOTHER CANTONESE SPECIALITY THAT EMPLOYS A RATHER UNUSUAL COOKING METHOD. THE
WHOLE CHICKEN IS WRAPPED IN CLOTH AND BAKED IN SALT, WHICH ACTS LIKE AN OVEN, KEEPING IN
THE HEAT TO PRODUCE VERY SUCCULENT CHICKEN MEAT.

1.5 kg (3 lb 5 oz) chicken
2 tablespoons light soy sauce
2 kg (4 lb 8 oz) sea salt or
   coarse salt

FILLING
1 spring onion (scallion), chopped
1 teaspoon grated ginger
2 star anise, crushed
1/2 teaspoon salt
4 tablespoons Mei Kuei Lu Chiew
   or brandy

DIPPING SAUCE
1 tablespoon oil
1 spring onion (scallion), chopped
1 teaspoon chopped ginger
1/2 teaspoon salt
21/2 tablespoons chicken and
   meat stock (page 281)

SERVES 4

RINSE the chicken, drain, and remove any fat
from the cavity opening and around the neck.
Cut off and discard the parson's nose. Blanch the
chicken in a pan of boiling water for 2–3 minutes,
then refresh under cold water and dry well. Brush
the chicken with the soy sauce and hang it up to
dry in a cool and airy place for a couple of hours,
or leave it uncovered in the fridge.

MEANWHILE, TO make the filling, combine the
spring onion, ginger, star anise, salt and Mei Kuei
Lu Chiew. Pour the filling into the cavity of the
chicken. Wrap the chicken tightly with a large
sheet of cheesecloth or fine muslin.

HEAT the salt in a large clay pot or casserole very
slowly until very hot, then turn off the heat and
remove about half. Make a hole in the centre of
the salt and place the chicken in it, breast side
up, then cover with the salt removed earlier so
that the chicken is completely buried. Cover the
clay pot or casserole and cook over medium heat
for 15–20 minutes, then reduce the heat to low
and cook for about 45–50 minutes. Leave for at
least 15–20 minutes before taking the chicken
out. (The salt can be reused.)

TO MAKE the dipping sauce, heat the oil in a
small wok or saucepan. Fry the spring onion and
ginger for 1 minute, then add the salt and stock.
Bring to the boil, then reduce the heat and
simmer for a couple of minutes.

REMOVE the chicken from the casserole and
unwrap it. Using a cleaver, cut the chicken
through the bones into bite-size pieces. Arrange
on a serving dish and serve hot or cold with the
dipping sauce.

Make sure every part of the
chicken is covered in salt to seal
in the flavour completely. The salt
does not affect the flavour of the
chicken as the wrapping and
skin keep it from coming into
contact with the flesh.

Table tennis played at an outside
recreation area in Beijing.

RED-COOKED CHICKEN

RED-COOKING LIQUID
2 cinnamon or cassia sticks
1¹/₂ star anise
2 pieces dried tangerine or orange
  peel, about 5 cm (2 inches) long
¹/₂ teaspoon fennel seeds
375 ml (1¹/₂ cups) dark soy sauce
90 g (3¹/₂ oz) sugar
125 ml (¹/₂ cup) Shaoxing rice wine

1.5 kg (3 lb 5 oz) chicken
1 tablespoon roasted sesame oil

SERVES 6

TO MAKE the red-cooking liquid, place all the ingredients in a clay pot or casserole with 1.5 litres (6 cups) water, bring to the boil, then reduced the heat and simmer for 30 minutes.

RINSE the chicken, drain, and remove any fat from the cavity opening and around the neck. Cut off and discard the parson's nose. Place the chicken, breast side down, in the cooking liquid and cook for 1¹/₂ hours, turning two or three times. Turn off the heat and leave in the liquid for 30 minutes. Brush the chicken with the sesame oil then cut the chicken through the bones into bite-size pieces. Spoon over a little liquid. Serve hot or cold.

THE SAUCE can be reused as a 'Master Sauce' (see page 290).

RED-COOKED CHICKEN

SOY CHICKEN

1.5 kg (3 lb 5 oz) chicken
1 tablespoon ground Sichuan
  peppercorns
2 tablespoons grated ginger
2 tablespoons sugar
3 tablespoons Shaoxing rice wine
310 ml (1¹/₄ cups) dark soy sauce
185 ml (³/₄ cup) light soy sauce
625 ml (2¹/₂ cups) oil
440 ml (1³/₄ cups) chicken and
  meat stock (page 281)
2 teaspoons roasted sesame oil

SERVES 4

RINSE the chicken, drain, and remove any fat from the cavity opening and around the neck. Cut off and discard the parson's nose. Rub the Sichuan peppercorns and ginger all over the inside and outside of the chicken. Combine the sugar, rice wine and soy sauces, add the chicken and marinate in the fridge for at least 3 hours, turning occasionally.

HEAT a wok over high heat, add the oil and heat until very hot. Drain the chicken, reserving the marinade, and fry for 8 minutes until browned. Put in a clay pot or casserole with the marinade and stock. Bring to the boil, then simmer, covered, for 35–40 minutes. Leave off the heat for 2–3 hours, transferring to the fridge once cool. Drain the chicken, brush with oil and refrigerate for 1 hour.

USING a cleaver, chop the chicken through the bones into bite-size pieces, pour over a couple of tablespoons of sauce and serve.

THE SAUCE can be reused as a 'Master Sauce' (see page 290).

The soy sauce and sugar in the marinade turn the chicken skin a rich dark brown when cooked.

DEEP-FRIED QUAILS WITH SPICY SALT

FRESH QUAILS ARE BEST FOR THIS RECIPE BECAUSE ONCE FROZEN, QUAIL CAN BECOME QUITE DRY
AND BLAND, AND TENDERNESS AND SUCCULENCE ARE THE MAIN CHARACTERISTICS OF THIS DISH.

Erhai Lake in Yunnan.

4 quails
1 teaspoon spicy salt and pepper
  (page 285)
1 teaspoon sugar
1 tablespoon light soy sauce
1 tablespoon Shaoxing rice wine
2–3 tablespoons plain (all-purpose)
  flour
oil for deep-frying
1 spring onion (scallion), finely
  chopped
1 red chilli, finely chopped

SERVES 4

SPLIT EACH quail in half down the middle and
clean well. Marinate with the spicy salt and
pepper, the sugar, soy sauce and rice wine for
2–3 hours in the fridge, turning frequently. Coat
each quail piece in the flour.

FILL a wok one-quarter full of oil. Heat the oil to
190°C (375°F), or until a piece of bread fries
golden brown in 10 seconds when dropped in
the oil. Reduce the heat and fry the quail for
2–3 minutes on each side. Remove from the wok
and drain on paper towels.

SOAK the spring onion and chilli in the hot oil
(with the heat turned off) for 2 minutes. Remove
with a wire sieve or slotted spoon and drain, then
sprinkle over the quail pieces. Serve hot.

Marinate the quail for long
enough for the flavours to
penetrate the meat.

LACQUERED SQUAB

THIS COOKING METHOD GIVES THE SKIN OF THE SQUAB A SHINY, DEEP REDDISH-BROWN GLAZE. THE
SIMMERING GIVES THE FLAVOUR AND THE FINAL DEEP-FRYING CRISPS THE SKIN.

2 x 500 g (1 lb 2 oz) squab
4 slices ginger
4 spring onions (scallions), chopped
4 tablespoons light soy sauce
3 tablespoons dark soy sauce
3 tablespoons Shaoxing rice wine
4 tablespoons rock (lump) sugar
1 teaspoon salt
2 cinnamon sticks
2 star anise
1 litre (4 cups) chicken stock
  (page 281)
oil for deep-frying

SERVES 4

BLANCH the squab in a pan of boiling water for
2 minutes, then remove and drain.

COMBINE the remaining ingredients except the oil
in a clay pot or casserole and bring to a simmer.
Add the squab, cover and simmer for 20 minutes.
Remove from the heat, take out the squab and
leave to dry for at least 1 hour.

FILL a wok one-quarter full of oil. Heat the oil to
190°C (375°F), or until a piece of bread fries golden
brown in 10 seconds when dropped in the oil. Fry
the squab until they are very crisp and brown. Drain
well and sprinkle with salt. Using a cleaver, cut the
squabs through the bones into bite-size pieces.

LACQUERED SQUAB

A chicken-seller in Chengdu.

In China, rice wine can be bought directly out of the earthenware pots it is matured in.

柠檬鸡

LEMON CHICKEN

LEMON CHICKEN IS A POPULAR CANTONESE DISH OF FRIED CHICKEN GLAZED WITH A TART, LEMONY SAUCE. HERE THE LEMON SAUCE IS HOME-MADE AND QUITE UNLIKE THE GLUGGY SAUCES OFTEN SERVED WITH THIS DISH. CHICKEN WINGS OR DUCK ARE ALSO DELICIOUS PREPARED IN THIS WAY.

500 g (1 lb 2 oz) skinless chicken
  breast fillet
1 tablespoon light soy sauce
1 tablespoon Shaoxing rice wine
1 spring onion (scallion), finely
  chopped
1 tablespoon finely chopped ginger
1 garlic clove, finely chopped
1 egg, lightly beaten
90 g (3/4 cup) cornflour (cornstarch)
oil for deep-frying

LEMON SAUCE
2 tablespoons lemon juice
2 teaspoons sugar
1/2 teaspoon salt
1/2 teaspoon roasted sesame oil
3 tablespoons chicken stock
  (page 281) or water
1/2 teaspoon cornflour (cornstarch)

SERVES 6

CUT the chicken into slices. Place in a bowl, add the soy sauce, rice wine, spring onion, ginger and garlic, and toss lightly. Marinate in the fridge for at least 1 hour, or overnight.

ADD the egg to the chicken mixture and toss lightly to coat. Drain any excess egg and coat the chicken pieces with the cornflour. The easiest way to do this is to put the chicken and cornflour in a plastic bag and shake it.

FILL a wok one-quarter full of oil. Heat the oil to 190°C (375°F), or until a piece of bread fries golden brown in 10 seconds when dropped in the oil. Add half the chicken, a piece at a time, and fry, stirring constantly, for 3 1/2–4 minutes, or until golden brown. Remove with a wire sieve or slotted spoon and drain. Repeat with the remaining chicken. Reheat the oil and return all the chicken to the wok. Cook until crisp and golden brown. Drain the chicken. Pour off the oil and wipe out the wok.

TO MAKE the lemon sauce, combine the lemon juice, sugar, salt, sesame oil, stock and cornflour.

REHEAT the wok over medium heat until hot, add the lemon sauce and stir constantly until thickened. Add the chicken and toss lightly in the sauce.

醉鸡

DRUNKEN CHICKEN

THERE ARE SEVERAL VERSIONS OF THIS POPULAR DISH, BUT IN THIS SIMPLE RECIPE, THE CHICKEN IS

STEAMED IN THE 'DRUNKEN' SAUCE, WHICH IS THEN POURED OVER TO SERVE.

1.5 kg (3 lb 5 oz) chicken
150 ml (5 fl oz) Shaoxing rice wine
3 tablespoons Chinese spirit (Mou
    Tai) or brandy
3 slices ginger
3 spring onions (scallions), cut into
    short lengths
2 teaspoons salt
1/4 teaspoon freshly ground
    black pepper
coriander (cilantro) leaves

SERVES 4

RINSE the chicken, drain, and remove any fat from the cavity opening and around the neck. Cut off and discard the parson's nose. Blanch the chicken in a pan of boiling water for 2–3 minutes, then refresh in cold water.

PLACE the chicken, breast side down, in a bowl. Add the rice wine, Chinese spirit, ginger, spring onion and half the salt. Place the bowl in a steamer. Cover and steam over simmering water in a wok for 1 1/2 hours, replenishing with boiling water during cooking. Transfer the chicken to a dish, breast side up, reserving the cooking liquid.

POUR half the liquid into a wok or saucepan and add the remaining salt and the pepper. Bring to the boil, then pour the sauce over the chicken. Using a cleaver, cut the chicken through the bones into bite-size pieces. Garnish with the coriander.

DRUNKEN CHICKEN

三杯鸡

THREE-CUP CHICKEN

THREE-CUP CHICKEN IS SO CALLED BECAUSE THE ORIGINAL RECIPE USES ONE CUP EACH OF RICE

WINE, SOY SAUCE AND LARD. CHRISTINE YAN OF YMING RESTAURANT IN LONDON MODIFIED IT HERE

BY SUBSTITUTING THE LARD WITH STOCK, AND THE RESULT IS A MUCH HEALTHIER DISH.

450 g (1 lb) skinless chicken thigh fillet
1 tablespoon cornflour (cornstarch)
1 tablespoon oil
2 spring onions (scallions), chopped
4 small pieces ginger
3 tablespoons Shaoxing rice wine
3 tablespoons light soy sauce
125 ml (1/2 cup) chicken and meat
    stock (page 281)
1/2 teaspoon roasted sesame oil

SERVES 4

CUT the chicken into 2 cm (3/4 inch) cubes. Combine the cornflour with water to make a paste. Toss the chicken cubes in the paste to coat.

HEAT the oil in a small clay pot or casserole, lightly brown the chicken with the spring onion and ginger, then add the rice wine, soy and stock. Bring to the boil, then reduce the heat and simmer, covered, for 20–25 minutes. There should be a little liquid left—if there is too much, boil it off. Add the sesame oil and serve the chicken hot from the pot.

A sign proclaims 'Thai-style chicken feet' for sale at an outside stall in Chengdu.

A shopping street in central Shanghai.

Ducks hanging up to dry after they have been plucked.

上海酱鸭

SHANGHAI SOY DUCK

THIS DUCK, SIMILAR TO CANTONESE SOY CHICKEN, IS TRADITIONALLY SERVED AT ROOM TEMPERATURE AS A FIRST COURSE, THOUGH THERE IS NO REASON WHY IT CAN'T BE SERVED AS A MAIN COURSE, HOT OR COLD. YOU CAN ALSO USE JOINTED PIECES OR DUCK BREASTS, JUST REDUCE THE COOKING TIME.

2.25 kg (5 lb) duck
2 teaspoons salt
4 spring onions (scallions), each
    tied in a knot
4 x 1 cm (1/2 inch) slices ginger,
    smashed with the flat side of
    a cleaver
6 star anise
3 cinnamon or cassia sticks
1 tablespoon Sichuan peppercorns
100 ml (31/2 fl oz) Shaoxing
    rice wine
200 ml (7 fl oz) light soy sauce
100 ml (31/2 fl oz) dark soy sauce
100 g (31/2 oz) rock (lump) sugar

SERVES 4

RINSE the duck, drain, and remove any fat from the cavity opening and around the neck. Cut off and discard the parson's nose. Blanch the duck in a pan of boiling water for 2–3 minutes, then refresh in cold water, pat dry and rub the salt inside the cavity.

PLACE the duck, breast side up, in a clay pot or casserole, and add the spring onion, ginger, star anise, cinnamon, peppercorns, rice wine, soy sauces, rock sugar and enough water to cover. Bring to the boil, then reduce the heat and simmer, covered, for 40–45 minutes. Turn off the heat and leave the duck to cool in the liquid for 2–3 hours, transferring the clay pot to the fridge once it is cool enough. Leave in the fridge until completely cold (you can keep the duck in the liquid overnight and serve it the next day).

TO SERVE, remove the duck from the liquid and drain well. Using a cleaver, cut the duck through the bones into bite-size pieces.

TRADITIONALLY this dish is served at room temperature, but if you would like to serve it hot, put the clay pot with the duck and the liquid back on the stove and bring it to the boil. Simmer for 10 minutes, or until the duck is completely heated through.

THE SAUCE can be reused as a 'Master Sauce' (see page 290).

棒棒鸡

BANG BANG CHICKEN

THIS CLASSIC SICHUANESE COLD PLATTER IS MADE FROM CHICKEN, CUCUMBER AND BEAN THREAD

NOODLES, MIXED IN A SESAME OR PEANUT SAUCE. THE SESAME DRESSING IS THE AUTHENTIC ONE

BUT THE PEANUT VERSION IS ALSO VERY GOOD.

1 1/2 cucumbers
1 teaspoon salt
30 g (1 oz) bean thread noodles
1 teaspoon roasted sesame oil
250 g (9 oz) cooked chicken, cut
    into shreds
2 spring onions (scallions), green
    part only, finely sliced

SESAME DRESSING
1/4 teaspoon Sichuan peppercorns
3 garlic cloves
2 cm (3/4 inch) piece ginger
1/2 teaspoon chilli sauce
3 tablespoons toasted sesame paste
2 tablespoons roasted sesame oil
2 1/2 tablespoons light soy sauce
1 tablespoon Shaoxing rice wine
1 tablespoon Chinese black
    rice vinegar
1 tablespoon sugar
3 tablespoons chicken stock
    (page 281)

OR

PEANUT DRESSING
60 g (1/4 cup) smooth peanut butter
1 teaspoon light soy sauce
1 1/2 tablespoons sugar
2 teaspoons Chinese black
    rice vinegar
1 tablespoon Shaoxing rice wine
1 tablespoon roasted sesame oil
1 spring onion (scallion), finely
    chopped
1 tablespoon finely chopped ginger
1 teaspoon chilli sauce
2 1/2 tablespoons chicken stock
    (page 281)

SERVES 6

SLICE the cucumbers lengthways and remove most of the seeds. Cut each half crossways into thirds, then cut each piece lengthways into thin slices that are 5 cm (2 inches) long and 1 cm (1/2 inch) wide. Place the slices in a bowl, add the salt, toss lightly, and set aside for 20 minutes. Pour off the water that has accumulated.

TO MAKE the sesame dressing, put the Sichuan peppercorns in a frying pan and cook over medium heat, stirring occasionally, for 7–8 minutes, or until golden brown and very fragrant. Cool slightly, then crush into a powder. Combine the garlic, ginger, chilli sauce, sesame paste, sesame oil, soy sauce, rice wine, vinegar, sugar and stock in a blender, food processor or mortar and pestle. Blend to a smooth sauce the consistency of thick cream. Stir in the Sichuan peppercorn powder. Pour into a bowl and set aside.

TO MAKE the peanut dressing, combine the peanut butter, soy sauce, sugar, vinegar, rice wine, sesame oil, spring onion, ginger, chilli sauce and stock in a blender, food processor or mortar and pestle. Blend until the mixture is the consistency of thick cream, adding a little water if necessary. Pour into a bowl and set aside.

SOAK the bean thread noodles in hot water for 10 minutes, then drain and cut into 8 cm (3 inch) lengths. Blanch the noodles in a pan of boiling water for 3 minutes, then refresh in cold water and drain again. Toss the noodles in the sesame oil and arrange them on a large platter. Arrange the cucumber slices on top. Place the chicken shreds on top of the cucumber. Just before serving, pour the sesame or peanut dressing over the chicken. Sprinkle with the spring onion and serve.

Peeling garlic in Sichuan.

白斩鸡

WHITE CUT CHICKEN

'WHITE CUT' IS A POACHING METHOD USED ALL OVER CHINA, WHERE A WHOLE CHICKEN IS COOKED IN A RELATIVELY SHORT TIME IN A WATER-BASED BROTH, THEN THE HEAT IS TURNED OFF AND THE RETAINED HEAT CARRIES OUT THE REMAINDER OF THE COOKING.

1.25 kg (2 lb 12 oz) chicken
2 spring onions (scallions), each tied in a knot
3 slices ginger, smashed with the flat side of a cleaver
3 tablespoons Shaoxing rice wine
1 tablespoon salt

DIPPING SAUCE
4 tablespoons dark soy sauce
1 tablespoon sugar
1 spring onion (scallion), finely chopped
1 garlic clove, finely chopped
1 teaspoon finely chopped ginger
1 teaspoon roasted sesame oil

SERVES 4

RINSE the chicken, drain, and remove any fat from the cavity opening and around the neck. Cut off and discard the parson's nose. Bring 1.5 litres (6 cups) water to a rolling boil in a clay pot or casserole, and gently lower the chicken into the water with the breast side facing up. Add the spring onion, ginger and rice wine, return to the boil, then add the salt and simmer, covered, for 15 minutes.

TURN OFF the heat and leave the chicken to cool in the liquid for 5–6 hours, without lifting the lid.

ABOUT 30 minutes before serving time, remove and drain the chicken. Using a cleaver, cut the chicken through the bones into bite-size pieces.

TO MAKE the dipping sauce, combine the soy sauce, sugar, spring onion, garlic, ginger and sesame oil with a little of the cooking liquid. Divide the sauce among small saucers, one for each person. Each piece of the chicken is dipped before eating.

ALTERNATIVELY, pour the sauce over the chicken before serving, but use light soy sauce instead of dark soy sauce so as not to spoil the 'whiteness' of the chicken.

Old men take their song birds out with them to the park when they meet their friends. The cages are hung up so the birds can sing together while their owners chat.

MEAT

You may find it easier to cut the meat into thin slices if you freeze it for 15 minutes first to firm it up.

木薯炒肉

MU SHU PORK

SINCE WHEAT IS THE STAPLE CROP IN NORTHERN CHINA, MEAT AND VEGETABLE DISHES ARE COMMONLY SERVED THERE WITH STEAMED BREAD OR PANCAKES INSTEAD OF RICE. THIS BEIJING DISH IS SERVED ROLLED IN MANDARIN PANCAKES, WHICH ARE FIRST SPREAD WITH HOISIN SAUCE.

250 g (9 oz) centre-cut pork loin, trimmed
60 ml ($^1/_4$ cup) light soy sauce
2$^1/_2$ tablespoons Shaoxing rice wine
$^1/_2$ teaspoon roasted sesame oil
2 teaspoons cornflour (cornstarch)
5 dried Chinese mushrooms
20 g ($^3/_4$ oz) dried black fungus (wood ears)
4 tablespoons oil
2 eggs, lightly beaten
4 garlic cloves, finely chopped
2 tablespoons finely chopped ginger
1 leek, white part only, finely shredded
$^1/_4$ small Chinese cabbage, shredded, stem sections and leafy sections separated
$^1/_2$ teaspoon sugar
$^1/_4$ teaspoon freshly ground black pepper
80 ml ($^1/_3$ cup) hoisin sauce
12 Mandarin pancakes (page 277)

SERVES 4

CUT the pork across the grain into slices about 5 mm ($^1/_4$ inch) thick, then cut into thin, matchstick-size shreds about 2 cm ($^3/_4$ inch) long. Put the shreds in a bowl, add 1 tablespoon of the soy sauce, 1 tablespoon of the rice wine, the sesame oil and 1 teaspoon of the cornflour, and toss lightly to coat. Cover with plastic wrap and marinate in the fridge for 30 minutes.

SOAK the dried mushrooms in boiling water for 30 minutes, then drain and squeeze out any excess water. Remove and discard the stems and shred the caps. Soak the dried black fungus in cold water for 20 minutes, then drain and squeeze out any excess water. Shred the black fungus.

HEAT a wok over high heat, add 2 tablespoons of the oil and heat until very hot. Stir-fry the pork mixture for 2–3 minutes, until the meat is brown and cooked. Remove with a wire sieve or slotted spoon and drain. Rinse out and dry the wok.

REHEAT the wok over high heat, add 1 tablespoon of the oil and heat until hot. Stir-fry the egg to scramble, then move to the side of the wok. Add 1 tablespoon of oil, heat until very hot, and stir-fry the garlic, ginger, mushrooms and black fungus for 10 seconds, or until fragrant. Add the leek and toss lightly for 1$^1/_2$ minutes, then add the cabbage stems and stir-fry for 30 seconds. Add the leafy cabbage sections, and cook for 1 minute, or until the vegetables are just tender. Combine 1$^1/_2$ tablespoons of the soy sauce, the remaining rice wine and cornflour, the sugar, black pepper and the meat, add to the sauce and simmer until thickened.

COMBINE the hoisin sauce, remaining soy sauce and 1$^1/_2$ tablespoons water in a small bowl. Serve the pork with the pancakes and sauce.

Harvesting bok choy in Liugan.

狮子头肉丸

LION'S HEAD MEATBALLS

THIS DISH IS SO NAMED BECAUSE THE LARGE MEATBALLS ARE SAID TO LOOK LIKE LION'S HEADS SURROUNDED BY A MANE OF BOK CHOY (PAK CHOI). ORIGINALLY THE MEATBALLS TENDED TO BE MADE FROM PORK AND PORK FAT AND WERE COARSER IN TEXTURE.

450 g (1 lb) minced (ground) pork
1 egg white
4 spring onions (scallions), finely
    chopped
1 tablespoon Shaoxing rice wine
1 teaspoon grated ginger
1 tablespoon light soy sauce
2 teaspoons sugar
1 teaspoon roasted sesame oil
300 g (10¹/₂ oz) bok choy
    (pak choi)
1 tablespoon cornflour (cornstarch)
oil for frying
500 ml (2 cups) chicken and meat
    stock (page 281)

SERVES 4

PUT the pork and egg white in a food processor and process briefly until you have a fluffy mixture, or mash the pork in a large bowl and gradually stir in the egg white, beating the mixture well until it is fluffy. Add the spring onion, rice wine, ginger, soy sauce, sugar and sesame oil, season with salt and white pepper, and process or beat again briefly. Fry a small portion of the mixture and taste it, reseasoning if necessary. Divide the mixture into walnut-size balls.

SEPARATE the boy choy leaves and place in the bottom of a clay pot or casserole.

DUST the meatballs with cornflour. Heat a wok over high heat, add 1 cm (¹/₂ inch) oil and heat until very hot. Cook the meatballs in batches until they are browned all over. Drain well and add to the clay pot in an even layer. Pour off the oil and wipe out the wok.

REHEAT the wok over high heat until very hot, add the chicken stock and heat until it is boiling. Pour over the meatballs. Cover and bring very slowly to the boil. Simmer gently with the lid slightly open for 1¹/₂ hours, or until the meatballs are very tender. Serve the meatballs in the dish they were cooked in.

Roll the mixture into balls using the palms of your hands, then dust with cornflour (cornstarch) to prevent them from sticking when you cook them.

A pickle stall in Sichuan.

Deep-frying the pork gives it a crispy, well-browned outside while keeping the meat inside very tender.

酸甜肉

SWEET-AND-SOUR PORK

ALTHOUGH SWEET-AND-SOUR PORK IS OFTEN THOUGHT OF AS A WESTERN INVENTION, IT IS IN FACT CHINESE. IN THE ORIGINAL VERSION, THE PORK IS LIGHT AND CRISPY AND SERVED IN A PIQUANT SWEET-AND-SOUR SAUCE. IF YOU LIKE IT WITH PINEAPPLE, ADD 320 G (2 CUPS) CUBED PINEAPPLE.

600 g (1 lb 5 oz) centre-cut pork loin, trimmed
1 egg
100 g (3¹/₂ oz) cornflour (cornstarch)
1 tablespoon oil
1 onion, cubed
1 red capsicum (pepper), cubed or cut into small triangles
2 spring onions (scallions), cut into 2 cm (³/₄ inch) lengths
150 g (5¹/₂ oz) Chinese pickles
250 ml (1 cup) clear rice vinegar
80 ml (¹/₃ cup) tomato sauce (ketchup)
300 g (1¹/₃ cups) sugar
oil for deep-frying

SERVES 4

CUT the pork into 2 cm (³/₄ inch) cubes and put it in a bowl with the egg, 75 g (2¹/₂ oz) of the cornflour and 2 teaspoons water. Stir to coat all of the pieces of pork.

HEAT a wok over high heat, add the oil and heat until very hot. Stir-fry the onion for 1 minute. Add the capsicum and spring onion and cook for 1 minute. Add the pickles and toss together to combine. Add the rice vinegar, tomato sauce and sugar and stir over low heat until the sugar dissolves. Bring to the boil, then simmer for 3 minutes.

COMBINE the remaining cornflour with 80 ml (¹/₃ cup) water, add to the sweet-and-sour mixture and simmer until thickened. Set aside.

FILL a wok one-quarter full of oil. Heat the oil to 180°C (350°F), or until a piece of bread fries golden brown in 15 seconds when dropped in the oil. Cook the pork in batches until golden brown and crispy. Return all of the pork to the wok, cook until crisp again, then remove with a wire sieve or slotted spoon and drain well. Add the pork pieces to the sauce, stir to coat, and reheat until bubbling.

红烧排骨

RED-COOKED PORK

RED-COOKING, OR BRAISING IN A SOY-SAUCE BASED LIQUID, IS A TECHNIQUE USED ALL OVER CHINA
TO MAKE CHICKEN, MEAT OR FISH VERY TENDER WITH LITTLE EFFORT.

1.5 kg (3 lb 5 oz) pork leg, with
   bone in and rind on
4 spring onions (scallions), each
   tied in a knot
4 slices ginger, smashed with the
   flat side of a cleaver
185 ml (³/₄ cup) dark soy sauce
4 tablespoons Shaoxing rice wine
1 teaspoon five-spice powder
50 g (1³/₄ oz) rock (lump) sugar

SERVES 8

SCRAPE the pork rind to make sure it is free of
any bristles. Blanch the pork in a pan of boiling
water for 4–5 minutes. Rinse the pork and place
in a clay pot or casserole with 625 ml (2¹/₂ cups)
water, the spring onions, ginger, soy sauce, rice
wine, five-spice powder and sugar. Bring to the
boil, then reduce the heat and simmer, covered,
for 2¹/₂–3 hours, turning several times, until the
meat is very tender and falling from the bone.

IF THERE is too much liquid, remove the pork and
reduce the sauce by boiling it for 10–15 minutes.
Slice the pork and serve with the sauce poured
over it.

RED-COOKED PORK

东坡肉

DONG PO PORK

NAMED AFTER A GOURMET STATESMAN OF THE SONG DYNASTY, THE PORK IS FRIED TO GIVE THE SKIN
A GOOD COLOUR AND TEXTURE, THEN SLOW COOKED TO MELTINGLY TENDER.

1 kg (2 lb 4 oz) belly pork, rind on
2 tablespoons oil
6 spring onions (scallions), sliced
8 slices ginger
100 g (3¹/₂ oz) rock (lump) sugar
2¹/₂ tablespoons dark soy sauce
2¹/₂ tablespoons light soy sauce
125 ml (¹/₂ cup) Shaoxing rice wine

SERVES 6

SCRAPE the pork rind to make sure it is free of
any bristles. Blanch the pork in a pan of boiling
water for 10 minutes, then drain well and dry
thoroughly with paper towels.

HEAT a wok over high heat, add the oil and heat
until very hot. Cook the pork until well browned
and the skin is crisp and brown. Drain the pork.

PUT the spring onion, ginger, sugar, soy sauces,
rice wine and 125 ml (¹/₂ cup) water in a clay pot
or casserole. Bring to the boil, stirring until the
sugar has dissolved. Add the pork, cover and
simmer for 2¹/₂–3 hours, or until very tender.
Remove the pork and drain, straining the liquid.
Cut the pork into very thin slices and serve with
the sauce.

Make sure that the pork is very
well browned and that the skin is
crisp, otherwise it will be soggy
after the second cooking stage.

CHAR SIU

CHAR SIU, OR BARBECUE PORK, IS A CANTONESE SPECIALITY THAT CAN BE SEEN HANGING IN CHINESE

RESTAURANTS. CHAR SIU MEANS 'SUSPENDED OVER FIRE' AND IS TRADITIONALLY DYED A RED COLOUR.

Hanging the char siu to roast above a tray of water creates a steamy atmosphere which helps keep the meat moist. Generally in China, char siu is bought from take-aways as most homes do not have an oven.

MARINADE
1 tablespoon rock (lump) sugar
1 tablespoon yellow bean sauce
1 tablespoon hoisin sauce
1 tablespoon oyster sauce
1 tablespoon red fermented tofu
1 tablespoon Chinese spirit
   (Mou Tai) or brandy
1/2 teaspoon roasted sesame oil

750 g (1 lb 10 oz) centre-cut pork
   loin, trimmed and cut into four
   20 cm (8 inch) strips
2 tablespoons maltose or honey,
   dissolved with a little water

SERVES 4

TO MAKE the marinade, combine the ingredients. Add the pork to the marinade and leave in the fridge for at least 6 hours.

PREHEAT the oven to 220°C (425°F/Gas 7). Put a baking dish with 625 ml (2¹/₂ cups) boiling water in the bottom of the oven. Drain the pork, reserving the marinade. Put an S-shaped meat hook through one end of each strip and hang from the top rack.

COOK FOR 10–15 minutes, then baste with the marinade. Reduce the heat to 180°C (350°F/Gas 4) and cook for 8–10 minutes. Cool for 2–3 minutes, then brush with the maltose and lightly brown under a grill (broiler) for 4–5 minutes, turning to give a charred look around the edges.

CUT the meat into slices. Add 185 ml (³/₄ cup) cooking liquid to the marinade. Bring to the boil and cook for 2 minutes. Strain and pour over the pork.

SPICY CRISPY PORK

750 g (1 lb 10 oz) belly pork, rind on
1 teaspoon salt
1 teaspoon five-spice powder

DIPPING SAUCE
2 tablespoons light soy sauce
1 tablespoon dark soy sauce
1 tablespoon chilli sauce (optional)

SERVES 6

SCRAPE the pork rind to make sure it is free of any bristles. Dry, then rub with the salt and five-spice powder. Leave uncovered in the fridge for at least 2 hours.

TO MAKE the dipping sauce, combine all of the ingredients.

PREHEAT the oven to 240°C (475°F/Gas 9). Place the pork, skin side up, on a rack in a roasting tin. Roast for 20 minutes, reduce the heat to 200°C (400°F/Gas 6) and cook for 40–45 minutes until crispy. Cut into pieces and serve with the sauce.

SPICY CRISPY PORK

芥菜焖三尘肉

BRAISED PORK BELLY WITH MUSTARD CABBAGE

MEAT FROM THE BELLY IS A CUT OF MEAT THAT NEEDS LONG, SLOW COOKING TO MAKE IT TENDER. THE RED TOFU AND PRESERVED MUSTARD CABBAGE TEMPER THE RICHNESS OF THE MEAT BECAUSE THEY ARE BOTH STRONGLY FLAVOURED.

200 g (7 oz) preserved mustard
    cabbage
1 kg (2 lb 4 oz) belly pork, rind on
2 tablespoons dark soy sauce
oil for frying

SAUCE
1 1/2 pieces fermented red tofu
1 tablespoon yellow bean sauce
1 1/2 tablespoons oyster sauce
2 tablespoons dark soy sauce
2 teaspoons sugar
4 star anise
2 tablespoons oil
2 garlic cloves, bruised
4 slices ginger, smashed with the
    flat side of a cleaver

SERVES 6

SOAK the preserved mustard cabbage in cold water for 4 hours. Drain and wash well in a sink full of water until the water is clear of grit. Drain again, then cut the cabbage into short lengths.

SCRAPE the pork rind to make sure it is free of any bristles. Bring a large clay pot or casserole full of water to the boil and add the pork belly. Simmer, covered, for 40 minutes, or until tender. Drain the pork and, when cool enough to handle, prick holes over the skin with a fork. Rub the soy sauce over the skin.

HEAT a wok with a lid over medium heat, add 2 cm (3/4 inch) of the oil and heat until hot. Add the pork belly, skin side down, and cook for 5–8 minutes, or until the skin is crispy, then turn over to brown the meat. Cover the wok slightly with the lid to protect you from the fat—the pork will sizzle violently as it cooks. Place the pork in a bowl of hot water for 30 minutes to make the skin bubble up and soften. Remove the pork from the bowl and cut it into 2 cm (3/4 inch) wide strips. Set aside.

TO MAKE the sauce, put the fermented tofu, yellow bean sauce, oyster sauce, soy sauce, sugar and star anise in a bowl. Heat a wok over medium heat, add the oil and heat until hot. Cook the garlic for 30 seconds, then add the sauce mixture and the ginger. Cook for 1–2 minutes, or until aromatic.

A cured meat shop in Guangzhou.

ADD the pork and coat with the sauce, then add 750 ml (3 cups) water and mix well. Cover and bring to the boil, then reduce the heat and simmer for 40 minutes. Add the mustard cabbage and cook for 15 minutes. If the sauce is too thin, boil it, uncovered, for a few minutes, until it thickens.

焖猪蹄

PICKLED PIG'S TROTTERS

THIS RECIPE IS TRADITIONALLY SERVED TO NEW MOTHERS—THE GINGER IS SAID TO BE A RESTORATIVE AND THE DISH SUPPOSEDLY HELPS MOTHERS PRODUCE PLENTY OF MILK FOR THEIR BABIES. THE HARD-BOILED EGGS ARE A SYMBOL OF LIFE AND CAN BE EATEN WITH THE MEAT.

450 g (1 lb) young ginger, peeled and cut into 2.5 cm (1 inch) pieces
1.5 kg (3 lb 5 oz) pig's trotters, front and back legs
1 litre (4 cups) Chinese black rice vinegar
115 g (4 oz) rock (lump) sugar
6 hard-boiled eggs (optional)

SERVES 6

PUT the ginger in a bowl of water. Bring a wok or saucepan of water to the boil, add the trotters, return to the boil, then drain. Scrape the skin to make sure it is free of any bristles. Using a cleaver, cut each trotter through the bone into three or four pieces.

DRAIN the ginger and lightly smash each piece with the side of a cleaver. Blanch the ginger in a pan of boiling water for 2 minutes, refresh in cold water and leave to cool.

PUT the vinegar and sugar in a wok or saucepan and bring to the boil, stirring to dissolve the sugar. Add the trotters and ginger and simmer, covered, for 2 hours, then simmer, uncovered, for 1–2 hours until tender. Add the unpeeled eggs and cook for 5 minutes. Cool, then refrigerate overnight. Lift off any fat and bring to the boil. Serve hot or cold.

Pig's trotters need to be cooked for several hours in order to break down all the connective tissue and make them tender.

CRYSTAL-BOILED PORK

水晶猪肉

CRYSTAL-BOILED PORK

1 kg (2 lb 4 oz) pork leg, boned and rind on
2 garlic cloves, finely chopped
1 spring onion (scallion), finely chopped
1 teaspoon sugar
4 tablespoons light soy sauce
1 teaspoon roasted sesame oil
1 teaspoon chilli oil (optional)

SERVES 8

SCRAPE the pork rind to make sure it is free of any bristles. Tie up like a parcel to hold its shape, then place in a clay pot or casserole of boiling water, return to the boil and skim off any scum. Simmer, covered, for 45–50 minutes.

TURN OFF the heat and let the pork cool in the water, without taking off the lid, for at least 4 hours, transferring the clay pot or casserole to the fridge once it is cool enough. Remove the pork from the liquid and drain, skin side up, for 2–3 hours.

CUT OFF the skin, leaving a thin layer of fat. Cut the pork across the grain into thin slices. Combine the remaining ingredients and pour over the pork.

A meat stall in an outdoor market in Sichuan.

酸甜红烧排骨

SPARERIBS WITH SWEET-AND-SOUR SAUCE

THIS DELICIOUS DISH IS CANTONESE IN ORIGIN. THE SAUCE SHOULD BE BRIGHT AND TRANSLUCENT, THE MEAT TENDER AND SUCCULENT, AND THE FLAVOUR NEITHER TOO SWEET NOR TOO SOUR. IF YOU PREFER YOU CAN USE A BONELESS CUT OF PORK SUCH AS LOIN.

500 g (1 lb 2 oz) Chinese-style
  pork spareribs
1/4 teaspoon salt
1/4 teaspoon freshly ground
  black pepper
1 teaspoon sugar
1 tablespoon Chinese spirit
  (Mou Tai) or brandy
1 egg yolk, beaten
1 tablespoon cornflour (cornstarch)
oil for deep-frying

SAUCE
1 tablespoon oil
1 small green capsicum (pepper),
  shredded
3 tablespoons sugar
2 tablespoons clear rice vinegar
1 tablespoon light soy sauce
1 tablespoon tomato paste (purée)
1/4 teaspoon roasted sesame oil
21/2 tablespoons chicken and meat
  stock (page 281)
2 teaspoons cornflour (cornstarch)

SERVES 4

ASK the butcher to cut the slab of spareribs crosswise into thirds that measure 5 cm (2 inches) in length, or use a cleaver to do so yourself. Cut the ribs between the bones to separate them. Put the pieces in a bowl with the salt, pepper, sugar and Chinese spirit. Marinate in the fridge for at least 35 minutes, turning occasionally.

MEANWHILE, blend the egg yolk with the cornflour and enough water to make a thin batter. Remove the spareribs from the marinade and coat them with the batter.

FILL a wok one-quarter full of oil. Heat the oil to 180°C (350°F), or until a piece of bread fries golden brown in 15 seconds when dropped in the oil. Fry the spareribs in batches for 5 minutes until they are crisp and golden, stirring to separate them, then remove and drain. Reheat the oil and fry the spareribs again for 1 minute to darken their colour. Remove and drain well on crumpled paper towels. Keep warm in a low oven.

TO MAKE the sauce, heat a wok over high heat, add the oil and heat until very hot. Stir-fry the green capsicum for a few seconds, then add the sugar, rice vinegar, soy sauce, tomato paste, sesame oil and stock, and bring to the boil. Combine the cornflour with enough water to make a paste, add to the sauce and simmer until thickened. Add the spareribs and toss to coat them with the sauce. Serve hot.

Chinese spirits are sold in fancy packaging. The Wuliangye shown here is made from five grains: sorghum, corn, wheat and two kinds of rice.

A tea-seller in Guangzhou.

豆瓣炒牛肉

BEEF WITH CAPSICUM AND BLACK BEAN SAUCE

LEAN STEAK IS A PARTICULARLY GOOD CUT OF BEEF FOR STIR-FRYING. THE TRADITIONAL VERSION OF THIS CANTONESE DISH CALLS FOR JUST GREEN CAPSICUM (PEPPER), BUT THIS RECIPE USES ALL DIFFERENT COLOURS TO MAKE A MORE ATTRACTIVE DISH.

750 g (1 lb 10 oz) rump or sirloin
  steak, trimmed
1 tablespoon light soy sauce
2 teaspoons Shaoxing rice wine
1/2 teaspoon roasted sesame oil
1 teaspoon cornflour (cornstarch)
250 ml (1 cup) oil

BLACK BEAN SAUCE
1 tablespoon oil
30 g (1 oz) finely chopped spring
  onion (scallion)
1 tablespoon finely chopped garlic
1 tablespoon salted, fermented
  black beans, rinsed and coarsely
  chopped
1 tablespoon finely chopped ginger
1 green capsicum (pepper),
  shredded
1 red capsicum (pepper), shredded
1 orange or yellow capsicum
  (pepper), shredded
2 teaspoons light soy sauce
1 tablespoon Shaoxing rice wine
1 teaspoon sugar
2 tablespoons chicken stock
  (page 281)
1/2 teaspoon roasted sesame oil
2 teaspoons cornflour (cornstarch)

SERVES 6

CUT the beef across the grain into slices 1 mm (1/12 inch) thick. Cut each slice of beef into thin strips and place in a bowl. Add the soy sauce, rice wine, sesame oil, cornflour and 1 tablespoon water, toss lightly to combine, then marinate in the fridge for 30 minutes. Drain the beef.

HEAT a wok over high heat, add the oil and heat until almost smoking. Add a third of the beef and cook, stirring constantly, for 1 minute, or until the pieces brown. Remove with a wire sieve or slotted spoon, then drain. Repeat with the remaining beef.

TO MAKE the black bean sauce, heat a wok over high heat, add the oil and heat until very hot. Stir-fry the spring onion, garlic, black beans and ginger for 10 seconds, or until fragrant. Add the peppers and stir-fry for 1 minute, or until cooked.

COMBINE the soy sauce, rice wine, sugar, stock, sesame oil and cornflour, add to the sauce and simmer until thickened. Add the beef and toss lightly to coat with the sauce.

红烧牛肉

RED-COOKED BEEF

THIS IS BASICALLY A STEW, SLOW-COOKED IN AN EQUAL MIXTURE OF SOY SAUCE, RICE WINE AND GINGER. THIS DISH IS A VERY HOME-STYLE ONE, MORE LIKELY FOUND IN SOMEONE'S KITCHEN THAN ON A RESTAURANT MENU.

500 g (1 lb 2 oz) shin of beef or
   stewing or braising beef, trimmed
3 tablespoons Shaoxing rice wine
3 slices ginger
3 tablespoons dark soy sauce
50 g (1³/₄ oz) rock (lump) sugar
300 g (10¹/₂ oz) carrots
1 teaspoon salt

SERVES 4

CUT the beef into 1.5 cm (⁵/₈ inch) cubes and put in a clay pot or casserole with enough water to cover. Add the rice wine and ginger, bring to the boil, skim off any scum, then simmer, covered, for 35–40 minutes. Add the soy and sugar and simmer for 10–15 minutes.

CUT the carrots into pieces roughly the same size as the beef, add to the saucepan with the salt and cook for 20–25 minutes.

RED-COOKED BEEF

五香牛肉

FIVE-SPICE BEEF

THIS IS A DELICIOUS BEEF RECIPE THAT IS VERY SIMPLE TO PREPARE. THE LIQUID IN WHICH THE BEEF HAS BEEN COOKED CAN BE REUSED FOR COOKING OTHER TYPES OF MEAT OR POULTRY, AND IS KNOWN AS LUSHUI ZHI—A 'MASTER SAUCE'.

750 g (1 lb 10 oz) shin of beef or
   stewing or braising beef, trimmed
2 spring onions (scallions), each tied
   in a knot
3 slices ginger, smashed with the
   flat side of a cleaver
4 tablespoons Chinese spirit
   (Mou Tai) or brandy
1.5 litres (6 cups) chicken and meat
   stock (page 281)
1 teaspoon salt
4 tablespoons light soy sauce
3 tablespoons dark soy sauce
1 tablespoon five-spice powder
150 g (5¹/₂ oz) rock (lump) sugar
1 spring onion (scallion), finely sliced
1 teaspoon roasted sesame oil

SERVES 8

CUT the beef into two to three long strips and place in a clay pot or casserole with the spring onions, ginger, Chinese spirit and stock. Bring to the boil and skim off any scum. Simmer, covered, for 15–20 minutes.

ADD the salt, soy sauces, five-spice powder and sugar to the beef, return to the boil, then simmer, covered, for 25–30 minutes.

LEAVE the beef in the liquid to cool for 1 hour, then remove, drain, and cool for 3–4 hours. Just before serving, slice thinly across the grain and sprinkle with the spring onion and sesame oil.

THE SAUCE can be reused as a 'Master Sauce' (see page 290).

Tying the spring onions (scallions) into knots bruises the flesh and allows more flavour to come out.

FIVE-SPICE BEEF

蒙古火锅

MONGOLIAN HOTPOT

THE HOTPOT WAS INTRODUCED TO NORTHERN CHINA BY THE MONGOLIANS, BUT IT SOON BECAME SO POPULAR THAT REGIONAL VARIATIONS EVOLVED. TRADITIONALLY LAMB OR BEEF IS USED, AS IN THIS SLIGHTLY ADAPTED VERSION OF THE NORTHERN CLASSIC.

The Great Wall of China.

350 g (12 oz) rump or sirloin steak, trimmed
1 tablespoon light soy sauce
80 ml (1/3 cup) Shaoxing rice wine
1/2 teaspoon roasted sesame oil
250 g (9 oz) Chinese cabbage, stems removed and leaves cut into 5 cm (2 inch) squares
1 tablespoon oil
2 garlic cloves, smashed with the flat side of a cleaver
750 ml (3 cups) chicken stock (page 281)
1/2 teaspoon salt
30 g (1 oz) bean thread noodles
225 g (8 oz) Chinese mushrooms (shiitake) or button mushrooms
180 g (6 oz) baby English spinach

DIPPING SAUCE
2 tablespoons light soy sauce
1 tablespoon Shaoxing rice wine
1 teaspoon Chinese black rice vinegar
1 teaspoon sugar
1/2 teaspoon chilli sauce or dried chilli flakes (optional)
1/2 spring onion (scallion), finely chopped
1 teaspoon finely chopped ginger
1 garlic clove, finely chopped

SERVES 6

CUT the beef across the grain into paper-thin slices. Place in a bowl and add the soy sauce, 1 tablespoon of the rice wine and the sesame oil, toss lightly, and arrange the slices on a platter.

SEPARATE the hard cabbage pieces from the leafy ones. Heat a wok over high heat, add the oil and heat until very hot. Stir-fry the hard cabbage pieces and garlic for several minutes, adding 1 tablespoon of water. Add the leafy cabbage pieces and stir-fry for several minutes. Add the remaining rice wine, chicken stock and salt, and bring to the boil. Reduce the heat and simmer for 20 minutes.

SOAK the bean thread noodles in hot water for 10 minutes, then drain and cut into 15 cm (6 inch) lengths. Arrange the mushrooms, spinach and noodles on several platters and place on a table where a heated Mongolian hotpot has been set up. (If you do not have a Mongolian hotpot, use a pot and a hot plate, or an electric frying pan or an electric wok.)

COMBINE the dipping sauce ingredients and divide among six bowls. Put a bowl of dipping sauce at each diner's place.

POUR the cabbage soup mixture into the hotpot and bring to the boil. To eat, each diner takes a slice of meat, dips it into the hot stock until the meat is cooked, then dips the meat into the dipping sauce, and eats. The mushrooms, noodles and spinach are cooked in the same way and dipped in the sauce before eating. Supply small wire strainers to cook the noodles so they stay together. The mushrooms and noodles should cook for 5 to 6 minutes, but the spinach should only take about 1 minute. Once all the ingredients have been eaten, the soup is eaten.

A hotpot restaurant in Yunnan.

香脆牛肉片

CRISPY SHREDDED BEEF

THE ORIGINS OF THIS DISH ARE A BIT OBSCURE, THOUGH SOME CLAIM THAT IT IS FROM SICHUAN OR

HUNAN, PROBABLY BECAUSE IT IS SPICY. MAKE SURE THE BEEF IS REALLY CRISPY WHEN YOU FRY IT.

400 g (14 oz) rump or sirloin steak,
    trimmed
2 eggs, beaten
1/2 teaspoon salt
4 tablespoons cornflour (cornstarch)
oil for deep-frying
2 carrots, finely shredded
2 spring onions (scallions), shredded
1 garlic clove, finely chopped
2 red chillies, shredded
80 g (1/3 cup) caster (superfine) sugar
3 tablespoons Chinese black
    rice vinegar
2 tablespoons light soy sauce

SERVES 4

CUT the beef into thin shreds. Combine the eggs, salt and cornflour, then coat the shredded beef with the batter. Mix well.

FILL a wok one-quarter full of oil. Heat the oil to 180°C (350°F), or until a piece of bread fries golden brown in 15 seconds when dropped in the oil. Cook the beef for 3–4 minutes, stirring to separate, then remove and drain. Cook the carrot for 1 1/2 minutes, then remove and drain. Pour the oil from the wok, leaving 1 tablespoon.

REHEAT the reserved oil over high heat until very hot and stir-fry the spring onion, garlic and chilli for a few seconds. Add the beef, carrot, sugar, vinegar and soy and stir to combine.

CRISPY SHREDDED BEEF

青葱炒牛肉

STIR-FRIED BEEF WITH SPRING ONIONS

THIS NORTHERN DISH COMBINES DELICIOUSLY TENDER BEEF WITH A GLAZE OF SOY SAUCE AND SUGAR

AND FRIED SPRING ONIONS (SCALLIONS). YOU CAN SERVE IT WITH MANDARIN PANCAKES OR RICE.

500 g (1 lb 2 oz) rump or sirloin steak
2 garlic cloves, finely chopped
2 tablespoons light soy sauce
1 tablespoon Shaoxing rice wine
2 teaspoons sugar
1 tablespoon cornflour (cornstarch)
3 tablespoons oil
5 spring onions (scallions), green
    part only, cut into thin strips

SAUCE
3 tablespoons light soy sauce
2 teaspoons sugar
1/2 teaspoon roasted sesame oil

SERVES 6

CUT the beef across the grain into 2 mm (1/8 inch) thick slices, then cut into bite-size pieces. Combine with the garlic, soy, rice wine, sugar and cornflour. Marinate in the fridge for at least 1 hour. Drain.

TO MAKE the sauce, combine all the ingredients.

HEAT a wok over high heat, add the oil and heat until very hot. Cook the beef in two batches for 1 1/2 minutes, or until brown. Remove and drain. Pour the oil from the wok, leaving 1 tablespoon.

REHEAT the reserved oil over high heat until very hot and stir-fry the spring onion for 1 minute. Add the beef and the sauce. Toss to coat the meat and spring onion with the sauce.

STIR-FRIED BEEF WITH SPRING ONIONS

蚝油炒牛肉

BEEF WITH OYSTER SAUCE

300 g (11 oz) rump or sirloin steak, trimmed
1 teaspoon sugar
1 tablespoon dark soy sauce
2 teaspoons Shaoxing rice wine
2 teaspoons cornflour (cornstarch)
4 dried Chinese mushrooms
oil for deep-frying
4 slices ginger
1 spring onion (scallion), cut into short lengths
75 g (2¹/₂ oz) snowpeas (mangetout), ends trimmed
1 small carrot, thinly sliced
¹/₂ teaspoon salt
2–3 tablespoons chicken and meat stock (page 281)
2 tablespoons oyster sauce

SERVES 4

CUT the beef across the grain into thin bite-size slices. Combine with half the sugar, the soy sauce, rice wine, cornflour and 2 tablespoons water. Marinate in the fridge for several hours, or overnight.

SOAK the dried mushrooms in boiling water for 30 minutes, then drain and squeeze out any excess water. Remove and discard the stems and cut the caps in half, or quarters if large.

FILL a wok one-quarter full of oil. Heat the oil to 180°C (350°F), or until a piece of bread fries golden brown in 15 seconds when dropped in the oil. Cook the beef for 45–50 seconds, stirring to separate the pieces, and remove as soon as the colour changes. Drain well in a colander. Pour the oil from the wok, leaving 2 tablespoons.

REHEAT the reserved oil over high heat until very hot and stir-fry the ginger and spring onion for 1 minute. Add the snowpeas, mushrooms and carrot and stir-fry for 1 minute, then add the salt, stock and remaining sugar and stir-fry for 1 minute. Toss with the beef and oyster sauce.

蒸面粉牛肉

STEAMED BEEF WITH RICE FLOUR

450 g (1 lb) rump or sirloin steak
2 tablespoons soy sauce
1 tablespoon chilli bean paste (toban jiang)
1 tablespoon Shaoxing rice wine
1 tablespoon finely chopped ginger
¹/₄ teaspoon freshly ground white pepper
1 tablespoon oil
125 g (4¹/₂ oz) glutinous rice flour
¹/₂ teaspoon ground cinnamon
1 teaspoon roasted sesame oil
1 spring onion (scallion), shredded

SERVES 4

CUT the beef into 2 mm (¹/₈ inch) slices and cut the slices into bite-size pieces. Combine with the soy sauce, chilli bean paste, rice wine, ginger, pepper and oil. Marinate in the fridge for 30 minutes.

DRY-FRY the rice flour in a wok until it is brown and smells roasted. Add the cinnamon. Drain the beef and toss in the rice flour to coat the slices.

PLACE the beef slices in a steamer lined with greaseproof paper punched with holes. Cover and steam over simmering water in a wok for 20 minutes. Sprinkle with the sesame oil and garnish with the spring onion.

STEAMED BEEF WITH RICE FLOUR

蒙古羊肉

MONGOLIAN LAMB

300 g (10 1/2 oz) lamb fillet
2 teaspoons finely chopped ginger
1 spring onion (scallion), chopped
2 teaspoons ground Sichuan
  peppercorns
1 teaspoon salt
2 tablespoons light soy sauce
1 tablespoon yellow bean sauce
1 tablespoon hoisin sauce
1 teaspoon five-spice powder
2 tablespoons Shaoxing rice wine
oil for deep-frying
crisp lettuce leaves
80 ml (1/3 cup) hoisin sauce, extra
1/2 cucumber, shredded
6 spring onions (scallions),
  shredded

SERVES 4

CUT the lamb along the grain into six long strips. Combine with the ginger, spring onion, pepper, salt, soy, yellow bean and hoisin sauces, five-spice powder and rice wine. Marinate in the fridge for at least 2 hours. Put the lamb and marinade in a heatproof dish in a steamer. Cover and steam for 2 1/2–3 hours over simmering water in a wok, replenishing with boiling water during cooking. Remove the lamb from the liquid and drain well.

FILL a wok one-quarter full of oil. Heat the oil to 180°C (350°F), or until a piece of bread fries golden brown in 15 seconds when dropped in the oil. Cook the lamb for 3–4 minutes, then remove and drain. Cut the lamb into bite-size shreds.

TO SERVE, place some lamb in the lettuce leaves with some hoisin sauce, cucumber and spring onion and roll up into a parcel.

Making bread and pancakes at a street stall in Beijing.

韭菜炒羊肉

STIR-FRIED LAMB AND LEEKS

300 g (10 1/2 oz) lamb fillet
1/4 teaspoon ground Sichuan
  peppercorns
1/2 teaspoon sugar
1 tablespoon light soy sauce
2 teaspoons Shaoxing rice wine
2 teaspoons cornflour (cornstarch)
1/2 teaspoon roasted sesame oil
3 tablespoons dried black fungus
  (wood ears)
625 ml (2 1/2 cups) oil
4 small pieces ginger
200 g (7 oz) young leeks, white part
  only, cut into short lengths
2 tablespoons yellow bean sauce

SERVES 4

CUT the lamb into thin slices and combine with the Sichuan peppercorns, sugar, soy sauce, rice wine, cornflour and sesame oil. Marinate in the fridge for at least 2 hours.

SOAK the dried black fungus in cold water for 20 minutes, then drain and squeeze out any excess water.

HEAT a wok over high heat, add the oil and heat until very hot. Stir-fry the lamb for 1 minute, or until the colour changes. Remove and drain. Pour the oil from the wok, leaving 2 tablespoons.

REHEAT the reserved oil over high heat until very hot and stir-fry the ginger, leek and black fungus for 1 minute, then add the yellow bean sauce, blend well, and add the lamb. Continue stirring for 1 minute.

STIR-FRIED LAMB AND LEEKS

TOFU

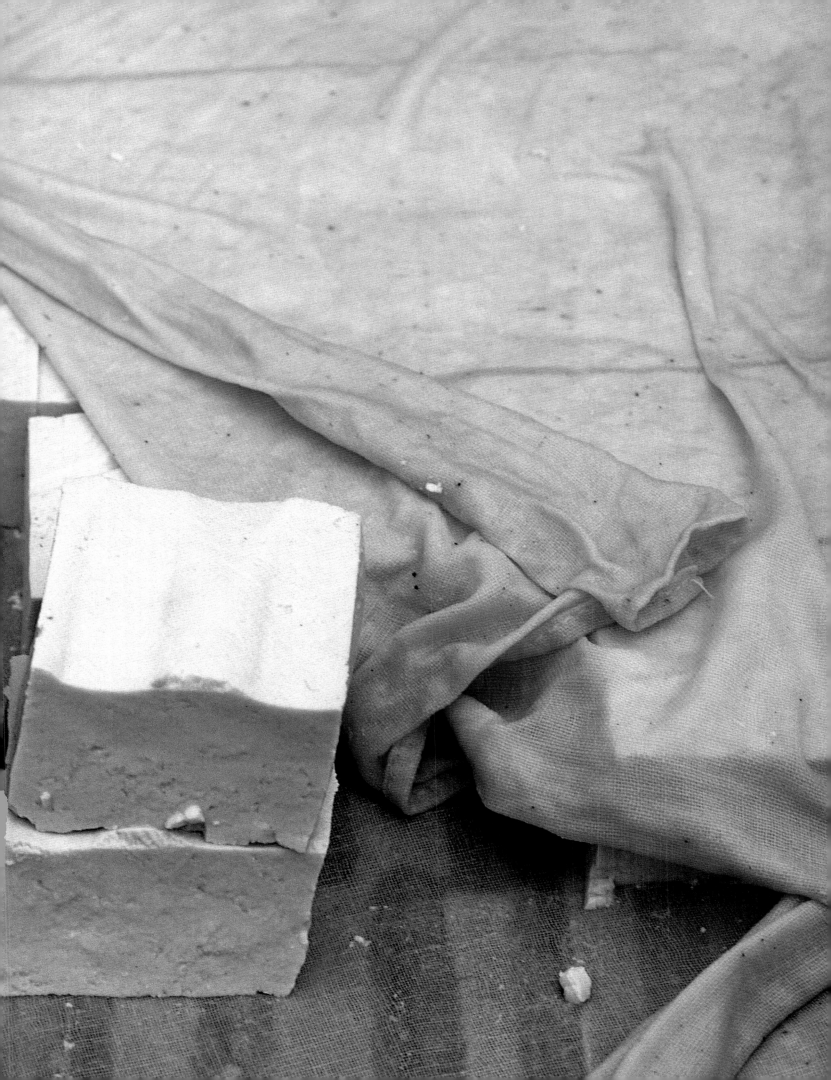

香菇焖豆腐

BRAISED TOFU WITH CHINESE MUSHROOMS

SOME PEOPLE FIND TOFU BLAND, BUT BY COOKING IT WITH STRONGLY FLAVOURED MUSHROOMS, YOU

HAVE A WELL-BALANCED DISH WITH A CONTRAST IN COLOUR, AROMA, FLAVOUR AND TEXTURE.

300 g (10^1/$_2$ oz) firm tofu, drained
50 g (1^3/$_4$ oz) dried Chinese
  mushrooms
4 tablespoons oil
1 teaspoon salt
1 teaspoon sugar
1 tablespoon Shaoxing rice wine
^{1}/$_2$ teaspoon roasted sesame oil
1 teaspoon cornflour (cornstarch)
1 tablespoon light soy sauce

SERVES 4

CUT the drained tofu into strips. Soak the dried mushrooms in boiling water for 30 minutes, then drain, reserving the soaking liquid, and squeeze out any excess water. Remove and discard the stems. Cut the caps in half.

HEAT a wok over high heat, add the oil and heat until very hot. Stir-fry the mushrooms for 35 seconds, then add 125 ml (^{1}/$_2$ cup) of the reserved liquid and bring to the boil. Add the tofu, salt, sugar and rice wine to the wok, and stir very gently to blend well. Braise for 2 minutes, making sure there is enough liquid to prevent the tofu from sticking to the wok, then sprinkle with the sesame oil.

COMBINE the cornflour and soy with enough of the reserved liquid to make a paste. Add to the sauce and simmer to form a clear, light glaze.

青菜炒腐酱

FERMENTED TOFU WITH ASIAN GREENS

USE ANY SELECTION OF ASIAN GREENS THAT YOU WISH—CHOY SUM, BOK CHOY (PAK CHOI), CHINESE

CABBAGE, CHINESE BROCCOLI AND WATER SPINACH ARE ALL SUITABLE. FERMENTED WHITE TOFU IS

STRONG, ESPECIALLY IF IT CONTAINS CHILLI, SO DON'T BE TEMPTED TO ADD ANY MORE TO THE RECIPE.

FERMENTED TOFU WITH
ASIAN GREENS

600 g (1 lb 5 oz) choy sum
250 g (9 oz) bok choy (pak choi)
1 tablespoon oil
3 garlic cloves, crushed
3 tablespoons fermented white tofu
1 teaspoon light soy sauce
3 tablespoons oyster sauce
2 teaspoons sugar
1 teaspoon roasted sesame oil

SERVES 4

CUT the choy sum horizontally into thirds and the bok choy into thirds and then quarters. Trim off any roots that may hold the pieces together, then wash well and dry thoroughly.

HEAT a wok over high heat, add the oil and heat until very hot. Stir-fry the garlic and tofu for 1 minute. Add the choy sum stems and stir-fry for 1 minute, then add the leaves and bok choy and stir-fry for 1–2 minutes, or until the vegetables just start to wilt. Add the soy and oyster sauces, sugar and sesame oil and toss everything together.

Selling snacks in Yunnan.

麻婆豆腐

MA PO TOFU

A QUINTESSENTIAL SICHUANESE DISH, SUPPOSEDLY NAMED AFTER AN OLD WOMAN WHO SERVED THIS IN HER RESTAURANT AND WHOSE POCKMARKED COMPLEXION LED TO THE DISH BEING CALLED MA PO TOFU, 'POCKMARKED GRANDMOTHER'S TOFU'. SOFT TOFU IS TRADITIONALLY USED.

750 g (1 lb 10 oz) soft or firm
    tofu, drained
250 g (9 oz) minced (ground) beef
    or pork
2 tablespoons dark soy sauce
1¹/2 tablespoons Shaoxing
    rice wine
¹/2 teaspoon roasted sesame oil
2 teaspoons Sichuan peppercorns
1 tablespoon oil
2 spring onions (scallions), finely
    chopped
2 garlic cloves, finely chopped
2 teaspoons finely chopped ginger
1 tablespoon chilli bean paste
    (toban jiang), or to taste
250 ml (1 cup) chicken and meat
    stock (page 281)
1¹/2 teaspoons cornflour
    (cornstarch)
1 spring onion (scallion), finely
    shredded

SERVES 6

CUT the tofu into cubes. Place the meat in a bowl with 2 teaspoons of the soy sauce, 2 teaspoons of the rice wine and the sesame oil, and toss lightly. Dry-fry the peppercorns in a wok or pan until brown and aromatic, then crush lightly.

HEAT a wok over high heat, add the oil and heat until very hot. Stir-fry the meat until browned, mashing and chopping to separate the pieces. Remove the meat with a wire sieve or slotted spoon and heat the oil until any liquid from the meat has evaporated. Add the spring onion, garlic and ginger and stir-fry for 10 seconds, or until fragrant. Add the chilli bean paste and stir-fry for 5 seconds.

COMBINE the stock with the remaining soy sauce and rice wine. Add to the wok, bring to the boil, then add the tofu and meat. Return to the boil, reduce the heat to medium and cook for 5 minutes, or until the sauce has reduced by a quarter. If you are using soft tofu, do not stir or it will break up.

COMBINE the cornflour with enough water to make a paste, add to the sauce and simmer until thickened. Season if necessary. Serve sprinkled with the spring onion and Sichuan peppercorns.

Fresh tofu and chilli pastes are readily available at the markets in China.

焖豆腐

BRAISED TOFU

TOFU PICKS UP ITS FLAVOUR FROM THE INGREDIENTS IT IS COOKED WITH. THE VEGETABLES SHOULD BE COOKED THROUGH, BUT NOT SO MUCH THAT THEY ARE SOFT AND MUSHY.

8 dried Chinese mushrooms
150 g (5½ oz) Chinese cabbage or choy sum
225 g (8 oz) firm tofu, drained
100 g (3½ oz) carrots
100 g (3½ oz) baby corn
3–4 tablespoons oil
2 tablespoons light soy sauce or oyster sauce
1 teaspoon salt
½ teaspoon sugar
1 tablespoon Shaoxing rice wine
2 spring onions (scallions), cut into short lengths
1 teaspoon roasted sesame oil

SERVES 4

SOAK the dried mushrooms in boiling water for 30 minutes, then drain, reserving the liquid, and squeeze out any excess water. Remove and discard the stems and cut the caps in half.

CUT the cabbage into large pieces and the tofu into 12 cubes. Diagonally cut the carrots. Leave the corn whole if small, or cut into pieces.

LINE a clay pot, casserole or saucepan with the Chinese cabbage and pour in 2½ tablespoons of the reserved liquid. Heat a wok over high heat, add half the oil and heat until very hot. Lightly brown the tofu for 2–3 minutes, transfer to the pot and add the soy or oyster sauce.

REHEAT the wok over high heat, add the remaining oil and heat until very hot. Stir-fry the carrot, corn and mushrooms for 1 minute. Add the salt, sugar and rice wine, blend well, then transfer to the pot. Bring to the boil, place the spring onion on top, then simmer, covered, for 15–20 minutes. Sprinkle with the sesame oil.

BRAISED TOFU

Soft tofu is sold by shops and travelling carts and is eaten as a snack. Here it is dressed with honey.

小葱辣椒拌豆腐

SOFT TOFU WITH CHILLI AND SPRING ONION

THIS RECIPE PERFECTLY SETS OFF THE SOFT, COOL SMOOTHNESS OF THE TOFU BY ADDING A HOT, HIGHLY SPICED DRESSING. SERVE WITH RICE AND STIR-FRIED GREENS FOR A HEALTHY MEAL.

250 g (9 oz) soft tofu, drained
2 spring onions (scallions), sliced
1 red chilli, thinly sliced
2 tablespoons chopped coriander (cilantro)
2 tablespoons soy sauce
80 ml (⅓ cup) oil
1 teaspoon roasted sesame oil

SERVES 4

CUT the drained tofu into cubes and put it on a heatproof plate.

SCATTER the spring onion, chilli, coriander and soy sauce over the tofu. Put the oils in a small saucepan and heat until they are smoking, then immediately pour the oils over the tofu.

THE LEE KUM KEE factory at Xinhui, China, makes soy sauce according to traditional methods. It uses premium soya beans, wheat flour and its own unique starter culture *(left)* rather than chemicals. The resulting soy sauce is analyzed for quality by a soy sauce master before bottling. To make the sauce, the beans are first cleaned, soaked, defatted and cooked by steaming *(middle and right)*.

SOY

SOYA BEANS ARE RARELY EATEN WHOLE, BUT WHEN TRANSFORMED INTO SOY SAUCE, TOFU, SOY MILK, VEGETABLE OIL, FERMENTED BEANS, BEAN PASTES OR SHAPED INTO NOODLES, THEY BECOME ONE OF THE ESSENTIAL INGREDIENTS OF CHINESE COOKING.

Soya beans have grown in China for perhaps 5,000 years, and it is from here that they spread to the rest of Asia. Importantly, they provide a valuable source of protein in a country where the diet sometimes includes little meat. Soya beans are sprouted as bean sprouts, which benefit from being cooked as they have a strong flavour, and sometimes eaten from the pod as a snack or thrown into stir-fries, but the protein in them can generally only be unlocked through processing the relatively undigestable beans in various ways.

SOY SAUCE

Invented in China over 2,000 years ago, soy sauce *(jiang you)* is one of the traditional seven necessities of a Chinese household, along with tea, salt, oil, vinegar, rice and firewood. First brought to Europe in the seventeenth century, soya beans are actually called after the sauce rather than the other way around, though the name is really a misnomer, as it is not so much a sauce as a flavouring extracted from fermented beans. Properly prepared soy sauce is made from mixing the beans with wheat flour to form a paste. This mixture is then fermented using two different *Aspergillus* moulds. Once the maturing process is complete, the sauce is strained and bottled. The fermentation produces a mix of flavours—salt, amino acids, sugars, acids, esters and alcohols—and the final flavour of each batch is controlled by the soy sauce master.

AT THE KUNG WO BEAN CURD FACTORY in Sham Shui Po, Hong Kong, 100 kg of beans a day are soaked for 5 hours, then ground up with water to make soy milk. This milk is boiled, left to settle, and the milk separated from the sediment. Finally the milk is coagulated *(far left)*. Curds are put into a mould and drained to form blocks *(middle)*, or poured into vats to set as soft tofu and scooped into bowls *(right)* and

After spraying with the starter culture and wheat flour *(left)*, they are left to ferment for a few days. The mixture is then put in a fermentation tank with brine *(middle)* and fermented for 3 months, circulating it by drawing liquid from the bottom and spraying it back in at the top *(right)*. The raw soy is drawn off, and the sediment is allowed to settle. The soy sauce is then analyzed, filtered, sterilized and bottled.

Chinese cooking uses both light and dark soy sauces. Light soy *(shengchou)* comes from the first pressing and has a light colour and a delicate, salty flavour. It is often just labelled as soy sauce and is used with white meat, fish and vegetables. Dark soy *(laochou)* is aged for longer than light, giving it a brownish-black colour and thicker texture. It sometimes has caramel added as well and is used with red meats and for red-cooking and braising. Chinese food is seasoned in the kitchen, so both types are often mixed within recipes. In Guangzhou, soy is always provided at the table as a condiment, unlike in the rest of China.

TOFU

Tofu or dofu is eaten all over China. Fresh tofu does not have much flavour of its own and is very versatile—it absorbs the flavourings and seasonings of the ingredients it is mixed with and can be cooked by any method. The Chinese also prize its unique texture. Tofu is made in a similar way to cheese. Dried beans are soaked, then crushed with water to make soy 'milk', boiled and coagulated. The curd is left to set and drain like fresh cheese. Soft tofu is allowed to retain a lot of moisture, while firm tofu is better drained, and pressed tofu has had almost all of its moisture removed.

TOFU PRODUCTS

Tofu can also be processed into other forms:

FERMENTED TOFU a seasoning ingredient made from fermented, dried cubes of curd, marinated with chillies, spices and alcohol (white tofu) and served as a spicy side dish, or coloured red with red fermented rice (red tofu) and used as a potent condiment or to flavour congee.

MOULDY TOFU rancid tofu with a strong taste that has been left to develop blue veins or a furry white rind. It is used as a pungent ingredient in cooking.

TOFU SKIN made by lifting off the skin that forms on top of boiling soy milk before coagulation and drying it. The brittle sheets and rolled sticks need to be soaked before use.

served warm to the breakfast trade with syrup. Later in the day, bowls of refrigerated soft tofu are served as a savoury or sweet snack *(left)*. Soy milk, which has been strained after the milk is boiled and not coagulated, is sold as a cold drink *(middle)* and the blocks *(right)* are sold by weight and also turned into fermented tofu, deep-fried puffs and a snack of fried, stuffed tofu in the shop.

Transporting tofu in Hangzhou.

The Temple of Heaven in Beijing.

北方豆腐

NORTHERN-STYLE TOFU

THIS DISH WAS APPARENTLY A FAVOURITE OF DOWAGER EMPRESS TZU-HSI IN THE NINETEENTH CENTURY, AND IT'S STILL A POPULAR CLASSIC IN CHINA TODAY. THE TOFU IS FIRST FRIED, THEN SIMMERED SO THAT IT MELTS IN YOUR MOUTH.

An outdoor haircut in Beijing.

1 kg (2 lb 4 oz) firm tofu, drained
oil for deep-frying
125 g (1 cup) cornflour (cornstarch)
2 eggs, lightly beaten
1 tablespoon finely chopped ginger
330 ml (1¹⁄₃ cups) chicken stock
  (page 281)
2 tablespoons Shaoxing rice wine
1 teaspoon salt, or to taste
¹⁄₂ teaspoon sugar
1¹⁄₂ teaspoons roasted sesame oil
2 spring onions (scallions), green
  part only, finely chopped

SERVES 6

HOLDING a cleaver parallel to the cutting surface, slice each tofu cake in half horizontally. Cut each piece into 3 cm (1¹⁄₄ inch) squares.

FILL a wok one-quarter full of oil. Heat the oil to 190°C (375°F), or until a piece of bread fries golden brown in 10 seconds when dropped in the oil. Coat each piece of tofu in the cornflour, then dip in the beaten egg to coat. Cook the tofu in batches for 3–4 minutes on each side, or until golden brown. Remove with a wire sieve or slotted spoon and drain in a colander. Pour the oil from the wok, leaving 1 teaspoon.

REHEAT the reserved oil over high heat until very hot and stir-fry the ginger for 5 seconds, or until fragrant. Add the stock, rice wine, salt and sugar, and bring to the boil. Add the fried tofu and pierce the pieces with a fork so that they will absorb the cooking liquid. Cook over medium heat for 20 minutes, or until all the liquid is absorbed. Drizzle the sesame oil over the tofu, toss carefully to coat, sprinkle with the spring onion and serve.

豆干包

STUFFED TOFU

SEVERAL VERSIONS EXIST OF THIS HIGHLY POPULAR DISH, WHICH IS THOUGHT TO BE A HAKKA RECIPE FROM THE SOUTHEAST OF CHINA. THE STUFFING HERE IS A MIXTURE OF PRAWNS (SHRIMP) AND PORK AND THOUGH THE RECIPE MAY APPEAR RATHER COMPLICATED, IT IS WORTH THE EFFORT.

Push the stuffing fairly firmly into the slit in the tofu—the pocket should be open at one end and the stuffing showing.

6 x 5 cm (2 inch) square cakes firm tofu, drained
2 dried Chinese mushrooms
50 g (1³/₄ oz) prawns (shrimp)
50 g (1³/₄ oz) minced (ground) pork
a pinch of salt
¹/₂ egg white, beaten
1 teaspoon Shaoxing rice wine
1 teaspoon light soy sauce
1–2 teaspoons cornflour (cornstarch)
3–4 tablespoons oil
2¹/₂ tablespoons chicken and meat stock (page 281)
2 tablespoons oyster sauce
1 spring onion (scallion), sliced

SERVES 4

PARBOIL the tofu cakes in a pan of lightly salted boiling water for 2–3 minutes to harden them, then drain. Cut each cake into two triangular pieces and make a slit at the base of each triangle.

SOAK the dried mushrooms in boiling water for 30 minutes, then drain and squeeze out any excess water. Remove and discard the stems and finely chop the caps. Peel and devein the prawns and chop them finely until they are almost a paste. Put the mushrooms and prawns in a bowl with the pork, salt, egg white, rice wine, soy sauce and enough cornflour to hold the mixture together. Fill the slit of each tofu piece with stuffing (the pieces will gape open and show the stuffing).

HEAT a wok over high heat, add the oil and heat until very hot. Cook the stuffed tofu for 2 minutes on each side, or until golden. Pour off any excess oil. Add the stock and oyster sauce, bring to the boil and braise for 5–6 minutes. Sprinkle with the spring onion.

STIR-FRIED TOFU IN YELLOW BEAN SAUCE

豆瓣酱炒豆腐

STIR-FRIED TOFU IN YELLOW BEAN SAUCE

400 g (14 oz) firm tofu, drained
2 tablespoons oil
1 garlic clove, crushed
1¹/₂ tablespoons yellow bean sauce
2 teaspoons oyster sauce
2 teaspoons sugar
2 teaspoons cornflour (cornstarch)
1 spring onion (scallion), cut into 2 cm (³/₄ inch) lengths
5 coriander (cilantro) sprigs

SERVES 4

CUT the drained tofu into bite-size pieces. Heat the wok over medium heat, add the oil and heat until hot. Cook the tofu until it is golden brown on both sides.

ADD the garlic, yellow bean sauce, oyster sauce and sugar and toss until well combined. Combine the cornflour with 170 ml (²/₃ cup) water, add to the sauce with the spring onion and simmer until the sauce has thickened and the spring onion has softened slightly. If the sauce is still a little thick, add a little water. Garnish with coriander sprigs.

焖面筋

BRAISED GLUTEN

GLUTEN IS A WHEAT FLOUR DOUGH THAT HAS HAD THE STARCH WASHED AWAY SO IT IS SPONGY AND POROUS RATHER LIKE TOFU, BUT MUCH FIRMER. IN CHINA, GLUTEN IS USED AS A MOCK MEAT BECAUSE IT CAN BE COOKED IN THE SAME WAY. YOU CAN USE READY-MADE GLUTEN IN THIS RECIPE.

1 kg (2 lb 4 oz) plain (all-purpose) flour
1¹/₂ teaspoons salt
oil for deep-frying
1 teaspoon sugar
1 tablespoon light soy sauce
3–4 tablespoons vegetable stock (page 281)
¹/₄ teaspoon roasted sesame oil

SERVES 4

SIFT the flour into a bowl with 1 teaspoon of the salt and gradually add 560 ml (2¹/₄ cups) warm water to make a dough. Knead until smooth, then cover with a damp cloth and leave in a warm place for 55–60 minutes.

RINSE the dough under cold water and wash off the starch by pulling, stretching and squeezing the dough with your hands. You should have about 300 g (10¹/₂ oz) gluten after 10–15 minutes of washing and squeezing. Extract as much water as you can by squeezing the dough hard, then cut the dough into bite-size pieces. Dry thoroughly.

FILL a wok one-quarter full of oil. Heat the oil to 180°C (350°F), or until a piece of bread fries golden brown in 15 seconds when dropped in the oil. Cook the gluten pieces for 3 minutes, or until golden. Remove and drain. Pour the oil from the wok, leaving 1 teaspoon.

REHEAT the reserved oil over high heat until very hot and add the gluten, remaining salt, sugar, soy sauce and stock, bring to the boil and braise for 2–3 minutes, or until the liquid has evaporated. Sprinkle with the sesame oil. Serve hot or cold.

Wash the gluten thoroughly under running water to get rid of the starch. You should end up with a firm, sliceable piece of gluten.

A Buddhist temple in Sichuan.

MOCK DUCK

GLUTEN IS USED IN VEGETARIAN CHINESE COOKING TO TAKE THE PLACE OF MEAT IN RECIPES. RATHER THAN RESEMBLING DUCK, THIS DISH IS COOKED AS DUCK WOULD BE COOKED. YOU CAN MAKE THE GLUTEN OR USE READY-MADE GLUTEN—PLAIN OR SHAPED LIKE PIECES OF DUCK.

1 kg (2 lb 4 oz) plain (all-purpose) flour
1 teaspoon salt
1 1/2 tablespoons cornflour (cornstarch)
2 tablespoons oil
1 green capsicum (pepper), diced
125 ml (1/2 cup) vegetable stock (page 281)
2 tablespoons light soy sauce
2 teaspoons Shaoxing rice wine
1 teaspoon sugar
1 teaspoon roasted sesame oil

SERVES 4

SIFT the flour into a bowl with the salt and gradually add 560 ml (2 1/4 cups) warm water to make a dough. Knead until smooth, then cover with a damp cloth and leave in a warm place for 55–60 minutes.

RINSE the dough under cold water and wash off all the starch by pulling, stretching and squeezing the dough with your hands. You should have about 300 g (10 1/2 oz) gluten after 10–15 minutes of washing and squeezing. Extract as much water as you can by squeezing the dough hard, then cut the dough into bite-size pieces. Dry thoroughly.

TOSS the gluten in 1 tablespoon of the cornflour. Heat a wok over high heat, add the oil and heat until very hot. Quickly stir-fry the gluten until it is browned all over, then remove from the wok. Stir-fry the capsicum until it starts to brown around the edges, then remove. Pour off any excess oil.

ADD the stock, soy sauce, rice wine and sugar to the wok and bring to the boil. Return the gluten and capsicum and simmer for 1 minute.

COMBINE the remaining cornflour with enough water to make a paste, add to the sauce and simmer until thickened. Sprinkle with the sesame oil and serve.

VEGETABLES

Lighting candles at a Buddhist temple.

Tiger lily buds, or golden needles, are dried unopened lilies. When reconstituted they resemble limp bean sprouts.

BUDDHA'S DELIGHT

THE ORIGINAL RECIPE FOR THIS WELL-KNOWN VEGETARIAN DISH USED NO LESS THAN EIGHTEEN DIFFERENT INGREDIENTS TO REPRESENT THE EIGHTEEN BUDDHAS. NOWADAYS, ANYTHING BETWEEN SIX TO EIGHT INGREDIENTS IS USUAL PRACTICE.

25 g (1 oz) tiger lily buds (golden needles)
6–8 dried Chinese mushrooms
10 g (1 cup) dried black fungus (wood ears)
150 g (5¹/₂ oz) braised gluten (page 199) or ready-made braised gluten, drained
50 g (1³/₄ oz) tofu puffs (deep-fried cubes of tofu)
100 g (1 cup) bean sprouts
1 carrot
4 tablespoons oil
50 g (¹/₂ cup) snowpeas (mangetout), ends trimmed
1 teaspoon salt
¹/₂ teaspoon sugar
4 tablespoons vegetable stock (page 281)
2 tablespoons light soy sauce
¹/₂ teaspoon roasted sesame oil

SERVES 4

SOAK the tiger lily buds in boiling water for 30 minutes. Rinse and drain the tiger lily buds, and trim off any roots if they are hard. Soak the dried mushrooms in boiling water for 30 minutes, then drain and squeeze out any excess water. Remove and discard the stems and cut the caps in half (or quarters if large). Soak the dried black fungus in cold water for 20 minutes, then drain and squeeze out any excess water. Cut any large pieces of fungus in half.

CUT the gluten and tofu into small pieces. Wash the bean sprouts, discarding any husks and straggly end pieces, and dry thoroughly. Diagonally cut the carrot into thin slices.

HEAT a wok over high heat, add the oil and heat until very hot. Stir-fry the carrot for 30 seconds, then add the snowpeas and bean sprouts. Stir-fry for 1 minute, then add the gluten, tofu, lily buds, mushrooms, black fungus, salt, sugar, stock and soy sauce. Toss everything together, then cover and braise for 2 minutes at a gentle simmer.

ADD the sesame oil, toss it through the mixture and serve hot or cold.

炒生菜

STIR-FRIED LETTUCE

LETTUCE IS GENERALLY EATEN COOKED IN CHINA AND LOTS OF DIFFERENT VARIETIES ARE AVAILABLE.
LETTUCE IS ADDED TO SOUPS, STIR-FRIES AND CASSEROLES, AS WELL AS COOKED ON ITS OWN AS A
VEGETABLE. YOU CAN USE ANY CRISP LETTUCE FOR THIS RECIPE.

750 g (1 lb 10 oz) crisp lettuce
1 tablespoon oil
4 tablespoons oyster sauce
1 teaspoon roasted sesame oil

SERVES 4

CUT the lettuce in half and then into wide strips,
trimming off any roots that may hold the pieces
together. Wash well and dry thoroughly (if too
much water clings to the lettuce it will cause it
to steam rather than fry).

HEAT a wok over high heat, add the oil and heat
until very hot. Toss the lettuce pieces around the
wok until they start to wilt, then add the oyster
sauce and toss everything together. Sprinkle with
the sesame oil, season and serve.

炒豆芽

BEAN SPROUTS STIR-FRY

BEAN SPROUTS CAN MEAN EITHER SOYA BEAN SPROUTS OR MUNG BEAN SPROUTS AND BOTH ARE
USED IN THIS RECIPE. SOYA BEAN SPROUTS ARE SLIGHTLY BIGGER AND MORE ROBUST FOR COOKING,
AS WELL AS BEING MORE COMMONLY FOUND IN CHINA.

200 g (7 oz) mung bean sprouts
200 g (7 oz) soya bean sprouts
1 tablespoon oil
1 red chilli, finely chopped
1 spring onion (scallion), finely
   chopped
2 tablespoons light soy sauce

SERVES 4

WASH the bean sprouts, discarding any husks
and straggly end pieces, and drain thoroughly.

HEAT a wok over high heat, add the oil and heat
until very hot. Stir-fry the chilli and spring onion for
30 seconds, add the bean sprouts and toss until
they start to wilt. Add the soy sauce and toss for
1 minute, then season and serve.

BEAN SPROUTS STIR-FRY

炒双冬

STIR-FRIED TWIN WINTER

THIS SIMPLE DISH IS CALLED 'TWIN WINTER' BECAUSE BOTH MUSHROOMS AND BAMBOO SHOOTS ARE AT THEIR BEST IN THE WINTER MONTHS. ANOTHER VERSION OF THIS DISH, TRIPLE WINTER, USES BAMBOO SHOOTS AND MUSHROOMS WITH CABBAGE.

Fresh bamboo shoots.

12 dried Chinese mushrooms
300 g (10^1/$_2$ oz) fresh or tinned bamboo shoots, rinsed and drained
3 tablespoons oil
2 tablespoons light soy sauce
2 teaspoons sugar
2 teaspoons cornflour (cornstarch)
^{1}/$_2$ teaspoon roasted sesame oil

SERVES 4

SOAK the dried mushrooms in boiling water for 30 minutes, then drain, reserving the liquid, and squeeze out any excess water. Remove and discard the stems and cut the caps in half (or quarters if large). Cut the bamboo shoots into small pieces the same size as the mushrooms.

HEAT a wok over high heat, add the oil and heat until very hot. Stir-fry the mushrooms and bamboo shoots for 1 minute. Add the soy sauce and sugar, stir a few times, then add 125 ml (^{1}/$_2$ cup) of the reserved liquid. Bring to the boil and braise for 2 minutes, stirring constantly.

COMBINE the cornflour with enough water to make a paste, add to the sauce and simmer until thickened. Sprinkle with the sesame oil, blend well and serve.

STIR-FRIED CHINESE CABBAGE

炒包菜

STIR-FRIED CHINESE CABBAGE

CHINESE CABBAGE IS A COOL-WEATHER CROP, BUT IT CAN NOW BE BOUGHT ALL YEAR ROUND. THERE ARE TWO KINDS; ONE HAS A PALE-GREEN, FINE LEAF, THE OTHER IS PALE YELLOW.

30 g (1 oz) dried shrimp
1 tablespoon oil
400 g (14 oz) Chinese cabbage, cut into 1 cm (^{1}/$_2$ inch) strips
1 tablespoon light soy sauce
2 teaspoons sugar
1 tablespoon clear rice vinegar
2 teaspoons roasted sesame oil

SERVES 4

SOAK the dried shrimp in boiling water for 1 hour, then drain.

HEAT a wok over high heat, add the oil and heat until very hot. Toss the Chinese cabbage for 2 minutes, or until wilted. Add the shrimp, soy sauce, sugar and rice vinegar and cook for 1 minute. Sprinkle with the sesame oil and serve.

Preserved mustard cabbage *(bottom, second from left)* for sale in Beijing.

回锅长豆

DOUBLE-COOKED YARD-LONG BEANS

THIS SICHUANESE RECIPE IS SO NAMED BECAUSE THE BEANS, AFTER BEING FRIED UNTIL TENDER, ARE THEN COOKED AGAIN WITH SEASONINGS AND A SAUCE. TRADITIONALLY YARD-LONG, OR SNAKE, BEANS ARE USED. THESE ARE AVAILABLE IN CHINESE SHOPS, BUT FRENCH BEANS ARE ALSO DELICIOUS.

1 kg (2 lb 4 oz) yard-long (snake) beans or French beans, trimmed
150 g (5^1/$_2$ oz) minced (ground) pork or beef
2 tablespoons light soy sauce
1^1/$_2$ tablespoons Shaoxing rice wine
^{1}/$_2$ teaspoon roasted sesame oil
oil for deep-frying
5 tablespoons finely chopped preserved mustard cabbage
3 spring onions (scallions), finely chopped
1^1/$_2$ teaspoons sugar

SERVES 6

DIAGONALLY cut the beans into 5 cm (2 inch) pieces. Lightly chop the meat with a cleaver until it goes slightly fluffy. Put the meat in a bowl, add 1 teaspoon of the soy sauce, 1 teaspoon of the rice wine and the sesame oil and stir vigorously to combine.

FILL a wok one-quarter full of oil. Heat the oil to 180°C (350°F), or until a piece of bread fries golden brown in 15 seconds when dropped in the oil. Add a third of the beans, covering the wok with the lid as they are placed in the oil to prevent the oil from splashing. Cook for 3^1/$_2$–4 minutes, stirring constantly, until they are tender and golden brown at the edges. Remove with a wire sieve or slotted spoon and drain. Reheat the oil and repeat with the remaining beans. Pour the oil from the wok, leaving 1 tablespoon.

REHEAT the reserved oil over high heat until very hot, add the meat and stir-fry until the colour changes, mashing and chopping to separate the pieces of meat. Push the meat to the side and add the preserved mustard cabbage and spring onion. Stir-fry over high heat for 15 seconds, or until fragrant. Add the beans with the remaining soy sauce and rice wine, sugar and 1 tablespoon water, and return the meat to the centre of the pan. Toss lightly to coat the beans with the sauce.

Meat, such as this pork, is minced by hand using two cleavers at a market.

蚝油炒西兰菜

CHINESE BROCCOLI IN OYSTER SAUCE

CHINESE BROCCOLI DIFFERS FROM ITS WESTERN RELATIVE IN THAT THE STEMS ARE LONG, THE FLORETS ARE TINY, AND THE FLAVOUR IS SLIGHTLY BITTER. SOME VERSIONS ARE PURPLE. CHINESE BROCCOLI IS AVAILABLE IN CHINESE GROCERS.

1 kg (2 lb 4 oz) Chinese broccoli (gai lan)
1 1/2 tablespoons oil
2 spring onions (scallions), chopped
1 1/2 tablespoons grated ginger
3 garlic cloves, finely chopped
3 tablespoons oyster sauce
1 1/2 tablespoons light soy sauce
1 tablespoon Shaoxing rice wine
1 teaspoon sugar
1 teaspoon roasted sesame oil
125 ml (1/2 cup) chicken stock (page 281)
2 teaspoons cornflour (cornstarch)

SERVES 6

WASH the broccoli well. Discard any tough stems and diagonally cut into 2 cm (3/4 inch) pieces through the stem and the leaf. Blanch the broccoli in a pan of boiling water for 2 minutes, or until the stems and leaves are just tender, then refresh in cold water and dry thoroughly.

HEAT a wok over high heat, add the oil and heat until very hot. Stir-fry the spring onion, ginger and garlic for 10 seconds, or until fragrant. Add the broccoli and cook until the broccoli is heated through. Combine the remaining ingredients, add to the wok, stirring until the sauce has thickened, and toss to coat the broccoli.

四川鱼香茄子

SICHUAN-STYLE SPICY EGGPLANT

THE CHINESE EGGPLANT (AUBERGINE) IS LONG, THIN AND ABOUT THE SIZE OF A ZUCCHINI (COURGETTE). ITS TENDER FLESH ABSORBS FLAVOURS AND IT IS THE PERFECT CARRIER FOR BOTH SPICY AND DELICATE SAUCES. IF THEY ARE UNAVAILABLE, USE SMALL, TENDER WESTERN ONES.

500 g (1 lb 2 oz) Chinese eggplants (aubergines) or thin eggplants
1/2 teaspoon salt
3 tablespoons light soy sauce
1 tablespoon Shaoxing rice wine
1 tablespoon roasted sesame oil
2 teaspoons clear rice vinegar
1 teaspoon sugar
1 spring onion (scallion), chopped
2 garlic cloves, finely chopped
1 teaspoon chilli bean paste (toban jiang)

PEEL the eggplants and trim off the ends. Cut the eggplants in half lengthways and cut each half into strips 2 cm (3/4 inch) thick. Cut the strips into 5 cm (2 inch) lengths. Place the eggplant in a bowl, add the salt and toss lightly, then set aside for 1 hour. Pour off any water that has accumulated.

ARRANGE the eggplant on a heatproof plate and place in a steamer. Cover and steam over simmering water in a wok for 20 minutes, or until tender. Combine the remaining ingredients in a bowl, then pour the sauce over the eggplant, tossing lightly to coat.

SICHUAN-STYLE
SPICY EGGPLANT

SERVES 6

蒜爆炒豆苗

FLASH-COOKED PEA SHOOTS WITH GARLIC

PEA SHOOTS ARE THE DELICATE LEAVES AT THE TOP OF PEA PLANTS. THEY ARE PARTICULARLY GOOD WHEN STIR-FRIED SIMPLY WITH A LITTLE OIL AND GARLIC. IF UNAVAILABLE, SPINACH OR ANY OTHER LEAFY GREEN MAY BE SUBSTITUTED.

350 g (12 oz) pea shoots
1 teaspoon oil
2 garlic cloves, finely chopped
1¹/₂ tablespoons Shaoxing
   rice wine
¹/₄ teaspoon salt

SERVES 6

TRIM the tough stems and wilted leaves from the pea shoots. Wash well and dry thoroughly.

HEAT a wok over high heat, add the oil and heat until very hot. Add the pea shoots and garlic and toss lightly for 20 seconds, then add the rice wine and salt, and stir-fry for 1 minute, or until the shoots are slightly wilted, but still bright green. Transfer to a platter, leaving behind most of the liquid. Serve hot, at room temperature, or cold.

Selling pea shoots in Dali.

炒莲藕

STIR-FRIED LOTUS ROOT

THE LOTUS IS A SYMBOL OF PURITY IN BUDDHIST CULTURE AS THE ROOTS, WHICH GROW IN MUD, ARE CLEAN AND PURE DESPITE THEIR MUDDY ORIGINS. LOTUS ROOT CAN BE EATEN RAW OR COOKED AND HAS A CRISP, CRUNCHY TEXTURE.

450 g (1 lb) fresh lotus root or
   350 g (12 oz) ready-prepared
   lotus root
1 tablespoon oil
1 garlic clove, thinly sliced
10 very thin slices ginger
2 spring onions (scallions), finely
   chopped
50 g (1³/₄ oz) Chinese ham, rind
   removed, diced
1 tablespoon Shaoxing rice wine
1 tablespoon light soy sauce
1 teaspoon sugar

SERVES 4

IF USING fresh lotus root, peel, cut into slices, wash well and drain thoroughly. Ready-prepared lotus root just needs to be washed, sliced and drained thoroughly.

HEAT a wok over high heat, add the oil and heat until very hot. Stir-fry the garlic and ginger for 30 seconds. Add the spring onion, ham and lotus root and stir-fry for 1 minute, then add the rice wine, soy sauce and sugar and cook for 2–3 minutes, or until the lotus root is tender but still crisp.

STIR-FRIED LOTUS ROOT

A market garden near Guilin.

STIR-FRIED EGGS
AND TOMATOES

STIR-FRIED EGGS AND TOMATOES

THIS IS A SIMPLE DISH OF SCRAMBLED EGGS FLAVOURED WITH TOMATOES, SPRING ONIONS (SCALLIONS) AND SESAME OIL, WHICH CAN BE EATEN ON ITS OWN OR AS A SIDE DISH. YOU CAN MAKE THIS IN A WOK OR IN A NON-STICK FRYING PAN.

4 eggs
2 teaspoons roasted sesame oil
1 tablespoon oil
2 spring onions (scallions), finely
  chopped
2 large very ripe tomatoes, chopped

SERVES 4

BEAT the eggs with the sesame oil and season with salt. Heat a wok or non-stick frying pan over high heat, add the oil and heat until very hot. Stir-fry the spring onion for 30 seconds, then add the tomato and stir-fry for 30 seconds. Add the egg and stir until the egg is set.

Chinese celery is similar to celery but has darker stems and a more pronounced flavour.

CELERY SALAD

YOU CAN OMIT THE DRIED SHRIMP USED AS A GARNISH FROM THIS DELICIOUS SALAD IF YOU ARE A VEGETARIAN. USE YOUNG CELERY THAT DOES NOT HAVE STRINGS RUNNING THROUGH IT IF YOU CAN, OTHERWISE PULL OUT THE STRINGS BEFORE SLICING.

2 tablespoons dried shrimp
2 tablespoons Shaoxing rice wine
8 Chinese celery or celery stalks
1 tablespoon light soy sauce
1 tablespoon sugar
1 tablespoon clear rice vinegar
1 teaspoon roasted sesame oil
1 tablespoon finely chopped ginger

SERVES 4

SOAK the dried shrimp in the rice wine for 1 hour.

CUT the celery into thin slices and blanch in a pan of boiling water for 1–2 minutes, then refresh in cold water and dry thoroughly. Arrange the celery on a serving dish.

COMBINE the soaked shrimp and rice wine with the soy sauce, sugar, rice vinegar, sesame oil and ginger. Blend well and pour over the celery just before serving.

酿苦瓜炒豆瓣酱

STUFFED BITTER MELON IN BLACK BEAN SAUCE

BITTER MELON LIVES UP TO ITS NAME—IT REALLY IS BITTER, AND SOMETHING OF AN ACQUIRED TASTE.

BUY RIPER MELONS, WHICH ARE MORE YELLOW IN COLOUR, AS THESE ARE A LITTLE SWEETER.

BLANCHING THE MELON IN BOILING WATER ALSO GETS RID OF A LITTLE BITTERNESS.

BLACK BEAN SAUCE

2 tablespoons salted, fermented black beans, rinsed and coarsely chopped

2 garlic cloves, finely chopped

2 teaspoons finely chopped ginger

2–3 small red chillies, seeded and thinly sliced

2 teaspoons oyster sauce

2 teaspoons soy sauce

3 teaspoons sugar

3 bitter melons

500 g (1 lb 2 oz) firm white fish fillets, such as cod, halibut or monkfish, skin removed

3 teaspoons finely chopped ginger

3 teaspoons light soy sauce

1 teaspoon roasted sesame oil

25 g (1/2 cup) finely chopped coriander (cilantro)

2 spring onions (scallions), thinly sliced

1/4 teaspoon freshly ground white pepper

2 1/2 tablespoons cornflour (cornstarch)

2 tablespoons oil

SERVES 4

TO MAKE the black bean sauce, combine the black beans, garlic, ginger, chilli, oyster sauce, soy sauce and sugar in a small bowl. Set aside.

SLICE the bitter melons into rings about 2.5 cm (1 inch) wide. Remove the seeds and membranes and blanch the pieces in a pan of boiling water for 2–3 minutes, then refresh in cold water and dry thoroughly.

FINELY CHOP the fish fillets with a cleaver or in a food processor and place in a bowl with the ginger, soy sauce, sesame oil, coriander, spring onion, pepper and 1 tablespoon of the cornflour, stirring to combine. Set aside in the fridge for up to 1 hour to allow the flavours to develop.

LIGHTLY COAT the bitter melon in 1 tablespoon of the cornflour to help the stuffing stick to it. Fill the centre of each piece with the fish mixture. Heat a wok over high heat, add the oil and heat until very hot. Cook the bitter melon in batches, without turning, until golden brown. Remove from the wok and keep warm.

ADD the black bean sauce to the wok and stir-fry over medium heat for 1 minute. Add the stuffed melon pieces and coat with the sauce.

COMBINE the remaining cornflour with about 170 ml (2/3 cup) water, add to the sauce and simmer until thickened.

Press the filling firmly into the hollow in each piece of melon so that it stays intact when the melon is fried.

炒西兰菜

CHINESE BROCCOLI WITH SOY SAUCE

CHINESE BROCCOLI (GAI LAN) IS A VERSATILE, HEALTHY VEGETABLE THAT IS QUICK TO PREPARE. THERE IS NO WASTE AS BOTH THE LEAVES AND STALKS ARE EATEN. IT CAN BE SERVED WITH MORE COMPLICATED SAUCES BUT GOES EQUALLY WELL WITH A LIGHT DRIZZLE OF SOY AND OYSTER SAUCE.

400–500 g (12 oz–1 lb 2 oz)
  Chinese broccoli (gai lan)
2 tablespoons oil
1 tablespoon oyster sauce
2 tablespoons light soy sauce

SERVES 4

WASH the broccoli well. Discard any tough-looking stems and cut the rest of the stems in half. Blanch the broccoli in a pan of boiling water for 2 minutes, or until the stems and leaves are just tender, then refresh in cold water and dry thoroughly. Arrange in a serving dish.

HEAT a wok over high heat, add the oil and heat until very hot. Carefully pour the hot oil over the Chinese broccoli (it will splatter). Gently toss the oil through the Chinese broccoli and drizzle with the oyster sauce and soy sauce. Serve hot.

Chinese broccoli (gai lan) comes in both the more common green and a dark purple variety.

炒菠菜

STIR-FRIED BOK CHOY

BOK CHOY (PAK CHOI) COMES IN SEVERAL VARIETIES AND SIZES. SOME TYPES HAVE LONG WHITE STEMS AND VERY GREEN LEAVES, WHEREAS OTHERS, SUCH AS SHANGHAI (BABY) BOK CHOY, HAVE SHORTER PALE-GREEN STEMS AND LEAVES. ALL TYPES ARE INTERCHANGEABLE IN RECIPES.

400 g (1 bunch) bok choy (pak choi)
2 tablespoons oil
2 garlic cloves, smashed with the
  flat side of a cleaver
3 thin slices ginger, smashed with
  the flat side of a cleaver
3 tablespoons chicken stock
  (page 281)
1 teaspoon sugar
salt or light soy sauce, to taste
1 teaspoon roasted sesame oil

SERVES 4

CUT the bok choy into 5–8 cm (2–3 inch) lengths. Trim off any roots that may hold the pieces together, then wash well and dry thoroughly.

HEAT a wok over high heat, add the oil and heat until very hot. Stir-fry the garlic and ginger for 30 seconds. Add the bok choy and stir-fry until it begins to wilt, then add the stock and sugar and season with the salt or soy sauce. Simmer, covered, for 2 minutes, or until the stems and leaves are tender but still green. Add the sesame oil and serve hot.

CHINESE BROCCOLI WITH
SOY SAUCE

酸辣包心菜

HOT-AND-SOUR CABBAGE

THIS SPICY PICKLE OR SIDE DISH IS WELL LOVED IN MANY PARTS OF CHINA, ALTHOUGH IT IS
ESPECIALLY POPULAR IN HANGZHOU, A CITY IN EAST CHINA THAT BOASTS GREAT FOOD. IT MAY BE
MADE WITH OTHER VEGETABLES BESIDES CABBAGE AND CAN BE EATEN HOT, WARM OR COLD.

Chinese cabbages for sale in a
Beijing market. The cabbages
are often covered in blankets to
protect them from frostbite.

1 small Chinese cabbage
3 tablespoons light soy sauce
1/2 teaspoon salt
2 tablespoons sugar
4 tablespoons Chinese black
   rice vinegar
1 tablespoon oil
1 red chilli, finely chopped
2 1/2 tablespoons finely chopped
   ginger
1 1/2 red capsicums (peppers),
   cut into 5 mm (1/4 inch) dice
1 1/2 tablespoons Shaoxing
   rice wine
1 teaspoon roasted sesame oil

SERVES 6

SEPARATE the cabbage leaves and trim off the
stems. Cut the leaves across their length into
1 cm (1/2 inch) wide strips, separating the stem
sections from the leafy sections.

COMBINE the soy sauce, salt, sugar and Chinese
black vinegar and set aside.

HEAT a wok over high heat, add the oil and heat
until very hot. Stir-fry the red chilli and ginger for
15 seconds. Add the red capsicum and stir-fry for
30 seconds, then add the rice wine and stir-fry
for 30 seconds. Add the stem sections of the
cabbage, toss lightly and cook for 1 minute. Add
the leafy sections and toss lightly, then pour in the
soy sauce mixture, tossing lightly to coat. Cook
for 30 seconds, then add the sesame oil. Serve
hot, at room temperature, or cold.

黑椒炒白菜

FLAT CABBAGE WITH BLACK PEPPER

FLAT CABBAGE (TAT SOI) HAS SMALL, DARK-GREEN, SHINY LEAVES WITH A WHITE STEM. IT IS
SOMETIMES CALLED ROSETTE CABBAGE. THE LEAVES NEED TO BE WASHED THOROUGHLY BEFORE
THEY ARE USED AS THEY HARBOUR A LOT OF DIRT.

1 flat cabbage (tat soi)
1 tablespoon oil
2 garlic cloves, sliced
1/4 teaspoon freshly ground
   black pepper
2 teaspoons Shaoxing rice wine
light soy sauce, to taste
2 teaspoons roasted sesame oil

SERVES 4

SEPARATE the cabbage leaves, wash well and
dry thoroughly.

HEAT a wok over high heat, add the oil and heat
until very hot. Stir-fry the garlic for a few seconds.
Add the cabbage leaves and stir-fry until they
have just wilted. Add the pepper and rice wine
and toss together. Season with the soy sauce and
add the sesame oil.

FLAT CABBAGE WITH
BLACK PEPPER

CABBAGE ROLLS WITH MUSTARD

MUSTARD SEEDS COME FROM PLANTS BELONGING TO THE CABBAGE FAMILY, WHICH HAVE GROWN IN CHINA FOR CENTURIES. ALTHOUGH IT WAS TRADITIONALLY GROWN FOR ITS LEAVES, MUSTARD IS ALSO SOMETIMES USED AS A SPICE IN ITS GROUND FORM, OR MADE UP INTO A PASTE AS A CONDIMENT.

1 Chinese cabbage
3 tablespoons English mustard
  powder
1 tablespoon light soy sauce
1 tablespoon clear rice vinegar
1 teaspoon roasted sesame oil

SERVES 4

SEPARATE the cabbage leaves and blanch them in a pan of boiling water for 1 minute, then refresh in cold water and dry thoroughly.

COMBINE the mustard powder, soy sauce, rice vinegar and sesame oil, then add enough cold water to make a stiff but spreadable paste.

TRIM the cabbage leaves into long strips about 5 cm (2 inches) wide. For each roll, use three strips. Lay a bottom strip on the work surface and cover with a thin layer of mustard, lay another strip on top covered with a layer of mustard, finish with a final strip and some mustard, then roll up. Repeat with the remaining cabbage to make four rolls. Put the rolls, standing upright, on a heatproof plate in a steamer. Cover and steam over simmering water in a wok for 20 minutes.

Blanching the leaves first makes them easier to roll. Make sure you only spread a thin layer of mustard on each.

STIR-FRIED WATER SPINACH WITH SHRIMP SAUCE

1 kg (2 lb 4 oz) water spinach
  (ong choy)
2½ tablespoons oil
2 teaspoons Chinese shrimp paste
3 garlic cloves, crushed
1–2 red chillies, seeded and
  chopped
2 teaspoons oyster sauce
2 teaspoons sugar

SERVES 4

WASH the water spinach well and dry thoroughly. Remove any tough lower stalks and only use the young stems and leaves.

HEAT a wok over high heat, add 1½ tablespoons of the oil and heat until very hot. Stir-fry the water spinach for 1 minute, or until it begins to wilt. Drain in a colander.

ADD the remaining oil to the wok with the shrimp paste, garlic and chilli, and toss over medium heat to release the flavours for 30 seconds to 1 minute. Add the water spinach, oyster sauce and sugar and toss for 1 minute.

STIR-FRIED WATER SPINACH
WITH SHRIMP SAUCE

RICE & NOODLES

EGG FRIED RICE

IN CHINA, PLAIN COOKED RICE IS SERVED WITH EVERYDAY MEALS, WHILE FRIED RICE IS ONLY EATEN AS A SNACK ON ITS OWN OR AT BANQUETS, WHEN IT IS SERVED AT THE END OF THE MEAL. THIS QUICK VERSION IS EXCELLENT TO SERVE AS A SIDE DISH.

4 eggs
1 spring onion (scallion), chopped
50 g (1/3 cup) fresh or frozen peas
  (optional)
3 tablespoons oil
1 quantity cooked rice (page 274)

SERVES 4

BEAT the eggs with a pinch of salt and 1 teaspoon of the spring onion. Cook the peas in a pan of simmering water for 3–4 minutes for fresh or 1 minute for frozen.

HEAT a wok over high heat, add the oil and heat until very hot. Reduce the heat, add the egg and lightly scramble. Add the rice before the egg is set too hard, increase the heat and stir to separate the rice grains and break the egg into small bits. Add the peas and the remaining spring onion and season with salt. Stir constantly for 1 minute.

EGG FRIED RICE

YANGZHOU FRIED RICE WITH PRAWNS

THIS WELL-KNOWN FRIED RICE DISH HAILS FROM YANGZHOU, A CITY IN THE EAST. IT CAN BE SERVED BY ITSELF AS A LIGHT MEAL OR WITH SOUP. THE SECRET TO NON-CLUMPY FRIED RICE IS USING COOKED RICE THAT HAS BEEN CHILLED, THEN LEFT OUT TO REACH ROOM TEMPERATURE.

125 g (4 1/2 oz) cooked prawns
  (shrimp)
150 g (1 cup) fresh or frozen peas
1 tablespoon oil
3 spring onions (scallions), chopped
1 tablespoon finely chopped ginger
2 eggs, lightly beaten
1 quantity cooked rice (page 274)
1 1/2 tablespoons chicken stock
  (page 281)
1 tablespoon Shaoxing rice wine
2 teaspoons light soy sauce
1/2 teaspoon salt, or to taste
1/2 teaspoon roasted sesame oil
1/4 teaspoon ground black pepper

SERVES 4

PEEL the prawns and cut then in half through the back, removing the vein. Cook the peas in a pan of simmering water for 3–4 minutes for fresh or 1 minute for frozen.

HEAT a wok over high heat, add the oil and heat until hot. Stir-fry the spring onion and ginger for 1 minute. Reduce the heat, add the egg and lightly scramble. Add the prawns and peas and toss lightly to heat through, then add the rice before the egg is set too hard, increase the heat and stir to separate the rice grains and break the egg into small bits.

ADD the stock, rice wine, soy sauce, salt, sesame oil and pepper, and toss lightly.

YANGZHOU FRIED RICE WITH PRAWNS

PEARL BALLS

THIS FAMOUS DISH ORIGINATED IN HUNAN PROVINCE, ONE OF CHINA'S MAJOR RICE BASINS. ONCE STEAMED, THE STICKY RICE THAT FORMS THE COATING FOR THESE MEATBALLS TURNS INTO PEARL-LIKE GRAINS. TRADITIONALLY, GLUTINOUS OR SWEET RICE IS USED, BUT YOU COULD USE RISOTTO RICE.

330 g (11½ oz) glutinous or
   sweet rice
8 dried Chinese mushrooms
160 g (1 cup) peeled water
   chestnuts
450 g (1 lb) minced (ground) pork
1 small carrot, grated
2 spring onions (scallions),
   finely chopped
1½ tablespoons finely chopped
   ginger
2 tablespoons light soy sauce
1 tablespoon Shaoxing rice wine
1½ teaspoons roasted sesame oil
2½ tablespoons cornflour
   (cornstarch)
soy sauce

SERVES 6

Roll the meatballs so they are completely coated in the glutinous rice, then press the rice on firmly so it sticks.

PUT the rice in a bowl and, using your fingers as a rake, rinse under cold running water to remove any dust. Drain the rice in a colander, then place it in a bowl with enough cold water to cover. Set aside for 1 hour. Drain the rice and transfer it to a baking tray in an even layer.

SOAK the dried mushrooms in boiling water for 30 minutes, then drain and squeeze out any excess water. Remove and discard the stems and chop the caps.

BLANCH the water chestnuts in a pan of boiling water for 1 minute, then refresh in cold water. Drain, pat dry and finely chop them.

PLACE the pork in a bowl, add the mushrooms, water chestnuts, carrot, spring onion, ginger, light soy sauce, rice wine, sesame oil and cornflour. Stir the mixture vigorously to combine.

ROLL the mixture into 2 cm (¾ inch) balls, then roll each meatball in the glutinous rice so that it is completely coated. Lightly press the rice to make it stick to the meatball. Place the pearl balls well apart in three steamers lined with greaseproof paper punched with holes or some damp cheesecloth or muslin. Cover and steam over simmering water in a wok, reversing the steamers halfway through, for 25 minutes. If the rice is still *al dente*, continue to cook for a little longer until it softens. Serve with the soy sauce.

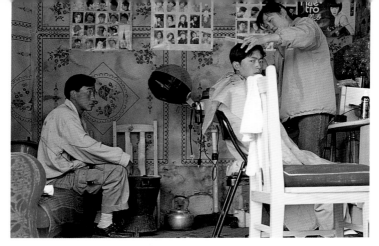

A haircut in Lijiang.

蒸鸡腊肠饭

STEAMED CHICKEN AND SAUSAGE RICE

THIS WARMING CANTONESE DISH IS TRADITIONALLY COOKED IN SMALL CLAY POTS SO THERE IS ONE

POT FOR EACH INDIVIDUAL. CHINESE SAUSAGE (LAP CHEONG) TASTES A LITTLE LIKE A SWEET SALAMI,

BUT IT MUST BE COOKED BEFORE EATING.

4 dried Chinese mushrooms
250 g (9 oz) skinless chicken
   thigh fillet
1 teaspoon Shaoxing rice wine
2 teaspoons cornflour (cornstarch)
3 Chinese sausages (lap cheong)
200 g (1 cup) long-grain rice
1 spring onion (scallion), chopped

SAUCE
2 tablespoons light soy sauce
1 tablespoon Shaoxing rice wine
1/2 teaspoon caster (superfine)
   sugar
1/2 garlic clove, chopped (optional)
1/2 teaspoon chopped ginger
1/2 teaspoon roasted sesame oil

SERVES 4

SOAK the dried mushrooms in boiling water for 30 minutes, then drain and squeeze out any excess water. Remove and discard the stems and shred the caps.

CUT the chicken into bite-size pieces and combine with a pinch of salt, the rice wine and cornflour.

PLACE the sausages on a plate in a steamer. Cover and steam over simmering water in a wok for 10 minutes, then thinly slice on the diagonal.

PUT the rice in a bowl and, using your fingers as a rake, rinse under cold running water to remove any dust. Drain the rice in a colander. Place in a large clay pot or casserole or four individual clay pots and add enough water so that there is 2 cm (3/4 inch) of water above the surface of the rice. Bring the water slowly to the boil, stir, then place the chicken pieces and mushrooms on top of the rice, with the sausage slices on top of them. Cook, covered, over very low heat for 15–18 minutes, or until the rice is cooked.

TO MAKE the sauce, combine the soy sauce, rice wine, sugar, garlic, ginger and sesame oil in a small saucepan and heat until nearly boiling. Pour the sauce over the chicken and sausage and garnish with the spring onion.

白粥加各样小菜

PLAIN CONGEE WITH ACCOMPANIMENTS

CONGEE IS EATEN IN CHINA FOR BREAKFAST OR AS AN ALL-DAY SNACK. PLAIN CONGEE IS SERVED

WITH LOTS OF DIFFERENT CONDIMENTS TO SPRINKLE OVER IT AND OFTEN A FRIED DOUGH STICK.

220 g (1 cup) short-grain rice
2.25 litres (9 cups) chicken stock
(page 281) or water
light soy sauce, to taste
sesame oil, to taste

TOPPINGS
3 spring onions (scallions), chopped
4 tablespoons chopped coriander
(cilantro)
30 g (1 oz) sliced pickled ginger
4 tablespoons finely chopped
preserved turnip
4 tablespoons roasted peanuts
2 one-thousand-year-old eggs,
cut into slivers
2 tablespoons toasted sesame seeds
2 fried dough sticks, diagonally sliced

SERVES 4

PUT the rice in a bowl and, using your fingers as a rake, rinse under cold running water to remove any dust. Drain the rice in a colander. Place in a clay pot, casserole or saucepan and stir in the stock or water. Bring to the boil, then reduce the heat and simmer very gently, stirring occasionally, for 1¾–2 hours, or until it has a porridge-like texture and the rice is breaking up.

ADD a sprinkling of soy sauce, sesame oil and white pepper to season the congee. The congee can be served plain, or choose a selection from the toppings listed and serve in bowls alongside the congee for guests to help themselves.

Fried dough sticks are available in Chinese shops and are sold as long thin sticks, best eaten fresh on the day they are made, or grilled until crisp again.

鱼粥

FISH CONGEE

EVERYDAY CONGEE, OR RICE PORRIDGE, IS USUALLY SERVED WITH A FEW SIMPLE ACCOMPANIMENTS,

BUT IT IS SOMETIMES COOKED INTO A MORE SUBSTANTIAL MEAL BY ADDING FISH OR MEAT.

FISH CONGEE

220 g (1 cup) short-grain rice
2.25 litres (9 cups) chicken stock
(page 281) or water
225 g (8 oz) firm white fish fillets,
such as cod, halibut or monkfish,
skin removed and cut into
small cubes
1 tablespoon finely shredded ginger
light soy sauce, to taste
2 spring onions (scallions), chopped

SERVES 4

PUT the rice in a bowl and, using your fingers as a rake, rinse under cold running water to remove any dust. Drain the rice in a colander. Place in a clay pot, casserole or saucepan and stir in the stock or water. Bring to the boil, then reduce the heat and simmer very gently, stirring occasionally, for 1¾–2 hours, or until it has a porridge-like texture and the rice is breaking up.

ADD the fish, ginger and a little soy and bring to the boil for 1 minute. Garnish with the spring onion.

Rice terraces at Longsheng.

什锦粥

RAINBOW CONGEE

TO THE CHINESE, CONGEE IS A VERSATILE DISH. IT IS A FAVOURITE COMFORT FOOD, A DISH PREPARED

FOR CONVALESCENTS BECAUSE IT IS SO SOOTHING TO EAT, AND A FILLING AND FLAVOURFUL SNACK.

A game of mahjong in Chengdu.

220 g (1 cup) short-grain rice
2 dried Chinese mushrooms
80 g (3 oz) snowpeas (mangetout),
  ends trimmed
2 Chinese sausages (lap cheong)
2 tablespoons oil
1/4 red onion, finely diced
1 carrot, cut into 1 cm (1/2 inch)
  dice
2–2.25 litres (8–9 cups) chicken
  stock (page 281) or water
1/4 teaspoon salt
3 teaspoons light soy sauce

SERVES 6

PUT the rice in a bowl and, using your fingers as a rake, rinse under cold running water to remove any dust. Drain the rice in a colander.

SOAK the dried mushrooms in boiling water for 30 minutes, then drain and squeeze out any excess water. Remove and discard the stems and chop the caps into 5 mm (1/4 inch) dice. Cut the snowpeas into 1 cm (1/2 inch) pieces.

PLACE the sausages on a plate in a steamer. Cover and steam over simmering water in a wok for 10 minutes, then cut them into small pieces.

HEAT a wok over medium heat, add the oil and heat until hot. Stir-fry the sausage until it is brown and the fat has melted out of it. Remove with a wire sieve or slotted spoon and drain. Pour the oil from the wok, leaving 1 tablespoon.

REHEAT the reserved oil over high heat until very hot. Stir-fry the red onion until soft and transparent. Add the mushrooms and carrot and stir-fry for 1 minute, or until fragrant.

PUT the mushroom mixture in a clay pot, casserole or saucepan and stir in 2 litres (8 cups) stock, the salt, soy sauce and the rice. Bring to the boil, then reduce the heat and simmer very gently, stirring occasionally, for 1 3/4–2 hours, or until it has a porridge-like texture and the rice is breaking up. If it is too thick, add the remaining stock and return to the boil. Toss in the snowpeas and sausage, cover and stand for 5 minutes before serving.

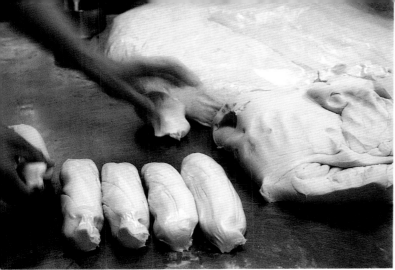
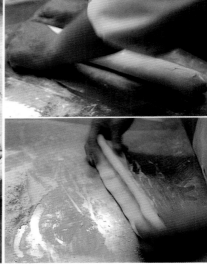

WHEAT NOODLES are still made by hand in China, and these 'pulled' or 'hand-drawn' noodles are an ancient art. At the Malan restaurants in Beijing, they follow a century-old recipe from Lanzhou in northwestern China. First, a large batch of dough is made from strong wheat flour, water and a little vegetable oil (to make the dough soft), left to rest, then worked to stretch the gluten. Portions are rolled into tubes and pulled

NOODLES

NOODLES GEOGRAPHICALLY DIVIDE CHINA, FROM THE COOL NORTH, WHERE HARDY WHEAT IS A STAPLE MADE INTO *MIAN*— WHEAT-FLOUR NOODLES—DOWN TO THE WARM, HUMID SOUTH, WHERE GROUND RICE IS TURNED INTO RICE NOODLES—*FEN*.

Though both kinds of noodles are now eaten all over China, noodles remain more of a staple in the North than the South, where a bowl of rice is the usual accompaniment to a meal.

TYPES OF NOODLES

Mian is the name for noodles made from wheat and barley, though it is often used as the general name for all noodles across China. They can be dried or fresh, made by machine or hand, and eggs can be added to the flour and water paste to make egg noodles, a Cantonese speciality.

Fen is the Chinese word for the flour made from millet and rice, and also refers to noodles made from ground rice. Popular in the South, they are also known as Sha He noodles after a town near Guangzhou, renowned for the quality of its noodles. Fresh rice noodles are formed in sheets and cut up after steaming to make the soft white noodles often found in dim sum. Dried rice noodles come in various thicknesses, from flat rice sticks to strand-like vermicelli, and are usually machine-made.

Fen also refers to non-grain noodles that are not regarded as 'true' noodles made from a staple ingredient such as wheat or rice. *Fen si,* or bean thread noodles, are made of mung bean flour, and their translucent appearance is reflected in their English names of cellophane or glass noodles. *Gan si* are made from pressed tofu.

amount of strands until the required thickness of noodle is reached (noodles for men are traditionally thicker than for women to provide more 'energy'). The thicker end of the noodles (the lump of dough that forms as the noodles are folded) is twisted off and the noodles gathered into a skein. The noodles must now be handled quickly and gently. They are dropped into a continually boiling pot of water and cooked for a couple of

horizontally to arm's length, folded back and stretched again until the dough is soft and elastic. The noodle-maker then starts to let the dough stretch to the floor in an arc, folding it just before it touches so the dough twists up like a coiled rope. Now strong enough to be split into strands, the dough is folded over and over, keeping each folded piece separate by dusting it in the flour on the work surface. Every fold doubles the

EATING NOODLES

Noodles are most often served up in bowls of soup or as roadside snacks in China, especially in the South, where they are rarely served in restaurants and are considered a home-cooking style dish. In the North, noodles are served with meals, and are also found in small restaurants or stalls dedicated to just a few noodle dishes, where the noodles are often hand-thrown to order, then boiled in large pots.

Noodles are a symbol of longevity in Chinese gastronomy and are sometimes eaten on special occasions. Very long, they are rarely cut as to do this may bring bad luck.

Most areas of China have a special noodle dish associated with the region. In Beijing, these are *la mian,* the pulled noodles *(shown above)* that are also known as Dragon's whiskers. In Sichuan, crossing-the-bridge noodles and ants climbing trees are favourite dishes, while fried Singapore noodles are actually from Fujian.

COOKING NOODLES

NOODLES IN SOUP the most common way to eat noodles, dropped into broth, sometimes topped with a little meat, vegetables or seafood, and always eaten as a snack, never as a soup or main course.

BRAISED NOODLES noodles in a thick sauce (which they may have been cooked in), with meat, vegetables or seafood.

FRIED NOODLES crisp- or soft-fried noodles, tossed with meat, vegetables or seafood and flavourings. Stir-fried noodles may be eaten as part of a meal—usually at home, as they are considered home-cooking style dishes. The Chinese name for fried noodles is *chao mian*, corrupted in English to *chow mein*.

TOSSED NOODLES plain boiled noodles, served with a meat sauce and fresh vegetables to mix through, and often eaten cold in the summer.

WON TONS made from an egg noodle dough, won ton wrappers are usually filled with meat and the dumplings poached in soup or fried.

minutes, then lifted out with chopsticks into a bowl. Malan's special recipe is based on five different colours, which are thought to influence the taste. The broth (transparent) is made with beef and chicken stock, Chinese herbs and a little MSG and is poured over the noodles. To this are added sliced turnip—white; chilli—red; coriander (cilantro) and spring onion (scallion)—green; and noodles—yellow. A little beef finishes the dish.

FRESH NOODLES WITH BEEF AND GARLIC CHIVES

250 g (9 oz) rump or sirloin steak
2 large garlic cloves, crushed
3 tablespoons oyster sauce
2 teaspoons sugar
1 tablespoon dark soy sauce
3 teaspoons cornflour (cornstarch)
1/4 teaspoon roasted sesame oil
3 tablespoons oil
1 red capsicum (pepper), thinly
   sliced
150 g (1 bunch) Chinese garlic
   chives, cut into short lengths
1 kg (2 lb 4 oz) fresh rice noodle
   rolls, cut into thick slices
chilli sauce

SERVES 6

CUT the beef across the grain into thin bite-size strips. Combine with the garlic, 1 tablespoon of the oyster sauce, 1 teaspoon of the sugar, 2 teaspoons of the soy sauce, the cornflour and sesame oil. Marinate in the fridge for at least 30 minutes, or overnight.

HEAT a wok over high heat, add the oil and heat until very hot. Stir-fry the capsicum for 1–2 minutes, or until it begins to soften. Add the beef and toss until it changes colour. Add the garlic chives and noodles and toss for 1–2 minutes, or until they soften. Add the remaining oyster sauce, sugar and soy sauce and toss well until combined.

SERVE with some chilli sauce on the side.

Slice the fresh noodle roll into thick slices, which will unroll and separate into noodles.

COLD TOSSED NOODLES

THIS IS A SUMMER DISH THAT PROVIDES A VERY REFRESHING SNACK FOR A HOT AFTERNOON OR EVENING. THE DRESSING CAN BE VARIED ACCORDING TO PERSONAL PREFERENCE BY ADDING MORE OR LESS CHILLI OR PRESERVED TURNIP. LEAVE OUT THE SHRIMP FOR A VEGETARIAN DISH.

DRESSING
20 g (3/4 oz) dried shrimp
3 tablespoons Shaoxing rice wine
3 tablespoons light soy sauce
2 tablespoons clear rice vinegar
1 teaspoon chilli sauce
1 tablespoon finely chopped ginger
2 tablespoons chopped preserved
   turnip
1 teaspoon roasted sesame oil

450 g (1 lb) fresh or 350 g (12 oz)
   dried egg noodles
1 tablespoon oil
2 spring onions (scallions), shredded

SERVES 6

TO MAKE the dressing, soak the dried shrimp in boiling water for 1 hour, then drain, coarsely chop and soak in the rice wine for 15 minutes. Combine the shrimp, soy sauce, rice vinegar, chilli sauce, ginger, preserved turnip and sesame oil.

COOK the noodles in a pan of salted boiling water for 2–3 minutes if fresh and 10 minutes if dried, then drain and rinse in cold water. Combine with the oil and spread the noodles out on a dish.

POUR the dressing over the top of the noodles and sprinkle with the spring onion. Toss at the table before serving.

COLD TOSSED NOODLES

牛肉炒面

CRISPY NOODLES WITH BEEF AND SNOWPEAS

THIS CANTONESE DISH IS A FAVOURITE ACROSS THE GLOBE. THE CRISP NOODLES WITH THEIR BEEF

AND SNOWPEA (MANGETOUT) TOPPING ARE DRENCHED IN A VELVETY OYSTER SAUCE.

275 g (9³/₄ oz) fresh or 175 g (6 oz)
  dried egg noodles
1¹/₂ teaspoons roasted sesame oil
350 g (12 oz) rump or sirloin
  steak, trimmed
1 tablespoon dark soy sauce
2 teaspoons Shaoxing rice wine
¹/₂ teaspoon sugar
1 garlic clove, finely chopped
1 teaspoon cornflour (cornstarch)
100 g (3¹/₂ oz) snowpeas
  (mangetout), ends trimmed
3 tablespoons oil

SAUCE
1 tablespoon finely chopped ginger
1 spring onion (scallion), finely
  chopped
330 ml (1¹/₃ cups) chicken stock
  (page 281)
3 tablespoons oyster sauce
1 tablespoon Shaoxing rice wine
¹/₂ teaspoon dark soy sauce
1 teaspoon sugar
¹/₂ teaspoon roasted sesame oil
1¹/₂ tablespoons cornflour
  (cornstarch)

SERVES 4

COOK the noodles in a pan of salted boiling water for 2–3 minutes if fresh and 10 minutes if dried, then drain and combine with 1 teaspoon of the sesame oil. Place the noodles in four small cake tins or flat-bottomed bowls and leave to cool.

CUT the beef across the grain into slices about 2 mm (¹/₈ inch) thick, then into 4 cm (1¹/₂ inch) squares. Combine the beef, soy sauce, rice wine, sugar, garlic, cornflour and the remaining sesame oil and toss lightly. Marinate in the fridge for at least 1 hour.

BLANCH the snowpeas in a pan of boiling water for 15 seconds. Drain and refresh immediately in cold water. Dry thoroughly.

HEAT a wok over high heat, add 2 tablespoons of the oil and heat until almost smoking. Invert the noodle cakes, one at a time, into the wok and fry on both sides until golden brown, swirling the pan from time to time to move the noodles so that they cook evenly. Put the noodles on a plate and keep warm and crisp in a low oven.

REHEAT the wok over high heat, add the remaining oil and heat until very hot. Drain the beef and stir-fry in batches for 1 minute, or until the beef changes colour. Remove with a wire sieve or slotted spoon, and drain. Pour the oil from the wok, leaving 2 tablespoons.

TO MAKE the sauce, reheat the reserved oil over high heat until very hot and stir-fry the ginger and spring onion for 10 seconds, or until fragrant. Add the remaining sauce ingredients, except the cornflour, and bring to the boil. Combine the cornflour with enough water to make a paste, add to the sauce and simmer until thickened.

ADD the beef and snowpeas, toss to coat with the sauce, and pour the mixture over the noodles.

A pot of boiling water for cooking noodles in Chengdu.

新加坡炒面

SINGAPORE NOODLES

2 tablespoons dried shrimp
300 g (10¹/₂ oz) rice vermicelli
100 g (3¹/₂ oz) barbecue pork
　(char siu)
100 g (1 cup) bean sprouts
4 tablespoons oil
2 eggs, beaten
1 onion, thinly sliced
1 teaspoon salt
1 tablespoon Chinese curry powder
2 tablespoons light soy sauce
2 spring onions (scallions),
　shredded
2 red chillies, shredded

SERVES 4

SOAK the dried shrimp in boiling water for 1 hour, then drain. Soak the noodles in hot water for 10 minutes, then drain. Thinly slice the pork. Wash the bean sprouts and drain thoroughly.

HEAT a wok over high heat, add 1 tablespoon of the oil and heat until very hot. Pour in the egg and make an omelette. Remove from the wok and cut into small pieces.

REHEAT the wok over high heat, add the remaining oil and heat until very hot. Stir-fry the onion and bean sprouts with the pork and shrimp for 1 minute, then add the noodles, salt, curry powder and soy sauce, blend well and stir for 1 minute. Add the omelette, spring onion and chilli and toss to combine.

SINGAPORE NOODLES

担担面

DAN DAN MIAN

A COMMON STREET FOOD SNACK IN SICHUAN, THIS DISH IS NOW POPULAR ALL OVER THE NORTH OF CHINA AND THE RECIPE VARIES FROM STALL TO STALL.

1 tablespoon Sichuan peppercorns
200 g (7 oz) minced (ground) pork
50 g (1³/₄ oz) preserved turnip,
　rinsed and finely chopped
2 tablespoons light soy sauce
2 tablespoons oil
2 garlic cloves, crushed
2 tablespoons grated ginger
4 spring onions (scallions), finely
　chopped
2 tablespoons sesame paste or
　smooth peanut butter
2 tablespoons light soy sauce
2 teaspoons chilli oil
185 ml (³/₄ cup) chicken stock
　(page 281)
400 g (14 oz) thin wheat flour noodles

SERVES 4

DRY-FRY the Sichuan peppercorns in a wok or pan until brown and aromatic, then crush lightly. Combine the pork with the preserved turnip and soy sauce and leave to marinate for a few minutes. Heat a wok over high heat, add the oil and heat until very hot. Stir-fry the pork until crisp and browned. Remove and drain well.

ADD the garlic, ginger and spring onion to the wok and stir-fry for 30 seconds, then add the sesame paste, soy sauce, chilli oil and stock and simmer for 2 minutes.

COOK the noodles in a pan of salted boiling water for 4–8 minutes, then drain well. Divide among four bowls, ladle the sauce over the noodles, then top with the crispy pork and Sichuan peppercorns.

Making wheat noodles by pulling them by hand. The noodles are made fresh for each customer and cooked immediately.

Lunch in Chengdu.

Make sure you separate all the minced meat as it cooks, or it will form large lumps and not resemble ants at all.

蚂 蚁 上 树

ANTS CLIMBING TREES

THE UNUSUAL NAME OF THIS SPICY SICHUANESE DISH IS SUPPOSED TO COME FROM THE FACT THAT IT BEARS A RESEMBLANCE TO ANTS CLIMBING TREES, WITH LITTLE PIECES OF MINCED PORK COATING LUSTROUS BEAN THREAD NOODLES.

125 g (4¹/2 oz) minced (ground)
  pork or beef
¹/2 teaspoon light soy sauce
¹/2 teaspoon Shaoxing rice wine
¹/2 teaspoon roasted sesame oil
125 g (4¹/2 oz) bean thread noodles
1 tablespoon oil
2 spring onions (scallions), finely
  chopped
1 tablespoon finely chopped ginger
1 garlic clove, finely chopped
1 teaspoon chilli bean paste
  (toban jiang), or to taste
2 spring onions (scallions), green
  part only, finely chopped

SAUCE
1 tablespoon light soy sauce
1 tablespoon Shaoxing rice wine
¹/2 teaspoon salt
¹/2 teaspoon sugar
¹/2 teaspoon roasted sesame oil
250 ml (1 cup) chicken stock
  (page 281)

SERVES 4

COMBINE the minced meat with the soy sauce, rice wine and sesame oil. Soak the bean thread noodles in hot water for 10 minutes, then drain.

HEAT a wok over high heat, add the oil and heat until very hot. Stir-fry the minced meat, mashing and separating it, until it changes colour and starts to brown. Push the meat to the side of the wok, add the spring onion, ginger, garlic and chilli paste and stir-fry for 5 seconds, or until fragrant. Return the meat to the centre of the pan.

TO MAKE the sauce, combine all the ingredients. Add the sauce to the meat mixture and toss lightly. Add the noodles and bring to the boil. Reduce the heat to low and cook for 8 minutes, or until almost all the liquid has evaporated. Sprinkle with the spring onion.

Making noodle dishes at a market in Yunnan.

什锦面

RAINBOW NOODLES

THIS DISH OF PRAWNS (SHRIMP), BEAN SPROUTS AND THIN RICE NOODLES IS ENLIVENED WITH A TOUCH OF CHINESE CURRY POWDER. MUCH MILDER THAN ITS INDIAN COUNTERPART AND SIMILAR TO FIVE-SPICE POWDER, YOU COULD USE A MILD INDIAN CURRY POWDER INSTEAD.

225 g (8 oz) prawns (shrimp)
1 tablespoon Shaoxing rice wine
2^1/$_2$ tablespoons finely chopped
   ginger
1 teaspoon roasted sesame oil
300 g (10^1/$_2$ oz) rice vermicelli
2 leeks, white part only
4 tablespoons oil
1^1/$_2$ tablespoons Chinese
   curry powder
200 g (2^1/$_4$ cups) bean sprouts
60 ml (^{1}/$_4$ cup) chicken stock
   (page 281) or water
2 tablespoons light soy sauce
1 teaspoon salt
^{1}/$_2$ teaspoon sugar
^{1}/$_2$ teaspoon freshly ground
   black pepper

SERVES 4

PEEL the prawns, leaving the tails intact. Using a sharp knife, score lengthways along the back and remove the vein. Place in a bowl, add the rice wine, 2 teaspoons of the ginger and the sesame oil, and toss to coat.

SOAK the noodles in hot water for 10 minutes, then drain. Cut the leeks into 5 cm (2 inch) lengths and shred finely. Wash well and dry thoroughly.

HEAT a wok over high heat, add 1 tablespoon of the oil and heat until very hot. Stir-fry the prawns in batches for 1^1/$_2$ minutes, or until they turn opaque. Remove with a wire sieve or slotted spoon and drain. Pour off the oil and wipe out the wok.

REHEAT the wok over high heat, add the remaining oil and heat until very hot. Stir-fry the curry powder for a few seconds, or until fragrant. Add the leek and remaining ginger and stir-fry for 1^1/$_2$ minutes. Add the bean sprouts and cook for 20 seconds, then add the prawns, stock or water, soy sauce, salt, sugar and pepper, and stir to combine.

ADD the noodles and toss until they are cooked through and have absorbed all the sauce. Transfer to a serving dish and serve.

Chinese, or black, mushrooms are also known as shiitake mushrooms. They can be bought fresh when in season and dried all year round.

BLACK MUSHROOM NOODLES

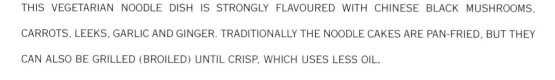

THIS VEGETARIAN NOODLE DISH IS STRONGLY FLAVOURED WITH CHINESE BLACK MUSHROOMS, CARROTS, LEEKS, GARLIC AND GINGER. TRADITIONALLY THE NOODLE CAKES ARE PAN-FRIED, BUT THEY CAN ALSO BE GRILLED (BROILED) UNTIL CRISP, WHICH USES LESS OIL.

275 g (9¾ oz) fresh or 175 g (6 oz) dried egg noodles
1½ teaspoons roasted sesame oil
5 dried Chinese mushrooms
2 leeks, white part only
2 carrots
1 tablespoon oil
2 garlic cloves, finely chopped
1 tablespoon finely chopped ginger
2 tablespoons Shaoxing rice wine
2 tablespoons light soy sauce
1 tablespoon oyster sauce
¼ teaspoon freshly ground black pepper
1½ tablespoons cornflour (cornstarch)

SERVES 4

COOK the noodles in a pan of salted boiling water for 2–3 minutes if fresh and 10 minutes if dried, then drain and combine with ½ teaspoon of the sesame oil.

PREHEAT the grill (broiler), shape the noodles into four mounds on a lightly oiled baking tray and grill (broil) for 10 minutes on each side, turning once, until golden brown. Keep warm in a low oven.

SOAK the dried mushrooms in boiling water for 30 minutes, then drain, reserving the liquid, and squeeze out any excess water. Remove and discard the stems and shred the caps. Cut the leeks into 5 cm (2 inch) lengths, then into 1 cm (½ inch) wide strips. Wash well and dry thoroughly. Cut the carrots to the same size as the leek.

HEAT a wok over high heat, add the oil and heat until very hot. Stir-fry the garlic and ginger until fragrant. Add the leek and carrot and stir-fry for 1 minute. Add the rice wine and mushrooms and cook for 1 minute.

ADD the soy and oyster sauces, pepper, remaining sesame oil and 80 ml (⅓ cup) of the reserved liquid. Combine the cornflour with water to make a paste, add to the sauce and simmer until thickened. Put the noodles on a plate and spoon the sauce over.

CROSSING-THE-BRIDGE NOODLES

LEGEND HAS IT THAT THIS DISH WAS INVENTED BY A WOMAN WHO HAD TO TAKE HER HUSBAND'S FOOD TO HIM EACH DAY. TO KEEP THE SOUP HOT FOR THE LONG JOURNEY, SHE FLOATED OIL ON TOP TO KEEP IN THE HEAT. THE SOUP MUST BE SERVED CLOSE TO BOILING AS YOU COOK THE FOOD IN IT.

100 g (3¹/₂ oz) prawns (shrimp)
100 g (3¹/₂ oz) skinless chicken
  breast fillet
100 g (3¹/₂ oz) squid tubes
115 g (4 oz) Chinese ham,
  thinly sliced
8 dried Chinese mushrooms
120 g (1¹/₃ cups) bean sprouts
350 g (12 oz) fresh rice noodles or
  250 g (9 oz) rice stick noodles
chilli sauce
light soy sauce
1 litre (4 cups) chicken stock
  (page 281)
4 spring onions (scallions),
  finely chopped

SERVES 4

PEEL the prawns and cut them in half through the back, removing the vein. Slice the prawns and the chicken breast thinly on the diagonal.

OPEN up the squid tubes by cutting down one side, scrub off any soft jelly-like substance and slice thinly on the diagonal. Arrange the prawns, chicken, squid and ham on a plate, cover and refrigerate until needed.

SOAK the dried mushrooms in boiling water for 30 minutes, then drain and squeeze out any excess water. Remove and discard the stems. Add the mushrooms to the plate. Wash the bean sprouts and drain thoroughly. Add to the plate.

SEPARATE the rice noodles into four bundles. If you are using dried rice noodles, soak in hot water for 10 minutes, then drain.

GIVE EACH guest a small saucer of chilli sauce and a saucer of soy sauce. Place the ingredients and dipping sauces on the table. Heat four soup bowls either in a low oven or by running them under very hot water for a few minutes. Put the chicken stock in a clay pot, casserole or saucepan with the spring onion and bring to the boil. When the stock has reached a rolling boil, fill the soup bowls.

GIVE EACH guest a hot bowl filled with stock and let them cook the meat, vegetables and noodles in the stock. You can be authentic and add a dash of oil to each bowl to seal in the heat, but it isn't really necessary.

A canal running through Lijiang.

桂皮牛肉面

CINNAMON BEEF NOODLES

1 teaspoon oil
10 spring onions (scallions), cut into
    short lengths, lightly smashed with
    the flat side of a cleaver
10 garlic cloves, thinly sliced
6 slices ginger, smashed with the
    flat side of a cleaver
1¹/₂ teaspoons chilli bean paste
    (toban jiang)
2 cassia or cinnamon sticks
2 star anise
125 ml (¹/₂ cup) light soy sauce
1 kg (2 lb 4 oz) chuck steak,
    trimmed and cut into cubes
250 g (9 oz) rice stick noodles
250 g (9 oz) baby English spinach
3 tablespoons finely chopped
    spring onion (scallion)

SERVES 6

HEAT a wok over medium heat, add the oil and heat until hot. Stir-fry the spring onion, garlic, ginger, chilli paste, cassia and star anise for 10 seconds, or until fragrant. Transfer to a clay pot, casserole or saucepan. Add the soy sauce and 2.25 litres (9 cups) water. Bring to the boil, add the beef, then return to the boil. Reduce the heat and simmer, covered, for 1¹/₂ hours, or until the beef is very tender. Skim the surface occasionally to remove impurities and fat. Remove and discard the ginger and cassia.

SOAK the noodles in hot water for 10 minutes, then drain and divide among six bowls. Add the spinach to the beef and bring to the boil. Spoon the beef mixture over the noodles and sprinkle with the spring onion.

In China for this recipe, cassia bark *(middle)* is used more often than cinnamon.

长寿面

LONGEVITY NOODLES

NOODLES SYMBOLIZE A LONG LIFE BECAUSE OF THEIR LENGTH AND ARE THEREFORE SERVED AT SPECIAL OCCASIONS SUCH AS BIRTHDAYS AND FEAST DAYS. THE NOODLES FOR THIS DISH ARE PARTICULARLY LONG AND CAN BE BOUGHT LABELLED AS LONGEVITY NOODLES.

250 g (9 oz) precooked longevity or
    dried egg noodles
100 g (1 cup) bean sprouts
100 g (¹/₃ cup) fresh or tinned
    bamboo shoots, rinsed
1 tablespoon oil
1 tablespoon finely chopped ginger
4 spring onions (scallions),
    thinly sliced
1 tablespoon light soy sauce
1 teaspoon roasted sesame oil
80 ml (¹/₃ cup) chicken stock
    (page 281)

SERVES 4

IF USING longevity noodles, cook in a pan of salted boiling water for 1 minute, drain, then rinse in cold water. If using dried egg noodles, cook in a pan of salted boiling water for 10 minutes, then drain. Wash the bean sprouts and drain thoroughly. Shred the bamboo shoots.

HEAT a wok over high heat, add the oil and heat until very hot. Stir-fry the ginger for a few seconds, then add the bean sprouts, bamboo shoots and spring onion and stir-fry for 1 minute. Add the soy sauce, sesame oil and stock and bring to the boil. Add the longevity or dried egg noodles and toss together until the sauce is absorbed.

LONGEVITY NOODLES

叉烧面／汤

CHAR SIU NOODLE SOUP

NOODLES IN SOUP ARE FAR MORE POPULAR THAN FRIED NOODLES (CHOW MEIN) IN CHINA. LIKE FRIED RICE, NOODLE DISHES ARE EATEN AS SNACKS RATHER THAN SERVED AS PART OF AN EVERYDAY MEAL. THIS IS A BASIC RECIPE—YOU CAN USE DIFFERENT INGREDIENTS FOR THE TOPPING.

4 dried Chinese mushrooms
200 g (7 oz) barbecue pork (char siu)
100 g (1/3 cup) fresh or tinned
  bamboo shoots, rinsed
100 g (3 1/2 oz) green vegetable,
  such as English spinach, bok choy
  (pak choi) or Chinese cabbage
2 spring onions (scallions)
450 g (1 lb) fresh or 350 g (12 oz)
  dried egg noodles
1 litre (4 cups) chicken and meat
  stock (page 281)
2–3 tablespoons oil
1 teaspoon salt
1/2 teaspoon sugar
1 tablespoon light soy sauce
1 teaspoon Shaoxing rice wine
1/4 teaspoon roasted sesame oil

SERVES 4

SOAK the dried mushrooms in boiling water for 30 minutes, then drain and squeeze out any excess water. Remove and discard the stems and shred the caps. Thinly shred the pork, bamboo shoots, green vegetable and spring onions.

COOK the noodles in a pan of salted boiling water for 2–3 minutes if fresh and 10 minutes if dried, then drain and place in four bowls. Bring the stock to the boil, then reduce the heat to simmering.

HEAT a wok over high heat, add the oil and heat until very hot. Stir-fry the pork and half the spring onion for 1 minute, then add the mushrooms, bamboo shoots and green vegetable and stir-fry for 1 minute. Add the salt, sugar, soy sauce, rice wine and sesame oil and blend well.

POUR the stock over the noodles and top with the meat mixture and the remaining spring onion.

烧鸭面／汤

ROAST DUCK NOODLE SOUP

THIS IS A QUICK AND EASY SNACK OR MEAL. CANTONESE-STYLE ROAST DUCK CAN BE BOUGHT AT CHINESE RESTAURANTS AND TAKE-AWAYS. ASK FOR IT TO BE CHOPPED INTO BITE-SIZE PIECES.

ROAST DUCK NOODLE SOUP

450 g (1 lb) fresh or 350 g (12 oz)
  dried egg noodles
1 litre (4 cups) chicken or chicken
  and meat stock (page 281)
400 g (14 oz) roast duck, chopped
100 g (3 1/2 oz) bok choy (pak choi),
  shredded
2 tablespoons soy sauce
1/4 teaspoon roasted sesame oil

SERVES 4

COOK the noodles in a pan of salted boiling water for 2–3 minutes if fresh and 10 minutes if dried, then drain and place in four bowls. Bring the stock to a boil, then reduce the heat and keep at simmering point.

TOP EACH bowl with the duck, bok choy, soy sauce and sesame oil, then pour on the stock.

Rice noodles being sold in a market in Yunnan.

Finely shred the steamed scallops. Because they have a strong flavour, they are best eaten in small pieces.

干贝海鲜面

NOODLES WITH SEAFOOD AND DRIED SCALLOPS

THIS NOODLE DISH IS RATHER GRAND TO BE A SIMPLE SNACK. NOT ONLY DOES IT INCLUDE FRESH SEAFOOD, IT ALSO HAS DRIED SCALLOPS AS AN ADDED FLAVOURING. DRIED SCALLOPS, ALSO KNOWN AS CONPOY, ARE REGARDED AS A DELICACY AND HAVE A RICH FLAVOUR.

4 dried scallops (conpoy)
12 prawns (shrimp)
200 g (7 oz) squid tubes
400 g (14 oz) thin rice stick noodles
1 tablespoon oil
2 tablespoons shredded ginger
2 spring onions (scallions),
    thinly sliced
150 g (5^1/2 oz) Chinese cabbage,
    finely shredded
250 ml (1 cup) chicken stock
    (page 281)
2 tablespoons light soy sauce
2 tablespoons Shaoxing rice wine
1 teaspoon roasted sesame oil

SERVES 4

PUT the dried scallops in a heatproof bowl with 1 tablespoon water and put them in a steamer. Cover and steam over simmering water in a wok for 30 minutes, or until they are completely tender. Remove the scallops and shred the meat.

PEEL the prawns and cut them in half through the back, removing the vein.

OPEN up the squid tubes by cutting down one side, scrub off any soft jelly-like substance, then score the inside of the flesh with a fine crisscross pattern, making sure you do not cut all the way through. Cut the squid tubes into 3 x 5 cm (1^1/4 x 2 inch) pieces.

SOAK the noodles in hot water for 10 minutes, then drain.

HEAT a wok over high heat, add the oil and heat until very hot. Stir-fry the ginger and spring onion for 1 minute, then add the prawns and squid and stir-fry until just opaque. Add the scallops and Chinese cabbage and toss together. Pour in the stock, soy sauce and rice wine and boil for 1 minute. Add the noodles and sesame oil, toss together and serve.

WON TON SOUP

WON TON LITERALLY TRANSLATED MEANS 'SWALLOWING A CLOUD'. WON TONS, KNOWN AS HUN TUN

OUTSIDE OF GUANGZHOU, ARE CATEGORIZED AS NOODLES AS THEY USE THE SAME DOUGH AS EGG

NOODLES. WON TON SOUP CAN ALSO INCLUDE EGG NOODLES—ADD SOME IF YOU LIKE.

250 g (9 oz) prawns (shrimp)
80 g (1/2 cup) peeled water
  chestnuts
250 g (9 oz) lean minced
  (ground) pork
3 1/2 tablespoons light soy sauce
3 1/2 tablespoons Shaoxing
  rice wine
1 1/2 teaspoons salt
1 1/2 teaspoons roasted sesame oil
1/2 teaspoon freshly ground
  black pepper
1 teaspoon finely chopped ginger
1 1/2 tablespoons cornflour
  (cornstarch)
30 square or round won ton
  wrappers
1.5 litres (6 cups) chicken stock
  (page 281)
450 g (1 lb) English spinach,
  trimmed (optional)
2 spring onions (scallions), green
  part only, finely chopped

SERVES 6

PEEL AND devein the prawns. Place in a tea towel and squeeze out as much moisture as possible. Mince the prawns to a coarse paste using a sharp knife or in a food processor.

BLANCH the water chestnuts in boiling water for 1 minute, then refresh in cold water. Drain, pat dry and roughly chop them. Place the prawns, water chestnuts, pork, 2 teaspoons of the soy sauce, 2 teaspoons of the rice wine, 1/2 teaspoon of the salt, 1/2 teaspoon of the sesame oil, the black pepper, ginger and cornflour in a mixing bowl. Stir vigorously to combine.

PLACE a teaspoon of filling in the centre of one won ton wrapper. Brush the edge of the wrapper with a little water, fold in half and then bring the two folded corners together and press firmly. Place the won tons on a cornflour-dusted tray.

BRING a saucepan of water to the boil. Cook the won tons, covered, for 5–6 minutes, or until they have risen to the surface. Using a wire sieve or slotted spoon, remove the won tons and divide them among six bowls.

PLACE the stock in a saucepan with the remaining soy sauce, rice wine, salt and sesame oil, and bring to the boil. Add the spinach and cook until just wilted. Pour the hot stock over the won tons and sprinkle with the spring onion.

The easiest way to make the won tons is to shape them in the same way as tortellini.

DESSERTS

Squeeze the juice out of the ginger by twisting it up in a piece of muslin.

生姜布丁

GINGER PUDDING

THIS DESSERT CAN ALSO BE EATEN AS A SNACK. THE GINGER JUICE CAUSES THE HOT MILK TO COAGULATE AND FORMS A GINGERY PUDDING WITH A SLIPPERY SMOOTH TEXTURE. IT IS IMPORTANT TO USE YOUNG, SWEET FRESH GINGER OR THE FLAVOUR WILL BE TOO HARSH.

200 g (7 oz) young ginger
1 tablespoon sugar
500 ml (2 cups) milk

SERVES 4

GRATE the ginger as finely as you can, collecting any juice. Place it in a piece of muslin, twist the top hard and squeeze out as much juice as possible. You will need 4 tablespoons. Alternatively, push the ginger through a juicer.

PUT 1 tablespoon of ginger juice and 1 teaspoon of sugar each into four bowls. Put the milk in a saucepan and bring to the boil, then divide among the bowls. Leave to set for 1 minute (the ginger juice will cause the milk to solidify). Serve warm.

杏仁豆腐（加水果）

ALMOND TOFU WITH FRUIT

DURING HOT WEATHER IN CHINA, REFRESHING FRUIT SALADS MADE FROM PINEAPPLE, MANGO, PAPAYA, MELON, LYCHEE AND LOQUAT ARE POPULAR SNACKS. THE MILKY SQUARE OF ALMOND JELLY THAT GOES WITH THIS FRUIT SALAD IS SAID TO RESEMBLE TOFU, HENCE THE TITLE.

2$\frac{1}{2}$ tablespoons powdered gelatine
  or 6 gelatine sheets
90 g ($\frac{1}{3}$ cup) caster (superfine)
  sugar
2 teaspoons almond extract
125 ml ($\frac{1}{2}$ cup) condensed milk
400 g (14 oz) tin lychees in syrup
400 g (14 oz) tin loquats in syrup
$\frac{1}{2}$ papaya, cut into cubes
$\frac{1}{2}$ melon, cut into cubes

SERVES 6

PUT 125 ml ($\frac{1}{2}$ cup) water in a saucepan. If you are using powdered gelatine, sprinkle it on the water and leave to sponge for 1 minute. If you are using sheets, soak in the water until floppy. Heat the mixture slightly, stirring to dissolve the gelatine.

PLACE the sugar, almond extract and condensed milk in a bowl and stir to combine. Slowly add 625 ml (2$\frac{1}{2}$ cups) water, stirring to dissolve the sugar. Stir in the dissolved gelatine. Pour into a chilled 23 cm (9 inch) square tin. Chill for at least 4 hours, or until set.

DRAIN HALF the syrup from the lychees and the loquats. Place the lychees, loquats and remaining syrup in a bowl. Add the papaya and melon. Cut the almond tofu into diamond-shaped pieces and arrange on plates. Spoon the fruit around the tofu.

ALMOND TOFU
WITH FRUIT

264

新年甜汤圆

NEW YEAR SWEET DUMPLINGS

THESE GLUTINOUS SWEET DUMPLINGS ARE MADE AT CHINESE NEW YEAR AND ARE OFTEN EATEN IN A
SWEET SOUP. THEY CAN BE FILLED WITH A NUT OR BEAN PASTE.

60 g (2¹/₄ oz) black sesame paste,
   red bean paste or smooth
   peanut butter
4 tablespoons caster (superfine)
   sugar
250 g (1¹/₂ cups) glutinous
   rice flour
30 g (1 oz) rock (lump) sugar

MAKES 24

COMBINE the sesame paste with the sugar.

SIFT the rice flour into a bowl and stir in 185 ml
(³/₄ cup) boiling water. Knead carefully (the dough
will be very hot) to form a soft, slightly sticky
dough. Dust your hands with extra rice flour, roll
the dough into a cylinder, then divide it into
cherry-size pieces. Cover the dough with a tea
towel and, using one piece at a time, form each
piece of dough into a flat round, then gather it into
a cup shape. The dough should be fairly thin.

FILL EACH cup shape with 1 teaspoon of paste
and fold the top over, smoothing the dough so
you have a round ball with no visible joins.

BRING 1 litre (4 cups) water to the boil, add the
rock sugar and stir until dissolved. Return to the
boil, add the dumplings in batches and simmer for
5 minutes, or until they rise to the surface. Serve
warm with a little of the syrup.

New Year dumplings are widely
available in the markets and night
markets of China during the New
Year celebrations.

炸香蕉

FRIED FRAGRANT BANANAS

125 g (1 cup) self-raising flour
2 tablespoons milk
1 tablespoon butter, melted
1 tablespoon caster (superfine)
   sugar
4 apple or lady finger bananas, or
   3 ordinary bananas
oil for deep-frying
honey (optional)

SERVES 4

COMBINE the flour, milk, butter and sugar, then
add enough water to make a thick batter.

CUT the bananas into 3 cm (1¹/₄ inch) chunks.

FILL a wok one-quarter full of oil. Heat the oil to
180°C (350°F), or until a piece of bread fries
golden brown in 15 seconds when dropped in the
oil. Dip the banana pieces, a few at a time, into
the batter and then fry them for 3 minutes, or until
they are well browned on all sides. Drain on paper
towels. Serve the bananas drizzled with honey for
extra sweetness.

FRIED FRAGRANT BANANAS

Ready-made eight-treasure rice.

Fresh longans.

八宝饭

EIGHT-TREASURE RICE

THIS CHINESE RICE PUDDING IS A FAVOURITE AT BANQUETS AND CHINESE NEW YEAR. THE EIGHT

TREASURES VARY, BUT CAN ALSO INCLUDE OTHER PRESERVED FRUITS.

12 whole blanched lotus seeds
12 jujubes (dried Chinese dates)
20 fresh or tinned gingko nuts,
   shelled
225 g (1 cup) glutinous rice
2 tablespoons sugar
2 teaspoons oil
30 g (1 oz) slab sugar
8 glacé cherries
6 dried longans, pitted
4 almonds or walnuts
225 g (8 oz) red bean paste

SERVES 8

SOAK the lotus seeds and jujubes in bowls of cold water for 30 minutes, then drain. Remove the seeds from the jujubes. If using fresh gingko nuts, blanch in a pan of boiling water for 5 minutes, then refresh in cold water and dry thoroughly.

PUT the glutinous rice and 310 ml (1¼ cups) water in a heavy-based saucepan and bring to the boil. Reduce the heat to low and simmer for 10–15 minutes. Stir in the sugar and oil.

DISSOLVE the slab sugar in 185 ml (¾ cup) water and bring to the boil. Add the lotus seeds, jujubes and gingko nuts and simmer for 1 hour, or until the lotus seeds are soft. Drain, reserving the liquid.

GREASE a 1 litre (4 cup) heatproof bowl. Decorate the base with the lotus seeds, jujubes, gingko nuts, cherries, longans and almonds. Smooth two-thirds of the rice over this to form a shell on the surface of the bowl. Fill with the bean paste, cover with the remaining rice and smooth the surface.

COVER the rice with a piece of greased foil and put the bowl in a steamer. Cover and steam over simmering water in a wok for 1–1½ hours, replenishing with boiling water during cooking.

TURN the pudding out onto a plate and pour the reserved sugar liquid over the top. Serve hot.

Eight-treasure rice can be made in any round dish. If you want it to sit higher on the plate, then choose a deep bowl. Remember that the pattern you make on the bottom will come out on top.

STEAMED PEARS IN HONEY

THIS RECIPE COMBINES SWEET PEARS WITH JUJUBES, SMALL RED DATES THAT ARE THOUGHT TO HAVE MEDICINAL BENEFITS. THEY ARE SOLD DRIED, BUT CAN BE LEFT OUT IF THEY ARE UNAVAILABLE.

STEAMED PEARS IN HONEY

100 g (3¹/₂ oz) jujubes (dried Chinese dates)
6 nearly ripe pears
6 tablespoons honey

SERVES 6

SOAK the jujubes in hot water for 1 hour, changing the water twice. Drain, stone and cut crosswise into strips.

CUT a slice off the bottom of each pear so that it will sit flat. Cut a 2.5 cm (1 inch) piece off the top and set it aside. Using a fruit corer or knife, remove the cores without cutting through to the bottom.

ARRANGE the pears upright on a heatproof plate. Place 1 tablespoon of honey and some jujubes into the cavity of each pear. Replace the tops and, if necessary, fasten with toothpicks.

PUT the plate in a steamer. Cover and steam over simmering water in a wok for 30 minutes, or until tender when pierced with a knife. Serve hot or cold.

ALMOND BISCUITS

ALMONDS ARE USED FOR SWEET RATHER THAN SAVOURY DISHES IN CHINA. THESE BISCUITS MAKE GREAT SNACKS AND CAN ALSO BE SERVED ALONGSIDE DESSERTS SUCH AS ALMOND TOFU.

Dip your thumb in some flour and make an indent in each biscuit to hold the almonds.

125 g (4¹/₂ oz) unsalted butter, softened
185 g (6 oz) sugar
1 egg, lightly beaten
200 g (7 oz) plain (all-purpose) flour
¹/₂ teaspoon baking powder
¹/₂ teaspoon salt
150 g (5¹/₂ oz) finely chopped almonds
1 teaspoon almond extract
1 egg, lightly beaten, extra
25 whole blanched almonds

MAKES 25

PREHEAT the oven to 180°C (350°F/Gas 4). Lightly grease a baking tray. Cream the butter and sugar for 5 minutes. Add the egg and beat until smooth. Sift together the flour, baking powder and salt and slowly add to the butter, stirring until smooth. Add the almonds and extract and stir until smooth.

DROP tablespoons of the mixture onto the baking tray, 3 cm (1¹/₄ inches) apart. Dip your thumb into some flour and make an indentation in the centre of each biscuit. Brush each biscuit with the beaten egg and place an almond in the centre of each indentation. Bake for 10–12 minutes, or until the biscuits are golden and puffed. Cool slightly, then transfer to a rack to cool completely.

ALMOND BISCUITS

BASICS

MANDARIN PANCAKES

THESE THIN PANCAKES ARE ALSO CALLED DUCK PANCAKES AND ARE USED FOR WRAPPING PEKING

DUCK (PAGE 134) AND OTHER NORTHERN DISHES, SUCH AS CRISPY SKIN DUCK (PAGE 129), MU SHU

PORK (PAGE 156) AND MONGOLIAN LAMB (PAGE 183).

450 g (1 lb) plain (all-purpose) flour
310 ml (1¼ cups) boiling water
1 teaspoon oil
roasted sesame oil

MAKES 24–30

SIFT the flour into a bowl, slowly pour in the boiling water, stirring as you pour, then add the oil and knead into a firm dough. Cover with a damp tea towel and set aside for 30 minutes.

TURN the dough out onto a lightly floured surface and knead for 8–10 minutes, or until smooth. Divide the dough into three equal portions, roll each portion into a long cylinder, then cut each cylinder into 8 to 10 pieces.

ROLL EACH piece of dough into a ball and press into a flat disc with the palm of your hand. Brush one disc with a little sesame oil and put another disc on top. Using a rolling pin, flatten each pair of discs into a 15 cm (6 inch) pancake.

HEAT an ungreased wok or frying pan over high heat, then reduce the heat to low and place the pairs of pancakes, one at a time, in the pan. Turn over when brown spots appear on the underside. When the second side is cooked, lift the pancakes out and carefully peel them apart. Fold each pancake in half with the cooked side facing inwards, and set aside under a damp cloth.

JUST BEFORE serving, put the pancakes on a plate in a steamer. Cover and steam over simmering water in a wok for 10 minutes.

TO STORE the pancakes, put them in the fridge for 2 days or in the freezer for several months. Reheat the pancakes either in a steamer for 4–5 minutes or a microwave for 30–40 seconds.

Mandarin pancakes are always rolled and cooked as a pair; the two pancakes are separated by a layer of sesame oil.

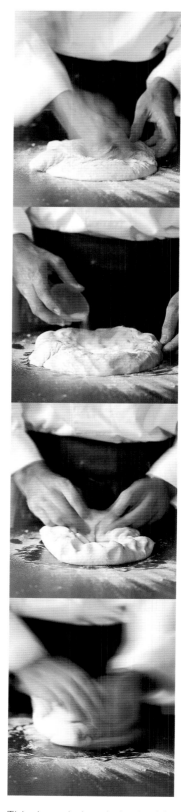

This bread dough is double risen, first with yeast and then with baking powder, which is kneaded into the dough, making it very light and fluffy.

BASIC YEAST DOUGH

CHINESE CHEFS USE TWO TYPES OF BREAD DOUGH FOR MAKING STEAMED BREADS, ONE MADE WITH YEAST AS HERE, THE OTHER MADE WITH A YEAST STARTER DOUGH.

3 tablespoons sugar
250 ml (1 cup) warm water
1¹/₂ teaspoons dried yeast
   or 10 g (¹/₄ oz) fresh yeast
400 g (3¹/₄ cups) plain (all-purpose)
   flour
2 tablespoons oil
1¹/₂ teaspoons baking powder

MAKES 1 QUANTITY

DISSOLVE the sugar in the water, then add the yeast. Stir lightly, then set aside for 10 minutes, or until foamy.

SIFT the flour into a bowl and add the yeast mixture and the oil. Using a wooden spoon, mix the ingredients to a rough dough. Turn the mixture out onto a lightly floured surface and knead for 8–10 minutes, or until the dough is smooth and elastic. If it is very sticky, knead in a little more flour—the dough should be soft. Lightly grease a bowl with the oil. Place the dough in the bowl and turn it so that all sides of the dough are coated. Cover the bowl with a damp cloth and set aside to rise in a draught-free place for 3 hours.

UNCOVER the dough, punch it down, and turn it out onto a lightly floured surface. If you are not using the dough straight away, cover it with plastic wrap and refrigerate.

WHEN YOU are ready to use the dough, flatten it and make a well in the centre. Place the baking powder in the well and gather up the edges to enclose the baking powder. Pinch the edges to seal. Lightly knead the dough for several minutes to evenly incorporate the baking powder, which will activate immediately.

USE the prepared dough as directed.

鸡汤

CHICKEN STOCK

1.5 kg (3 lb 5 oz) chicken
  carcasses, necks, pinions and feet
250 ml (1 cup) Shaoxing rice wine
6 slices ginger, smashed with the
  flat side of a cleaver
6 spring onions (scallions), ends
  trimmed, smashed with the flat
  side of a cleaver
4 litres (16 cups) water

MAKES 3 LITRES (12 CUPS)

REMOVE ANY excess fat from the chicken, then chop into large pieces and place in a stockpot with the rice wine, ginger, spring onions and water and bring to the boil. Reduce the heat and simmer gently for 3 hours, skimming the surface to remove any impurities.

STRAIN through a fine strainer, removing the solids, and skim the surface to remove any fat. If the stock is too weak, reduce it further. Store in the fridge for up to 3 days or freeze in small portions.

CHICKEN AND MEAT STOCK

排骨鸡汤

CHICKEN AND MEAT STOCK

650 g (1 lb 7 oz) chicken carcasses,
  necks, pinions and feet
650 g (1 lb 7 oz) pork spareribs
4 spring onions (scallions), each tied
  into a knot
12 slices ginger, smashed with the
  flat side of a cleaver
4 litres (16 cups) water
80 ml (1/3 cup) Shaoxing rice wine
2 teaspoons salt

MAKES 3 LITRES (12 CUPS)

REMOVE ANY excess fat from the chicken and meat, then chop into large pieces and place in a stockpot with the spring onions, ginger and water and bring to the boil. Reduce the heat and simmer gently for 3$\frac{1}{2}$–4 hours, skimming the surface to remove any impurities.

STRAIN through a fine strainer, removing the solids, and skim the surface to remove any fat. Return to the pot with the rice wine and salt. Bring to the boil and simmer for 3–4 minutes. Store in the fridge for up to 3 days or freeze in small portions.

VEGETABLE STOCK

菜汤

VEGETABLE STOCK

500 g (1 lb 2 oz) fresh soya
  bean sprouts
10 dried Chinese mushrooms
6 spring onions (scallions), each
  tied into a knot (optional)
4 litres (16 cups) water
3 tablespoons Shaoxing rice wine
2 teaspoons salt

MAKES 3 LITRES (12 CUPS)

DRY-FRY the sprouts in a wok for 3–4 minutes. Place the sprouts, mushrooms, spring onions and water in a stockpot and bring to the boil. Reduce the heat and simmer for 1 hour.

STRAIN through a fine strainer, removing the solids (keep the mushrooms for another use). Return to the pot with the rice wine and salt. Bring to the boil and simmer for 3–4 minutes. Store in the fridge for up to 3 days or freeze in small portions.

SOY AND VINEGAR

SOY, VINEGAR AND CHILLI

SOY, CHILLI AND SESAME

酱醋调味酱

SOY AND VINEGAR DIPPING SAUCE

SIMPLE DIPPING SAUCES ARE SERVED WITH FOODS SUCH AS STEAMED DUMPLINGS. THE ADDITION OF VINEGAR GIVES A MORE ROUNDED FLAVOUR THAN USING JUST SOY SAUCE.

125 ml (1/2 cup) light soy sauce
3 tablespoons Chinese black
rice vinegar

MAKES 225 ML (ABOUT 1 CUP)

COMBINE the soy sauce and vinegar with 2 tablespoons water in a small bowl, then divide among individual dipping bowls. This dipping sauce goes well with jiaozi (page 20) or dim sum like siu mai (page 38).

酱醋辣酱

SOY, VINEGAR AND CHILLI DIPPING SAUCE

125 ml (1/2 cup) light soy sauce
2 tablespoons Chinese black
rice vinegar
2 red chillies, thinly sliced

MAKES 200 ML (ABOUT 3/4 CUP)

COMBINE the soy sauce, vinegar and chilli in a small bowl, then divide among individual dipping bowls. This dipping sauce goes well with jiaozi (page 20) or dim sum like har gau (page 41) or tofu rolls (page 35).

红醋调味酱

RED VINEGAR DIPPING SAUCE

125 ml (1/2 cup) red rice vinegar
3 tablespoons shredded ginger

MAKES 225 ML (ABOUT 1 CUP)

COMBINE the rice vinegar, 21/2 tablespoons water and the ginger in a small bowl, then divide among individual dipping bowls. This dipping sauce goes well with jiaozi (page 20).

酱辣芝麻调味酱

SOY, CHILLI AND SESAME DIPPING SAUCE

125 ml (1/2 cup) light soy sauce
21/2 tablespoons chilli oil
1 tablespoon roasted sesame oil
1 spring onion (scallion), finely
chopped

MAKES 200 ML (ABOUT 3/4 CUP)

COMBINE the soy sauce, chilli oil, sesame oil and spring onion in a small bowl, then divide among individual dipping bowls. This dipping sauce goes well with jiaozi (page 20) and steamed breads (page 46).

辣椒盐和胡椒

SPICY SALT AND PEPPER

1 tablespoon salt
2 teaspoons ground Sichuan
  peppercorns
1 teaspoon five-spice powder

MAKES 2 TABLESPOONS

COMBINE the salt, Sichuan peppercorns and five-spice powder. Dry-fry over low heat, stirring constantly, for 2–3 minutes, or until aromatic. This mix can be used as an ingredient or as a dipping condiment for roast duck or chicken.

SPICY SALT AND PEPPER

辣酱

CHILLI SAUCE

1 kg (2 lb 4 oz) red chillies,
  stalks removed
3 teaspoons salt
4 tablespoons sugar
170 ml (²/₃ cup) clear rice vinegar

MAKES 400 ML (ABOUT 1¹/₂ CUPS)

PUT the chillies in a saucepan with 5 tablespoons water, cover and bring to the boil. Cook until the chillies are tender, then add the salt, sugar and vinegar. Blend the mixture to a paste in a blender or food processor, or push through a sieve. Store in the fridge for up to 1 month or freeze in small portions. Use as an ingredient or dipping sauce.

辣椒油

CHILLI OIL

50 g (1³/₄ oz) dried chilli flakes
125 ml (¹/₂ cup) oil
60 ml (¹/₄ cup) roasted sesame oil

MAKES 200 ML (ABOUT ³/₄ CUP)

PUT the chilli in a heatproof bowl. Put the oils in a saucepan and heat until they are very hot but not smoking. Pour onto the chilli and leave to cool. Try not to breathe in the fumes. When cool, transfer to a jar. Store in the fridge for up to 6 months. The oil can be used as a flavouring, and the chilli at the bottom of the jar can be used instead of fresh chilli.

CHILLI OIL

姜汁

GINGER JUICE

200 g (7 oz) young ginger

MAKES ABOUT 60 ML (¹/₄ CUP)

GRATE the ginger as finely as you can, collecting any juice. Combine the ginger with an equal volume of cold water and place it in a piece of muslin, twist the top hard and squeeze out as much juice as possible. Alternatively, push the ginger through a juicer, then combine with an equal quantity of cold water. Use as an ingredient.

GINGER JUICE

CHILLI SAUCE

TEA HOUSES are popular all over China. Some are a male domain where business is conducted, such as at this one in Yuyuan Bazaar, Shanghai *(top)*, while others, like this one at Wenshu Monastery, Chengdu *(bottom right)*, are family-orientated and allow patrons to sit all day over a constantly refilled cup of tea. Tea houses also offer snacks to accompany the tea, from melon seeds or oranges to more ornate sweet offerings *(bottom left)*.

TEA

TEA HAS BEEN POPULAR IN CHINA SINCE AT LEAST THE SIXTH CENTURY BC, AND IT WAS FROM CHINA THAT TEA TRAVELLED TO JAPAN, EUROPE AND INDIA. INTEGRAL TO FESTIVALS, A SIGN OF HOSPITALITY, A MEDICINE, AND STEEPED IN TRADITION, TEA IS BOTH A DRINK AND A PART OF CHINESE CULTURE ITSELF.

For the Chinese, tea is a drink to be savoured on its own or before or after a meal. The exception is tea with yum cha, which means to 'drink tea' and originated as a few snacks to complement the tea at tea houses, rather than the full meal it often is today. In China, hot water is provided in hotels, waiting rooms and on trains for people to make tea using their own screwtop jar or in a large cup with a lid that can be slid back just enough to drink the tea without the leaves coming too. Carrying a receptacle for tea is not a statement of class or rank, everyone does it.

ORIGINS OF TEA

Tea plants (*Camellia sinensis*) are native to the mountains of Southwest China, and are now grown all over the South, and in the East and North where conditions are favourable. Teas from Yunnan and Fujian are particularly treasured. Tea is made from the two top leaves and bud, picked every 7–10 days to gather the young shoots and to encourage more shoots to sprout, known as a flush. These small leaves are more prized than too large or broken leaves. Fannings (tea dust and broken leaves) are the lowest grades of all.

DRAGON WELL TEA is China's finest green tea, grown around the West Lake of Hangzhou, especially in the village of Longjing (Dragon Well). Here, the Wen family runs a small tea estate producing three pickings a year. The tea buds are hand-picked, then dried by rubbing the leaves around a heated metal basin to arrest any fermentation. The Wen family teas are sold by weight from their house in the village.

VARIETIES OF TEA

Tea is categorized by the different methods of its production:

GREEN an unfermented tea made by firing (drying) fresh leaves in a kind of wok to prevent them oxidizing (fermenting). The tea is usually rolled and twisted to uncurl in boiling water.

OOLONG the leaves are semi-fermented before firing to produce a tea halfway between green and black. The most famous oolong teas are from Fujian and Taiwan.

BLACK a fully fermented tea where the leaves are wilted and bruised by rolling, then fermented and dried.

WHITE a very rare, totally unfermented green tea from Fujian.

Chinese teas can also be categorized by other factors:

BRICK usually pu'er teas from Yunnan compressed into blocks. A piece is sliced off to make tea.

SCENTED tea leaves mixed with scented flowers.

FLOWER petal teas, which are not true teas but tisanes.

GLOSSARY OF CHINESE FOOD AND COOKING

abalone A single-shelled mollusc that is a delicacy in China. Sometimes available fresh from specialist fish shops, but more often used dried or tinned. Dried abalone, bought from Chinese dried goods shops, needs to be soaked for 6 hours, then simmered for 4. Tinned can be used as it is.

bamboo shoots A bamboo is a giant grass and its shoots are a common vegetable in China. Fresh shoots are cone-shaped and can contain a toxin called hydrocyanic acid, which is removed by boiling for 5 minutes. The more readily available tinned ones are usually cut into strips and need to be rinsed. Dried or preserved bamboo shoots may also be available. Dried ones should be soaked. Winter shoots are more highly prized than spring shoots as they are more tender. Bamboo is known as 'winter' in many dishes.

barbecue pork (char siu) A Cantonese speciality, these pork pieces are coated in maltose or honey and roasted until they have a red, lacquered appearance. Available at Chinese roast meat restaurants.

bean sprouts These can be sprouted mung or soya beans. Soya bean sprouts are bigger and more robust, but the two are usually interchangeable. Recipes may tell you to remove the straggly ends, but this is not necessary and is for aesthetic reasons. You can keep the sprouts in water in the fridge for several days. Change the water daily.

bean thread noodles Not true noodles, these are made from mung bean starch and are also labelled as cellophane or glass noodles. They come as vermicelli or slightly thicker strands and need to be soaked. They have no flavour of their own but soak up flavourings they are cooked with.

bitter melon Also known as a warty melon, this looks like a pale-green cucumber covered in a warty skin. The flesh is very bitter and needs to be blanched or degorged, then married with strong flavours.

black fungus Also known as wood or cloud ears, this is a cultivated wood fungus, which is dried in pieces and can be found in bags in Chinese shops. When reconstituted, it expands to up to five times its original size. It is used in recipes for both its colour and slightly crunchy, rubbery texture.

bok choy (pak choi) Also called a little Chinese white cabbage, this is a mild, open-leaved cabbage with a fat white or pale-green stem and dark-green leaves. A smaller variety is called Shanghai or baby bok choy. Bok choy is widely available.

cassia The bark of the cassia tree is similar to cinnamon, which can be used instead, though cassia has a more woody flavour. It is used as a flavouring, especially in braises, and is a component of five-spice powder.

chilli bean paste (toban jiang) Made from broad beans fermented with chillies and salt to give a browny-red sauce, this is an important ingredient in Sichuan cooking, but is never served as a dipping sauce. Other pastes, called hot or Sichuan bean pastes, can be substituted. These are made of fermented soya beans and sometimes other ingredients such as garlic. It is hard to judge their heat, so take care when adding a new one to a recipe. Chinese shops usually have a large number to choose from.

chilli oil A condiment made by pouring smoking hot oil over chilli flakes and seeds. Ready-made versions can be bought.

chilli sauce Made from fresh chillies and a variety of other ingredients, such as garlic and vinegar, the thicker version is good for cooking and the thinner for a dipping sauce.

Chinese broccoli (gai lan) This has dark-green stalks and leaves and tiny florets.

Chinese cabbage A white cabbage also known as Chinese leaf; Tianjin, Beijing or napa cabbage; or wong bok. There are two main types: one is long with pale-green leaves and a thick white stem, while the other is pale yellow with curlier leaves and a rounder shape. Both are widely available.

Chinese chives Garlic chives have a long, flat leaf and are green and very garlicky, or yellow with a milder taste. Flowering chives are round-stemmed with a flower at the top, which can be eaten. Both are used as a vegetable rather than as a herb.

Chinese curry powder A strong and spicy version of five-spice powder, with additional spices including turmeric and coriander, which lend the curry flavour.

Chinese ham A salted and smoked ham with a strong flavour and dryish flesh. Yunnan and Jinhua hams are the best known, and outside China, Yunnan ham can be bought in tins. You can substitute prosciutto if you can't find it.

Chinese mushrooms The fresh version, found as shiitake mushrooms, is cultivated by the Japanese. The Chinese, however, usually use dried ones, which have a strong flavour and aroma and need to be soaked to reconstitute them before they are used. The soaking liquid can be used to add flavour to dishes. These are widely available.

Chinese pickles These can be made from several types of vegetables, preserved in a clear brine solution or in a soy-based solution, which is called jiang cai. Both can be used where Chinese pickles are called for in a recipe. They are available in packets and jars from Chinese shops.

Chinese sausage There are two kinds of Chinese sausage: a red variety, lap cheong or la chang, which is made from pork and pork fat and dried; and a brown variety, yun cheung or xiang chang, which is made from liver and pork and also dried. Chinese sausages have to be cooked before eating.

Chinese shrimp paste Very pungent pulverized shrimp. Refrigerate after opening.

Chinese spirits Distilled from grains, these vary in strength but generally are stronger than Western spirits. Spirits are used for drinking and cooking and Mou Tai is a common brand. Brandy can be substituted.

Chinese-style pork spareribs These are the shorter, fatter ribs known as pai gwat and are cut into short lengths. If they are unavailable, use any spareribs but trim off any excess fat.

Chinese turnip Looking like a huge white carrot, this is actually a type of radish and is also called Chinese white radish. It has a crisp, juicy flesh and mild radish flavour. It is also known as mooli, or by the Japanese name daikon, and is widely available.

choy sum A green vegetable with tender pale-green stalks, small yellow flowers and dark-green leaves. It has a mild flavour and is often just blanched and eaten with a simple flavouring like garlic or oyster sauce.

clay pot Also known as a sand pot, these earthenware, lidded pots are used for braises, soups and rice dishes that need to be cooked slowly on the stove. The pots come in different shapes: the squatter ones are for braising and the taller ones for soups and rice. The pots can be fragile and should be heated slowly, preferably with a liquid inside.

cleaver A large, oblong, flat-bladed knife. In China, different cleavers are used for all chopping and cutting, but heavy-duty ones are good for chopping through bones as

they are very robust. They can be bought in Chinese shops and at kitchenware shops.

dang gui A bitter Chinese herb that is a relation of European Angelica and is valued for its medicinal properties. It can be found in Chinese shops or herbalists and looks like small bleached pieces of wood. It is generally added to braises or soups.

dried scallops (conpoy) Scallops dried to thick amber discs. They need to be soaked or steamed until soft and are often shredded before use. They have a strong flavour so you don't need many, and as they are expensive they are mostly eaten at banquets.

dried shrimps These are tiny, orange, saltwater shrimps that have been dried in the sun. They come in different sizes and the really small ones have their heads and shells still attached. Dried shrimp need to be soaked in water or rice wine to soften them before use and are used as a seasoning, not as a main ingredient.

dumpling wrappers Used for jiaozi, wheat wrappers, also called Shanghai wrappers or wheat dumpling skins, are white and can be round or square. Egg wrappers for siu mai are yellow and may also be round or square. They are sometimes labelled gow gee wrappers or egg dumpling skins. All are found in the refrigerated cabinets in Chinese shops and good supermarkets and can be frozen until needed.

fermented tofu A marinated tofu that is either red, coloured with red rice, or white, and may also be flavoured with chilli. It is sometimes called preserved tofu or tofu cheese and is used as a condiment or flavouring. It is sold in jars in Chinese shops.

five-spice powder A Chinese mixed spice generally made with star anise, cassia, Sichuan pepper, fennel seeds and cloves, which gives a balance of sweet, hot and aromatic flavours. Five-spice may also include cardamom, coriander, dried orange peel and ginger. Used ground together as a powder or as whole spices tied in muslin.

flat cabbage (tat soi) Also known as a rosette cabbage, this is a type of bok choy (pak choi). It looks like a giant flower with shiny, dark-green leaves that grow out flat.
gingko nuts These are the nuts of the

maidenhair tree. The hard shells are cracked open and the inner nuts soaked to loosen their skins. The nuts are known for their medicinal properties and are one of the eight treasures in dishes like eight-treasure rice. Shelled nuts can be bought in tins in Chinese shops and are easier to use.

glutinous rice A short-grain rice that, unlike other rice, cooks to a sticky mass and so is used in dishes where the rice is required to hold together. Glutinous rice is labelled as such and has plump, highly polished and shiny grains. Black or red glutinous rice, used mainly in desserts, is slightly different.

Guilin chilli sauce From the southwest of China, this sauce is made from salted, fermented yellow soya beans and chillies. It is used as an ingredient in cooking. If it is unavailable, use a thick chilli sauce instead.

hoisin sauce This sauce is made from salted, yellow soya beans, sugar, vinegar, sesame oil, red rice for colouring and spices such as five-spice or star anise. It is generally used as a dipping sauce, for meat glazes or in barbecue marinades.

jujubes Also known as Chinese or red dates, jujubes are an olive-sized dried fruit with a red, wrinkled skin, which are thought to build strength. They need to be soaked and are used in eight-treasure or tonic-type dishes. They are also thought to be lucky because of their red colour.

longans From the same family as lychees, these are round with smooth, buff-coloured skins, translucent sweet flesh and large brown pips. Available fresh, tinned or dried.

lotus leaves The dried leaves of the lotus, they need to be soaked before use and are used for wrapping up food like sticky rice to hold it together while it is cooking. They are sold in packets in Chinese shops.

lotus root The rhizome of the Chinese lotus, the root looks like a string of three cream-coloured sausages, but when cut into it has a beautifully lacy pattern. It is available fresh, which must be washed, tinned or dried. Use the fresh or tinned version as a fresh vegetable and the dried version in braises.

lotus seeds These seeds from the lotus are considered medicinal and are used in eight-treasure dishes as well as being roasted, salted or candied and eaten as a snack. Lotus seeds are also made into a sweet paste to fill buns and pancakes. Fresh and dried lotus seeds are both available and dried seeds need to be soaked before use.

maltose A sweet liquid of malted grains used to coat Peking duck and barbecued meats. Honey can be used instead.

master sauce This is a stock of soy sauce, rice wine, rock (lump) sugar, spring onions (scallions), ginger and star anise. Additional ingredients vary according to the chef. Meat, poultry or fish is cooked in the stock, then the stock is reserved so it matures, taking on the flavours of everything that is cooked in it. The spices are replenished every few times the sauce is used. Master sauce spices can be bought as a mix, or a ready-made liquid version. Freeze between uses.

Mei Kuei Lu Chiew A fragrant spirit known as Rose Dew Liqueur. Made from sorghum and rose petals. It is used in marinades, but brandy can be used instead.

noodles Egg noodles come fresh and dried in varying thicknesses. In recipes they are interchangeable, so choose a brand that you like and buy the thickness appropriate to the dish you are making. Wheat noodles are also available fresh and dried and are interchangeable in recipes. Rice noodles are made from a paste of ground rice and water and can be bought fresh or as dried rice sticks or vermicelli. The fresh noodles are white and can be bought in a roll.

one-thousand-year old eggs Also known as one-hundred-year old or century eggs, these are eggs that have been preserved by coating them in a layer of wood ash, slaked lime and then rice husks. The eggs are left to mature for 40 days to give them a blackish-green yolk and amber white. To eat, the coating is scraped off and the shell peeled. These eggs are eaten as an hors d'oeuvre or used to garnish congee.

oyster sauce A fairly recent invention, this is a Cantonese speciality made with oyster extract. Add to dishes at the end of cooking or use as a dipping sauce or marinade.

pepper Used as an ingredient rather than as a condiment, most hot dishes were originally flavoured with copious quantities of pepper rather than the chillies used now. White pepper is used rather than black.

plum sauce This comes in several varieties, with some brands sweeter than others and some adding chilli, ginger or garlic. It is often served with Peking duck rather than the true sauce and is a good dipping sauce.

preserved ginger Ginger pickled in rice vinegar and sugar, which is typically used for sweet-and-sour dishes. Japanese pickled ginger could be used as a substitute.

preserved mustard cabbage Also called Sichuan pickle or preserved vegetables, this is the root of the mustard cabbage preserved in chilli and salt. It is available whole and shredded in jars or tins.

preserved turnip This is Chinese turnip, sliced, shredded or grated, and usually preserved in brine. It has a crunchy texture and needs to be rinsed before using.

red bean paste Made from crushed adzuki beans and sugar, this sweet paste is used in soups and to fill dumplings and pancakes. There is a richer black version and this can be used instead.

rice flour This is finely ground rice, often used to make rice noodles. Glutinous rice flour, used for making sweet things, makes a chewier dough. Obtainable from Chinese shops or supermarkets.

rice vinegar Made from fermented rice, Chinese vinegars are milder than Western ones. Clear rice vinegar is mainly used for pickles and sweet-and-sour dishes. Red rice vinegar is a mild liquid used as a dipping sauce and served with shark's fin soup. Black rice vinegar is used in braises, especially in northern recipes—Chinkiang (Zhenjiang) vinegar is a good label. Rice vinegars can last indefinitely but may lose their aroma, so buy small bottles. If you can't find them, use cider vinegar instead of clear and balsamic instead of black.

roasted sesame oil Chinese sesame oil is made from roasted white sesame seeds and is a rich amber liquid, unlike the pale unroasted Middle Eastern sesame oil. Buy small bottles as it loses its aroma quickly. It does not fry well as it smokes at a low temperature, but sprinkle it on food as a seasoning or use it mixed with another oil for stir-frying.

rock (lump) sugar Yellow rock sugar comes as uneven lumps of sugar, which may need to be further crushed before use if very big. It is a pure sugar that gives a clear syrup and makes sauces it is added to shiny and clear. You can use sugar lumps instead.

salted, fermented black beans Very salty black soya beans that are fermented using the same moulds as are used for making soy sauce. Added to dishes as a flavouring, they must be rinsed before use and are often mashed or crushed. They are available in jars or bags from specialist shops. You can also use a black bean sauce.

sea cucumber A slug-like sea creature related to the starfish. Always sold dried, it needs to be reconstituted by soaking. It has a gelatinous texture and no flavour.

sesame paste Made from ground, roasted white sesame seeds, this is a fairly dry paste. It is more aromatic than tahini, which can be used instead by mixing it with a little Chinese sesame oil. Black sesame paste is used for sweets like New Year dumplings.

Shaoxing rice wine Made from rice, millet, yeast and Shaoxing's local water, this is aged for at least 3 years, then bottled either in glass or decorative earthenware bottles. Several varieties are available. As a drink, rice wine is served warm in small cups. Dry sherry is the best substitute.

shark's fin Prized for its texture more than for its flavour, shark's fin is very expensive. Preparing a dried fin takes several days, so using the ready-prepared version is much easier as it just needs soaking and then cooking. It looks like very thin dried noodles.

Sichuan peppercorns Not a true pepper, but the berries of a shrub called the prickly ash. Sichuan pepper, unlike ordinary pepper, has a pungent flavour and the aftertaste, rather than being simply hot, is numbing. The peppercorns should be crushed and dry-roasted to bring out their full flavour.

slab sugar Dark brown sugar with a caramel flavour sold in a slab. Soft brown sugar can be used instead.

soy sauce Made from fermented soya beans, soy sauce comes in two styles: light soy sauce, which is also known as just soy sauce or superior soy sauce, and is used with fish, poultry and vegetables, and dark soy sauce, which is more commonly used with meats. Chinese soy sauce, unlike Japanese, is not used as a condiment except with Cantonese cuisine. As it is not meant to be a dipping sauce, it is best to mix a tablespoon of dark with two tablespoons of light to get a good flavour for a condiment. It does not last forever so buy small bottles and store it in the fridge.

soya beans These are oval, pale-green beans. The fresh beans are cooked in their fuzzy pods and served as a snack. The dried beans can be yellow or black, and the yellow ones are used to make soy milk by boiling and then puréeing the beans with water before straining off the milk. Dried soya beans need to be soaked in water overnight.

spring roll wrappers Also called spring roll skins, these wrappers are made with egg and are a pale or dark yellow. They are found in the refrigerated cabinets of Chinese shops and supermarkets and can be frozen until needed.

star anise An aromatic ingredient in Chinese cooking, this is a star-shaped dried seed pod containing a flat seed in each point. It has a similar flavour and aroma to fennel seed and aniseed. It is used whole in braises or ground into five-spice powder.

steaming A method of cooking food in a moist heat to keep it tender and preserve its flavour. Bamboo steamers fit above a saucepan or wok and a 25 cm (10 inch) steamer is the most useful, although you will need a bigger one for cooking whole fish. Use as many as you need, stacked on top of each other, and reverse them halfway through cooking to ensure the cooking is even. Metal steamers are available, but bamboo ones are preferred in China as they absorb the steam, making the food a little drier.

stir-frying A method of cooking in a wok that only uses a little oil and cooks the food evenly and quickly, retaining its colour and texture. Everything to be cooked needs to be prepared beforehand, cut to roughly the same shape, dry and at room temperature. The wok is heated, then the oil added and heated before the ingredients are thrown in. Stir-frying should only take a couple of minutes, the heat should be high and the ingredients continually tossed.

tangerine peel Dried tangerine or orange peel is used as a seasoning. It looks like dark-brown strips of leather with a white underside, and is used mostly in braised dishes or master sauces. It is not soaked first but is added straight to the liquid in the dish. Sold in bags in Chinese shops.

tiger lily buds Sometimes called golden needles, these aren't from tiger lilies but are the unopened flowers from another type of lily. The buds are bought dried and then soaked. They have an earthy flavour and are used mainly in vegetarian dishes.

tofu Also known as bean curd, tofu is called doufu in China and it is made by coagulating soya bean milk. The curds are sold in blocks, either soft, firm or pressed, depending on their water content. Keep the blocks in water in the fridge, changing the water frequently, for up to 2 to 3 days. Japanese tofu can be used but the silken variety is softer than Chinese soft tofu. Available at supermarkets.

tofu puffs Deep-fried squares of tofu, crispy on the outside and spongy in the middle. Frying your own tofu will not be the same, but can be substituted. Puffs, sold in Chinese shops, can be frozen.

tofu skins Made by scooping the layer of skin off the top of boiling soya milk and drying it. Tofu skins come either as dried sheets, which need to be soaked in water, or already softened in vacuum packs. The skins are used as a wrapper or split into sticks and added to stir-fries and soups.

water chestnuts These are the rhizomes of a plant that grows in paddy fields in China. The nut has a dark-brown shell and a crisp white interior. The raw nuts need to be peeled with a knife and blanched, then stored in water. Tinned ones need to be drained and rinsed. Freshly peeled nuts are sometimes available from Chinese shops.

water spinach Called ong choy in Chinese, this vegetable has long, dark-green pointed leaves and long hollow stems. Often cooked with shrimp paste.

wheat starch A powder-like flour made by removing the protein from wheat flour. It is used to make dumpling wrappers.

winter melon A very large dark-green gourd or squash that looks like a watermelon. The skin is dark green, often with a white waxy bloom, and the flesh is pale green. You can usually buy pieces of it in Chinese shops.

wok A bowl-shaped cooking vessel that acts as both a frying pan and a saucepan in the Chinese kitchen. Choose one made from carbon steel about 35 cm (14 inches) in diameter. To season it, scrub off the layer of machine oil, then heat with 2 tablespoons of oil over low heat for several minutes. Rub the inside with paper towels, changing the paper until it comes out clean. The inside will continue to darken as it is used and only water should be used for cleaning. Use a different wok for steaming, as boiling water will strip off the seasoning. A metal spatula (charn) is perfect for moving ingredients around the wok.

won ton wrappers Also called won ton skins, these are square and yellow and slightly larger than dumpling wrappers. They can be found in the refrigerated cabinets in Chinese shops and good supermarkets and can be frozen until needed.

yard-long beans Also called snake or long beans, these are about 40 cm (16 inches) long. The darker green variety has a firmer texture.

yellow bean sauce This is actually brown in colour and made from fermented yellow soya beans, which are sweeter and less salty than black beans, mixed with rice wine and dark brown sugar. It varies in flavour and texture (some have whole beans in them) and is sold under different names—crushed yellow beans, brown bean sauce, ground bean sauce and bean sauce. It is mainly used in Sichuan and Hunan cuisine.

INDEX

A

abalone, 288
Abalone, snowpeas and oyster
    mushrooms, 72
Almond biscuits, 271
Almond tofu with fruit, 264
Ants climbing trees, 246

B

bamboo shoots, 288
bananas, Fried fragrant, 267
Bang bang chicken, 151
barbecue pork
    Char siu, 164, 288
    Char siu bau, 24
    Char siu noodle soup, 257
    Steamed rice noodle rolls, 31
Barbecue spareribs, 32
bean sauce, Stir-fried tofu in
    yellow, 196
bean sprouts, 288
Bean sprouts stir-fry, 207
beef
    Beef with capsicum and black
        bean sauce, 172
    Beef with oyster sauce, 180
    Cinnamon beef noodles, 254
    Crispy noodles with beef and
        snowpeas, 242
    Crispy shredded beef, 179
    Five-spice beef, 175
    Fresh noodles with beef and
        garlic chives, 241
    Mongolian hotpot, 176
    Red-cooked beef, 175
    Steamed beef with rice flour, 180
    Stir-fried beef with spring
        onions, 179
    West Lake beef soup, 64
biscuits, Almond, 271
bitter melon, 288
bitter melon in black bean sauce,
    Stuffed, 219

black bean, 290
    Beef with capsicum and black
        bean sauce, 172
    Scallops with black bean
        sauce, 114
    Steamed mussels with black
        bean sauce, 76
    Stuffed bitter melon in black
        bean sauce, 219
black fungus, 288
Black mushroom noodles, 250
bok choy, 288
bok choy, Stir-fried, 220
Braised chicken wings, 28
Braised gluten, 199
Braised pork belly with mustard
    cabbage, 167
braised prawns, Sichuan-style, 97
Braised tofu, 190
Braised tofu with Chinese
    mushrooms, 186
breads, Steamed, 46
Buddha's delight, 204

C

cabbage, Hot-and-sour, 223
Cabbage rolls with mustard, 224
Candied walnuts, 53
Cantonese corn soup, 56
Cantonese pickled vegetables, 50
Cantonese-style steamed fish, 75
capsicum and black bean sauce,
    Beef with, 172
capsicum, Stir-fried squid flowers
    with, 80
cassia, 288
Celery salad, 216
celery, Shredded chicken with, 126
char siu see barbecue pork
chicken
    Bang bang chicken, 151
    Braised chicken wings, 28
    Chicken and meat stock, 281

Chicken and mushroom soup, 56
Chicken stock, 281
Crossing-the-bridge noodles, 253
Drunken chicken, 147
Hainan chicken, 133
Jellyfish and chicken salad, 91
Kung pao chicken, 130
Lemon chicken, 144
Red-cooked chicken, 140
Salt-baked chicken, 139
Shredded chicken with celery, 126
Soy chicken, 140
Steamed chicken with
    mushrooms, 126
Steamed chicken and sausage
    rice, 232
Three-cup chicken, 147
White cut chicken, 152
Yunnan pot chicken, 122
chilli bean paste, 288
Chilli crab, 92
Chilli oil, 285, 288
Chilli sauce, 285, 288
chilli and spring onion, Soft tofu
    with, 190
Chinese broccoli, 288
Chinese broccoli in oyster sauce, 212
Chinese broccoli with soy sauce, 220
Chinese cabbage, 288
Chinese cabbage, Stir-fried, 208
Chinese chives, 288
Chinese curry powder, 288
Chinese ham, 288
    Winter melon and ham
        soup, 63
Chinese mushrooms see
    mushrooms
Chinese New Year, 95
Chinese pickles, 289
Chinese sausage, 289
    Steamed chicken and sausage
        rice, 232
Chinese shrimp paste, 289

Chinese spirits, 289
Chinese turnip, 289, 290
    Turnip cake, 42
choy sum, 289
Cinnamon beef noodles, 254
Clams in yellow bean sauce, 76
congee with accompaniments,
    Plain, 235
congee, Fish, 235
congee, Rainbow, 236
conpoy see scallops
coriander soup, Sliced fish and,
    64
corn soup, Cantonese, 56
crab
    Chilli crab, 92
    Crabmeat fu rong, 113
    Salt and pepper soft-shell
        crabs, 113
Crispy fried pig's ear, 49
Crispy noodles with beef and
    snowpeas, 242
Crispy rice, 274
Crispy shredded beef, 179
Crispy skin duck, 129
Crossing-the-bridge noodles, 253
Crystal-boiled pork, 168
cucumber, Sichuan pickled, 50
cucumber soup, Lamb and, 68
custards, Steamed mussel, 109
custards, Steamed prawn, 109

D

Dan dan mian, 245
dang gui, 289
Deep-fried quails with spicy salt, 143
Deep-fried squid flowers with spicy
    salt, 80
dipping sauces, 282
Dim sum, 36, 37
Dong po pork, 163
Double-cooked yard-long beans, 211
Drunken chicken, 147

duck
   Crispy skin duck, 129
   Peking duck, 134, 136, 137
   Roast duck noodle soup 257
   Shanghai soy duck, 148
dumpling wrappers, 289
dumplings, New Year sweet, 267

E
eggplant, Sichuan-style spicy, 212
eggs
   Egg fried rice, 228
   Tomato and egg soup, 60
   Tea eggs, 49
   Stir-fried eggs and tomatoes, 216
Eight-treasure rice, 268

F
Fermented tofu with Asian
   greens, 186
fish
   Cantonese-style steamed fish, 75
   Fish congee, 235
   Shanghai-style five-willow fish, 98
   Sichuanese braised fish in spicy
      sauce, 110
   Sliced fish and coriander soup, 64
   Smoked fish, 79
   Sole with mushrooms and rice
      wine, 118
   Sweet-and-sour fish, 117
   Sweet-and-sour fish fillets,
      105
   West Lake fish, 83
   Whole fish with yellow bean
      sauce, 106
Five-spice beef, 175
five-spice powder, 289
five-willow fish, Shanghai-style, 98
flat cabbage, 289
Flat cabbage with black
   pepper, 223
Fried fragrant bananas, 267
Fried peanuts, 53
fu rong, Crabmeat, 113
fu rong, Lobster, 88

G
gai lan see Chinese broccoli
garlic chives, Fresh noodles with
   beef and, 241
garlic, Flash-cooked pea shoots
   with, 215
Ginger juice, 285
ginger, preserved, 290
Ginger pudding, 264
gingko nuts, 289

gluten
   Braised gluten, 199
   Buddha's delight, 204
   Mock duck, 200
glutinous rice, 289
glutinous rice in lotus leaves,
   Steamed, 27
Guilin chilli sauce, 289

H
Hainan chicken, 133
ham see Chinese ham
Har gau, 41
hoisin sauce, 289
honey, Steamed pears in, 271
hotpot, Mongolian, 176
Hot-and-sour cabbage, 223
Hot-and-sour soup, 68

J
Jellyfish and chicken salad, 91
Jiaozi, 20
jujubes, 289

K
Kung pao chicken, 130

L
Lacquered squab, 143
Lamb and cucumber soup, 68
lamb and leeks, Stir-fried, 183
lamb, Mongolian, 183
lap cheong see Chinese sausage
leeks, Stir-fried lamb and, 183
Lemon chicken, 144
lettuce, Stir-fried, 207
Lion's head meatballs, 159
Lobster fu rong, 88
longans, 289
Longevity noodles, 254
lotus leaves, 289
lotus leaves, Steamed glutinous rice
   in, 27
lotus root, 289
lotus root, Stir-fried, 215
lotus seeds, 290
Love birds prawns, 102
lump sugar see rock sugar

M
Ma po tofu, 189
maltose, 290
Mandarin pancakes, 277
master sauce, 290
meatballs, Lion's head, 159
Mei Kuei Lu Chiew, 290
Mock duck, 200
Mongolian hotpot, 176

Mongolian lamb, 183
Mu shu pork, 156
mushrooms, 288
   Abalone, snowpeas and oyster
      mushrooms, 72
   Black mushroom noodles, 250
   Braised tofu with Chinese
      mushrooms, 186
   Chicken and mushroom soup, 56
   Sea cucumber with
      mushrooms, 101
   Sole with mushrooms and rice
      wine, 118
   Steamed chicken with
      mushrooms, 126
mussel custards, Steamed, 109
mussels with black bean sauce,
   Steamed, 76
mustard cabbage, Braised pork
   belly with, 167
mustard cabbage, preserved, 290
mustard, Cabbage rolls with, 224

N
New Year sweet dumplings, 267
noodles, 238, 239, 288, 290
   Ants climbing trees, 246
   Bang bang chicken, 151
   Black mushroom noodles, 250
   Char siu noodle soup, 257
   Cinnamon beef noodles, 254
   Cold tossed noodles, 241
   Crispy noodles with beef and
      snowpeas, 242
   Crossing-the-bridge noodles, 253
   Dan dan mian, 245
   Fresh noodles with beef and
      garlic chives, 241
   Longevity noodles, 254
   Mongolian hotpot, 176
   Noodles with seafood and dried
      scallops, 258
   Rainbow noodles, 249
   Roast duck noodle soup, 257
   Seafood clay pot, 114
   Singapore noodles, 245
   Steamed rice noodle rolls, 31
   Won ton soup, 261
Northern-style tofu, 195

O
one-thousand-year old eggs, 290
ong choy see water spinach
oyster sauce, 290
oyster sauce, Beef with, 180
oyster sauce, Chinese broccoli in, 212

P
pak choi see bok choy
pancakes, Mandarin, 277
pancakes, Spring onion, 45
pea shoots with garlic, Flash-
   cooked, 215
peanuts, Fried, 53
Pearl balls, 231
pears in honey, Steamed, 271
Peking duck, 134, 136, 137
pepper, 290
pepper, Flat cabbage with
   black, 223
Pickled pig's trotters, 168
pig's ear, Crispy fried, 49
pig's trotters, Pickled, 168
plum sauce, 290
pork see also barbecue pork
   Ants climbing trees, 246
   Barbecue spareribs, 32
   Braised pork belly with mustard
      cabbage, 167
   Chinese-style pork spareribs, 289
   Crystal-boiled pork, 168
   Dan dan mian, 245
   Dong po pork, 163
   Double-cooked yard-long
      beans, 211
   Hot-and-sour soup, 68
   Jiaozi, 20
   Lion's head meatballs, 159
   Mu shu pork, 156
   Pearl balls, 231
   Red-cooked pork, 163
   Siu mai, 38
   Spareribs with sweet-and-sour
      sauce, 171
   Spicy crispy pork, 164
   Spicy salt and pepper
      spareribs, 32
   Spring rolls, 23
   Stir-fried squab in lettuce
      leaves, 125
   Stuffed tofu, 196
   Sweet-and-sour pork, 160
   Won ton soup, 261
prawns
   Crossing-the-bridge noodles, 253
   Har gau, 41
   Love birds prawns, 102
   Noodles with seafood and dried
      scallops, 258
   Rainbow noodles, 249
   Seafood clay pot, 114
   Sichuan-style braised prawns, 97
   Siu mai, 38
   Steamed prawn custards, 109

Steamed rice noodle rolls, 31
Stuffed tofu, 196
Sweet-and-sour prawns with
    vegetables, 87
Won ton soup, 261
Yangzhou fried rice with
    prawns, 228
pudding, Ginger, 264

Q

quails with spicy salt, Deep-fried, 143

R

Rainbow congee, 236
Rainbow noodles, 249
red bean paste, 290
Red-cooked beef, 175
Red-cooked chicken, 140
Red-cooked pork, 163
Red vinegar dipping sauce, 282
rice, 274, 289
    Crispy rice, 274
    Egg fried rice, 228
    Eight-treasure rice, 268
    Fish congee, 235
    Plain congee with
        accompaniments, 235
    Rainbow congee, 236
    Steamed chicken and sausage
        rice, 232
    Steamed glutinous rice in lotus
        leaves, 27
    Yangzhou fried rice with
        prawns, 228
rice flour, 290
rice flour, Steamed beef with, 180
rice noodle rolls, Steamed, 31
rice vinegar, 290
rice wine, Sole with mushrooms
    and, 118
rock sugar, 290

S

salad, Celery, 216
salad, Jellyfish and chicken, 91
Salt-baked chicken, 139
Salt and pepper soft-shell crabs, 113
salt and pepper spareribs, Spicy,
32
salt and pepper, Spicy, 285
Salted soya bean pods, 53
sausage see Chinese sausage
scallops, 289
    Noodles with seafood and dried
        scallops, 258
    Scallops with black bean
        sauce, 114

Seafood clay pot, 114
Stir-fried scallops with Chinese
    greens, 84
sea cucumber, 290
Sea cucumber with mushrooms, 101
seafood
    Abalone, snowpeas and oyster
        mushrooms, 72
    Cantonese-style steamed fish, 75
    Chilli crab, 92
    Clams in yellow bean sauce, 76
    Crabmeat fu rong, 113
    Crossing-the-bridge noodles, 253
    Deep-fried squid flowers with
        spicy salt, 80
    Fish congee, 235
    Har gau, 41
    Jellyfish and chicken salad, 91
    Lobster fu rong, 88
    Love birds prawns, 102
    Noodles with seafood and dried
        scallops, 258
    Rainbow noodles, 249
    Salt and pepper soft-shell
        crabs, 113
    Scallops with black bean
        sauce, 114
    Sea cucumber with
        mushrooms, 101
    Seafood clay pot, 114
    Shanghai-style five-willow fish, 98
    Shark's fin soup, 59
    Sichuan-style braised prawns, 97
    Sichuanese braised fish in spicy
        sauce, 110
    Siu mai, 38
    Sliced fish and coriander soup, 64
    Smoked fish, 79
    Sole with mushrooms and rice
        wine, 118
    Steamed mussel custards, 109
    Steamed mussels with black
        bean sauce, 76
    Steamed prawn custards, 109
    Steamed rice noodle rolls, 31
    Stir-fried scallops with Chinese
        greens, 84
    Stir-fried squid flowers with
        capsicum, 80
    Stuffed bitter melon in black
        bean sauce, 219
    Stuffed tofu, 196
    Sweet-and-sour fish, 117
    Sweet-and-sour fish fillets, 105
    Sweet-and-sour prawns with
        vegetables, 87
    West Lake fish, 83

Whole fish with yellow bean
    sauce, 106
Won ton soup, 261
Yangzhou fried rice with
    prawns, 228
sesame oil, roasted, 290
sesame paste, 290
Shanghai soy duck, 148
Shanghai-style five-willow fish, 98
Shaoxing rice wine, 290
shark's fin, 290
Shark's fin soup, 59
shrimp sauce, Stir-fried water
    spinach with, 224
shrimps, dried, 289
Sichuan peppercorns, 290
Sichuan pickled cucumber, 50
Sichuan-style braised prawns, 97
Sichuan-style spicy eggplant, 212
Sichuanese braised fish in spicy
    sauce, 110
Singapore noodles, 245
Siu mai, 38
Smoked fish, 79
snowpeas, Crispy noodles with
    beef and, 242
snowpeas and oyster mushrooms,
    Abalone, 72
Sole with mushrooms and rice
    wine, 118
soup
    Cantonese corn soup, 56
    Char siu noodle soup, 257
    Chicken and mushroom soup, 56
    Hot-and-sour soup, 68
    Lamb and cucumber soup, 68
    Mixed vegetable soup, 63
    Roast duck noodle soup, 257
    Shark's fin soup, 59
    Sliced fish and coriander soup, 64
    Ten-treasure soup, 67
    Tofu and spinach soup, 60
    Tomato and egg soup, 60
    West Lake beef soup, 64
    Winter melon and ham soup, 63
    Won ton soup, 261
Soy chicken, 140
Soy, chilli and sesame dipping
    sauce, 282
soy duck, Shanghai, 148
soy sauce, 192, 193, 291
soy sauce, Chinese broccoli with, 220
Soy, vinegar and chilli dipping
    sauce, 282
Soy and vinegar dipping sauce, 282
soya bean pods, Salted, 53
soya beans, 291

spareribs, 289
    Barbecue spareribs, 32
    Spareribs with sweet-and-sour
        sauce, 171
    Spicy salt and pepper
        spareribs, 32
Spicy crispy pork, 164
spicy salt, Deep-fried quails with, 143
spicy salt, Deep-fried squid flowers
    with, 80
Spicy salt and pepper, 285
Spicy salt and pepper spareribs, 32
spinach soup, Tofu and, 60
Spring onion pancakes, 45
spring onion, Soft tofu with chilli
    and, 190
spring onions, Stir-fried beef with, 179
spring roll wrappers, 291
Spring rolls, 23
squab, Lacquered, 143
squab in lettuce leaves, Stir-fried,
    125
squid
    Crossing-the-bridge noodles, 253
    Deep-fried squid flowers with
        spicy salt, 80
    Noodles with seafood and dried
        scallops, 258
    Stir-fried squid flowers with
        capsicum, 80
star anise, 291
Steamed beef with rice flour, 180
Steamed breads, 46
Steamed chicken with
    mushrooms, 126
Steamed chicken and sausage
    rice, 232
steamed fish, Cantonese-style,
    75
Steamed glutinous rice in lotus
    leaves, 27
Steamed mussel custards, 109
Steamed mussels with black bean
    sauce, 76
Steamed pears in honey, 271
Steamed prawn custards, 109
steamed rice, Boiled or, 274
Steamed rice noodle rolls, 31
steaming, 291
Stir-fried beef with spring onions,
    179
Stir-fried bok choy, 220
Stir-fried Chinese cabbage, 208
Stir-fried eggs and tomatoes, 216
Stir-fried lamb and leeks, 183
Stir-fried lettuce, 207
Stir-fried lotus root, 215

Stir-fried scallops with Chinese greens, 84
Stir-fried squab in lettuce leaves, 125
Stir-fried squid flowers with capsicum, 80
Stir-fried tofu in yellow bean sauce, 196
Stir-fried twin winter, 208
Stir-fried water spinach with shrimp sauce, 224
stir-fry, Bean sprouts, 207
stir-frying, 291
stock, 281
Stuffed bitter melon in black bean sauce, 219
Stuffed tofu, 196
sweet-and-sour
    Sweet-and-sour fish, 117
    Sweet-and-sour fish fillets, 105
    Sweet-and-sour pork, 160
    Sweet-and-sour prawns with vegetables, 87
    sweet-and-sour sauce, Spareribs with, 171

T
tangerine peel, 291
tat soi see flat cabbage
tea, 286, 287
Tea eggs, 49
tea houses, 36, 286
Ten-treasure soup, 67
Three-cup chicken, 147
tiger lily buds, 291
toban jiang see chilli bean paste
tofu, 192, 193, 289, 291
    Almond tofu with fruit, 264
    Braised tofu, 190
    Braised tofu with Chinese mushrooms, 186
    Buddha's delight, 204
    Fermented tofu with Asian greens, 186
    Hot-and-sour soup, 68
    Ma po tofu, 189
    Northern-style tofu, 195
    Soft tofu with chilli and spring onion, 190
    Stir-fried tofu in yellow bean sauce, 196
    Stuffed tofu, 196
    Tofu rolls, 35
    Tofu and spinach soup, 60
Tomato and egg soup, 60
tomatoes, Stir-fried eggs and, 216
turnip see Chinese turnip
twin winter, Stir-fried, 208

V
vegetable soup, Mixed, 63
Vegetable stock, 281
vegetables, Cantonese pickled, 50

W
walnuts, Candied, 53
water chestnuts, 291
water spinach, 291
water spinach with shrimp sauce, Stir-fried, 224
West Lake beef soup, 64
West Lake fish, 83
wheat starch, 291
White cut chicken, 152
winter melon, 291
Winter melon and ham soup, 63
Won ton soup, 261
won ton wrappers, 291

Y
Yangzhou fried rice with prawns, 228
yard-long beans, 291
yard-long beans, Double-cooked, 211
yeast dough, Basic, 278
yellow bean sauce, 291
yellow bean sauce, Clams in, 76
yellow bean sauce, Stir-fried tofu in, 196
yellow bean sauce, Whole fish with, 106
Yunnan pot chicken, 122

BIBLIOGRAPHY

Bartlett, Frances and Lai, Ivan. *Hong Kong on a Plate*. Roundhouse Publications (Asia) Ltd, 1997.

Bender, Arnold and David. *Oxford Dictionary of Food and Nutrition*. Oxford University Press, 1995.

Davidson, Alan. *The Oxford Companion to Food*. Oxford University Press, 1999.

Halvorsen, Francine. *The Food and Cooking of China*. John Wiley & Sons, Inc., 1996.

Hom, Ken. *Easy Family Dishes*. BBC Books, 1998.

Hom, Ken. *Ken Hom's Asian Ingredients*. Ten Speed Press, 1996.

Hom, Ken. *The Taste of China*. Pavilion Books Limited, 1990.

Hsiung, Deh-Ta. *The Chinese Kitchen*. Kyle Cathie Limited, 1999.

Hsiung, Deh-Ta. *The Festive Food of China*. Kyle Cathie Limited, 1991.

Hutton, Wendy. *The Food of China*. Periplus Editions (HK) Ltd, 1996.

Lo, Vivienne and Jenny. *150 Recipes from the Teahouse*. Faber and Faber Limited, 1997.

Mowe, Rosalind. *Culinaria: Southeast Asian Specialties*. Könemann, 1999.

Passmore, Jacki. *The Encyclopedia of Asian Food & Cooking*. Doubleday, 1991.

Ross, Rosa Lo San. *Beyond Bok Choy A Cook's Guide to Asian Vegetables*. Artisan, 1996.

Shun Wah, Annette and Aitken, Greg. *Banquet Ten Courses to Harmony*. Doubleday, 1999.

Simonds, Nina. *China's Food, A Traveler's Guide to the Best Restaurants, Dumpling Stalls, Teahouses and Markets in China*. Harper Perennial, 1991.

Simonds, Nina. *Classic Chinese Cuisine*. Houghton Mifflin Company, 1994.

Sinclair, Charles. *International Dictionary of Food and Cooking*. Peter Collin Publishing Ltd, 1998.

Sinclair, Kevin. *China The Beautiful Cookbook*. The Knapp Press, 1987.

Solomon, Charmaine. *Encyclopedia of Asian Food*. William Heinemann, 1996.

Sterling, Richard, Chong, Elizabeth, Qin, Lushan Charles. *World Food Hong Kong*. Lonely Planet Publications Pty Ltd, 2001.

Yin-Fei Lo, Eileen. *The Dim Sum Dumpling Book*. Macmillan, 1995.

Yin-Fei Lo, Eileen. *The Chinese Kitchen*. William Morrow and Company, Inc, 1999.

Yiu, Hannah. *Easy Asian Vegetable Cooking*. Oriental Merchant Pty Ltd.

Young, Grace. *The Wisdom of the Chinese Kitchen*. Simon & Schuster Editions, 1999.

THE FOOD OF CHINA

This edition first published in Canada in 2005 by Whitecap Books,
351 Lynn Ave., North Vancouver, British Columbia, Canada, V7J 2C4.

www.whitecap.ca

ISBN 1 55285 683 6
ISBN 978 1 55285 683 3

First published in 2001 by Murdoch Books Pty Limited

Food Editor: Lulu Grimes
Design Concept: Marylouise Brammer
Designer: Susanne Geppert
Editor: Justine Harding
Photographer: Jason Lowe
Stylist: Sarah de Nardi
Stylist's Assistants: Ross Dobson, Shaun Arantz, Olivia Lowndes
Recipes: Deh-Ta Hsiung, Nina Simonds
Additional Recipes: Wendy Quisumbing
Interpreter: Anna Bryant
Map: Rosanna Vecchio
Production: Monika Paratore

Publisher: Kay Scarlett
Chief Executive: Juliet Rogers

IMPORTANT: Those who might be at risk from the effects of salmonella food poisoning
(the elderly, pregnant women, young children and those suffering from immune deficiency
diseases) should consult their GP with any concerns about eating raw eggs.

ACKNOWLEDGMENTS

The Publisher wishes to thank the following for all their help in making this book possible:

Bass Hotels and Resorts: Geoffrey Webb, Bradley Moody; Hong Kong Tourist Association: Liam Fitzpatrick, Peter Randall;
Oriental Merchant: Hannah Yiu; Chopstix Media: Ian Fenn.

Beijing: Chen Shi, Malan Restaurants, Beijing; Bob Ren, Jerrie Xuan, Crowne Plaza, Beijing; Niu Lihong, Beijing Wangfujing
Quanjude Roast Duck Restaurant, Beijing; Li Family Restaurant, Beijing; Lily Wei, Beijing Tourism Bureau; Kaman Ng,
Australian Embassy, Beijing. Shanghai: Alex; Maggie Wang, Julie Chan, Crowne Plaza, Shanghai; Mid-lake Pavilion Tea
House, Shanghai. Hangzhou: Anne Stackler, Marcel Holman, Kenneth Law, Holiday Inn, Hangzhou; Wen Family Tea,
Hangzhou. Chengdu: Valerie Tan, Lakshman T Perera, Willy Schnitzel, Richard Cheng, White Bai, Nancy Lu, Crowne Plaza,
Chengdu; Tea House, Wenshu Monastery, Chengdu. Dali: Li-yi He, Mr China's Son, Dali. Kunming: Clark Liu, Holiday Inn,
Kunming; Jacky Lee, Yunnan Tea Import and Export Corp., Kunming. Guilin: Tang Jun, Holiday Inn, Guilin. Guangzhou: Ida
Chan, Raymond Wong, Holiday Inn City Centre, Guangzhou. Hong Kong: F.C. Tang, W. C. Yip, Ann Wai Pik Wa, Wendy
Ko, Lee Kum Kee; Lee King Yin, Luk Yu Tea House, Hong Kong; Johnny Cheung, Ng Long, Wing Wah Noodles, Hong
Kong; Tina Jansen, Prudence Mak, Catherine McNabb, Leung Fai Hung, Grand Stanford Inter-Continental, Hong Kong;
Chan Janny, City Hall Chinese Restaurant, Hong Kong; So Shing Fung, Kung Wo Bean Curd Factory, Hong Kong.